INCREDIBLE
TALE

INCREDIBLE TALE

The Odyssey of the Average American
in the Last Half Century

By GERALD W. JOHNSON

HARPER & BROTHERS . PUBLISHERS
NEW YORK

PRINTED IN THE UNITED STATES OF AMERICA BY
KINGSPORT PRESS, INC., KINGSPORT, TENNESSEE

TO THE MEMORY OF

ARCHIBALD JOHNSON,

WHO BEQUEATHED FAITH TO HIS HEIRS

Contents

III. ROOSEVELT PASSES

IV. STALIN PASSES

V. ONE ABIDES

INCREDIBLE
TALE

I

Wilson Passes

I. Inexperienced Aeschines

*A*ESCHINES, *the orator, prosecuting a case in Athens in the year 330 B.C., had a pretty idea. To his speech he* added a rhetorical flourish that had nothing whatever to do with the case before the court, but that he thought would soothe and tickle the emotions of the jurymen, thereby rendering them more sympathetic to him and his side.

It was good. It was so good that more than two thousand years later an English historian, George Grote, picked it up and quoted it in his history of Greece as reflecting the spirit of the times with great felicity. For they were something more than merely troubled times; they were times remarkably like ours, stunned and bewildered. With his own eyes Aeschines

*had seen the world upheaved and civilization, if not overthrown,
at least altered beyond recognition. The storm had gathered
first in the north, where Philip of Macedon had developed
the phalanx, the ancient equivalent of the modern armored
division. Employing this novelty he had overwhelmed and
crushed one Greek city after another with little more trouble
than Hitler's* panzer *armies had in sweeping through Denmark,
the Netherlands, Belgium and Luxemburg.*

*Then his successor, Alexander the Great, had hurled the new
weapon against Persia, in the eyes of the Greeks immeasurably
the greatest power on earth, one that had stood from time
immemorial; yet before the impact of the phalanx Persia had
gone down like France in 1940. At the moment when Aeschines
spoke Alexander was just attaining the summit of his power.
The Battle of Arbela had been fought, and the Great King
was a fugitive, hunted like a rabbit by Alexander's cavalry.
Neither Aeschines nor the jurors had played any considerable
part in this, but they had seen it all, and it was to the natural
emotion of the man who had been a spectator when a mighty
drama was played that Aeschines appealed in the words that
impressed Grote:*

What is there in the list of strange and unexpected events that
has not occurred in our time? Our lives have transcended the limits
of humanity; we are born to serve as a theme of incredible tales
to posterity.[1]

*A smart lawyer, summing up in an important case, calculates
the effect of every word. Aeschines knew what he was about.
The pride of the spectator is an emotion as nearly universal,
perhaps, as any that is harbored in the human breast. It is the
great buckler against the tragedy of human existence, the*

---

[1] Aeschines, *Oration Against Ctesiphon*, 330 B.C., quoted by Grote, *History
of Greece*, A.D. 1857, vol. 12, p. 258.

recourse of the grandsire in the chimney corner and the veteran in the Old Soldiers' Home. It gives a man importance in his own eyes and in those of his children, if in no others; and there is always the chance, however slim, that the spectator has learned something from what he saw, in which case he really is important.

The generation that had seen Philip followed by Alexander, therefore, had some reason to hear Aeschines' words with gratification. Next to being a doer of memorable deeds, it is best to have seen them done; if one has not the gifts of mind and character to be a great man, it is yet something not ignoble to have been a contemporary of great men, and a witness of their achievements. The chorus at least is on the stage.

The members of the dicastery that tried Ctesiphon were by no means irrational if they heard Aeschines with pleasure.[2] It is probable that they left the court that day appreciably more self-respecting, appreciably less inclined to sit among the ashes, wailing, and more inclined to bestir themselves as becomes men who have seen things happen and who have a tale to tell. The oration, therefore, was not mere ranting; to the extent that it carried conviction, it also carried a certain comfort and a certain pride. For the wistfulness of one who says, "Et ego in Arcadia," is no more genuine than the sultry pride of one who says, "Et ego in Erebi." The Italian peasants crossed themselves when they saw Dante passing by, the man who had been to hell; and Dante was not displeased.

Then if Athenians of the fourth century before Christ could get a lift of the spirit from being reminded of the vastness of their experience, let Aeschines speak again; let him address Americans whose age runs close to that of the twentieth century, men and women who were born while Victoria reigned,

---

[2] For the delight of the cynical, however, let it be recorded that Aeschines lost his case.

and who have lived to see Truman become strangest of all Emperors of the West. Let him employ the same words, and they will carry greater force and clearer truth than when they were uttered twenty-two centuries ago. For he will be addressing an audience that has seen everything the ancient Athenians saw, but multiplied. Where they beheld two colossi bestride the world, we have seen four; where they saw one ancient and mighty empire crash, we have seen five; where they heard of one Arbela, we have heard of a dozen.

To say that all this has done us any good would be overbold. "Happy the people whose annals are poor," and the annals of the American people for the past fifty years have been inordinately rich. As the century reaches its halfway mark, they are certainly not to be described as a happy people. There are pessimists who see them as an utterly distracted people, nor is there any lack of evidence to support that view.

It is beyond dispute that people can be distracted by too much experience. There is a tale connected with a famous institution devoted to the cure of the unstrung, and therefore regarded by the inexact laity as a madhouse. Among the patients was the celebrated wife of a celebrated man, a pair who had had a meteoric joint career from relative poverty and definite obscurity to a dizzy height of wealth and fame, all in a few short years.

"I am astonished to find Mrs. X in this place," said a visitor to an outspoken woman who had known the celebrity from childhood. "Is it possible that she has lost her mind?"

"Lost her mind? Mina X? Nonsense!" exploded the outspoken friend. "There's nothing in the wide world the matter with Mina, except that she's done everything—twice!"

The American who has lived from Victoria to Truman, that is to say, the American who is fifty or more in 1950, is not far from Mina's condition. He has experienced pretty nearly everything at least twice, and if his stability is impaired, as compared with that of his father, the reason is not far to seek.

There is, however, one glaring omission in the list of his experiences. He has not seen his country invaded and conquered. But that this omission is any great help is doubtful; it merely means that he has not experienced the ultimate disaster, hence has no definite assurance that he can stand it. Yet he realizes, as his father never realized, that invasion and conquest are possible; so his escape thus far gives him no assurance for the future, while his experience as a spectator has taught him with horrible clarity what invasion and conquest mean.

This American is almost through. Another ten years, or fifteen at most, will see his withdrawal from effective participation in public affairs, for he will then be beyond the age of vigorous and efficient work. On the whole, this is doubtless fortunate, for the passing generation is a battered generation; even such victories as it has won have exacted a heavy price in the exhaustion of its mental and spiritual resources. The coming to the fore of new men, less scarred and twisted, less tired, ought to be a blessing to the world.

But it may involve some loss. After all, the men of fifty and more do possess one psychic asset not in possession of the younger generation. This is the experience of having lived in a world whose peace had been broken only by localized disturbances for ninety-nine years. The Crimean, the American Civil, and the Franco-Prussian wars were ferocious combats, but confined to restricted areas; the last upheaval threatening the whole of Western civilization had ended at Waterloo in 1815. A boy born in 1900 came to the age of puberty, one born in 1895 to adolescence, under conditions that have not subsisted since. They grew up in a mental and moral climate free of the killing frosts that have nipped activities of the mind and spirit since—the freezing fear of total war.

If all comprehension of what this means passes with the passing generation, the world will be the poorer. In the course of nature the time has come for the old guard to be relieved; far from being lamentable, that is right and proper and the old guard should march off briskly to the strains of a quickstep. But first it should transfer the colors to the new guard, not carry them off. Such faith, such hope, such serenity based on self-confidence as it has carried through the late campaigns are not its private property but, as Washington put it, "a standard to which the wise and honest can repair" in all generations.

To effect the transfer properly some ceremonial is in order, some ritual to inform the new guard and remind the old of what the colors mean, for to the eyes of the uninstructed the ideals of the passing generation may seem to be nothing more than bits of tattered and bloodstained silk.

One way to accomplish this is to take to heart the words of Aeschines: "Our lives have transcended the limits of humanity; we are born to serve as a theme for incredible tales to posterity."

One generation saw Philip of Macedon pass, followed by Alexander; one saw Julius pass, followed by Augustus; one saw Genghis pass, followed by Kublai. In each case the event was a double one, the work of the earlier leader being picked up and carried further by his successor, with the result that Philip, Julius and Genghis are all greater men in the eyes of posterity than any would have been without his great successor. In a similar order of succession, David passed, followed by Solomon; and the success of the religions derived from ancient Israel has made that event comparable in importance to the others. But all these were spaced centuries apart, and the generation that witnessed each has been the theme of incredible tales.

Now, our generation has seen Wilson pass, followed by Roosevelt; and Lenin pass, followed by Stalin. This is unique; so if the tale of the earlier generations is incredible, ours must be fabulous beyond all precedent.

In the nature of things it is difficult, extremely difficult, for a man to perceive anything resembling the legendary in the men and events of his own time. Storied Camelot with street-cars and asphalt paving, a Paladin in a blue serge suit, Semiramis with nylon stockings and a permanent wave—these are concepts at which imagination boggles and healthy common sense dismisses them with a snort of derision.

Yet healthy common sense is sometimes myopic. It cannot always take the long view and it frequently fails to perceive the true outline of the distant hills. Least of all can it estimate correctly the relations of things, even near-by things, things at hand. The first half of the twentieth century has been exceptionally hard on common sense. Seldom have any of its important events squared with the dicta of common sense, while the latest and one of the most startling, the development of atomic fission, is so far removed from the ordinary habits of thinking of the ordinary man that in his eyes it bears a strong resemblance to necromancy. Soon after it was revealed to the public, there was a widespread opinion that the warlocks who did it should be, if not hanged immediately, at least kept under jealous guard and debarred from any effective participation in public affairs.

The fact, therefore, that the common man of the twentieth century sees no touch of glamour in the harried life that has been his is no definite proof that the glamour isn't there. Perhaps what he needs is to take some other than the strictly common-sense view. Consider, for example, the philosophic view as expressed in Bertrand Russell's comment on modern man: "In power he is nearly as feeble as his minuteness suggests, but in contemplation he is boundless, and the equal of all that he can understand."[3]

This flat assertion that he who could understand the pageantry of the twentieth century would be equal to it is bold, so bold

[3] Bertrand Russell, *Human Knowledge*, New York: Simon and Schuster, 1949, p. 162.

*that all Russell's authority is hardly enough to justify its accept-
ance without caution; but it does justify an attempt to look at
this period in its larger outlines, for the discovery of any
semblance of a pattern in it might contribute something to better
understanding.*

2. The Voice

A VOICE and Teeth were the first signs manual in the
United States of the century that most of us erroneously
believe began as the clock struck twelve on the night of December 31, 1899.[4] The Voice was the voice of William Jennings
Bryan, the Teeth were the teeth of Theodore Roosevelt, and
both were phenomenal. Never was there such a voice before,
never such teeth. They became symbolic, they took on all sorts
of connotations, political, moral, economic, even religious, much
as the Horn of Roland and Excalibur, the sword of Arthur,
were more than merely an instrument and a weapon in the minds
of the common people of the Middle Ages.

William Jennings Bryan could speak to thirty thousand people
in the open air and make every word heard at the fringes of
the crowd without the aid of microphones and amplifiers or any
other mechanical device. He was a big man, somewhat spindle-
shanked, but with a chest like a beer keg and a mouth that could
have received a billiard ball with effortless ease. His head was

[4] Precise people say that the nineteenth century ended and the twentieth
began at midnight, December 31, 1900.

thickest through the jowls, slanting to a relatively narrow ridge at the top, but in his youth he wore a great mane of black hair that gave the casual observer a contrary impression; his head seemed to be widest at the brow, a triangle standing on its apex. Even in his last days the hair still clustered thickly above his ears, and although a pointed, bald dome loomed up through it, most people still failed to note how the power of the head was concentrated in the mouth and jaws, with a comparatively small brainpan above them.

But when Bryan spoke nobody was interested in such details. In later years his voice acquired a note of stridency, but at the height of his powers it was a superb musical instrument with never a wolf tone through all the register. Even when in volume it rose to thunder, still it caressed the ears, a thirty-two-foot open diapason, not a foghorn. This apparent ease was deceptive, of course; actually the man expended a terrific amount of energy in each of his orations, as is evidenced by the fabulous quantities of food he consumed on an active campaign without suffering any appreciable impairment of his health. A man who ate like Bryan had to expend energy at a furious rate; had he not done so, he would either have blown out every gasket in his internal mechanism, or he would have ended the tour weighing seven hundred pounds.

Yet at his most impassioned he seemed to be well within his limits, with plenty of reserve power still untouched, and this gave an extraordinary effect of mastery to his utterance. To the common man it seemed that whatever Bryan said had more behind it; at least this was so in the early days and measurably so up until 1908.

It was not the mastery of the Sultan, though, with the flash of the scimitar gleaming through it. It was the mastery of a man calmly certain of what he said, the mastery of superior knowledge to which the common man cheerfully yields when he would fight bitterly against mastery based on power. The ironical fact that Bryan actually knew less than almost any other man who figured prominently in public life at the time is beside the point. He seemed to know. The people thought he knew, and, as William A. Dunning pointed out long ago, what men think is true forms the basis on which they act, although it is not necessarily true at all.

Long years afterward it was brought out in court that Bryan didn't know that man is a mammal, or at least would not admit the fact. But as the century began, there was really no occasion for him to consider the matter. As we look back on those halcyon days it becomes apparent that there was little occasion for him to consider much of anything, because life was absurdly simple; but that is a deceptive appearance. Life was as complicated and perplexing in 1900 as it is in 1950, and if that seems incredible it is only because experience has given us the answers to some of the questions that seemed unanswerable then.

To do him justice, Bryan had the answers to some of those questions, to an astonishingly large number, in fact. His trouble was that when he had the answer he almost invariably had it by the wrong end and so could not make it fit. His knowledge was intuitive rather than empirical, which is to say, he played hunches oftener than he thought things through; but because his hunches were usually good, he has made an indelible impression upon United States history, and is today a major prophet, however he may have failed as a statesman.

Consider, as a shining example, the issue on which he first shook the country, the free coinage of silver at the ratio of sixteen to one. Modern schoolboys in the history class probably find one of the dreariest moments in the whole course that in which they confront the task of learning what was meant by "free silver" and "sixteen to one." It is a dreary task because, as a matter of fact, they didn't mean anything, being assertions that put effect

ahead of cause. One might as well seek to understand what is
meant by the assertion that "Thunder causes lightning," an
effort doomed to defeat from the start. Yet in the presidential
campaign of 1896 these slogans occupied the attention of the
country almost to the exclusion of anything else, and Bryan
employed them so effectively that he almost shattered the
Republican party a full generation ahead of its fated moment.

Obviously, then, the people who participated in that campaign thought that these expressions carried tremendous significance, and the reasons why they thought so are more interesting
than the fact. One of the reasons was that Bryan had the
answer, but had it by the wrong end. In the course of the campaign he thundered against "the Money Devil of Wall Street"
and threw bankers, brokers and industrialists into paroxysms
of wrath and fear. They accused him of being a fool, a liar, a
conscienceless demagogue, and a radical bent on subverting the
government.

The truth is, there *was* a Money Devil, but his habitat was not
Wall Street. His lair was in the colleges and universities, in the
textbooks on economics, in the minds of farmers, businessmen
and teachers, in the mind of Bryan himself. The devil of it was
that we were trying to manage an elastic economy with a rigid
currency. Every time the crops were harvested, money became
tight and borrowers had to pay through the nose; every time
business slacked off a bit, money lost value and lenders could
get little or no return. This was true because the dollar represented, not a true economic value, but a certain weight of gold;
since there was a fixed amount of gold in the world, there could
be only a certain number of dollars, no matter how much the
movement of business called for more money.

Bryan perceived the trouble plainly enough, but not the
remedy. He had the idea that the recurrent economic crises were
due to the fact that the dollar was stuck tight to the rare metal,

gold, and that it could be relieved by attaching it in part to the relatively more abundant metal, silver. He therefore proposed to enact into law the principle that the number of dollars equivalent to one ounce of gold should always be equivalent to sixteen ounces of silver.

But the trouble, of course, was not that gold had been selected as the standard. The trouble was that the currency had no elasticity and could have none as long as it was rigidly bound to any metal in limited supply. Twenty years later we turned Bryan's answer around and then it was so beautiful a fit that the currency system sustained the shock of two frightful wars with almost no trouble.[5]

So it was with Bryan's chief issue in his second campaign, that of 1900. This time it was Imperialism that Bryan opposed, and again his opposition itself was correct, but again it was badly aimed. Poor old William McKinley, the President in office, was no more imperialist than the bronze statue to which William Allen White compared him; McKinley was, indeed, so obviously the virtuous Methodist that even a country far from subtle in its judgments could see that it was preposterous to cast him for the role of Caesar or Genghis Khan. So Bryan's second campaign was less successful than his first, although he was assailing an enemy more vicious than the Money Devil.

For imperialism was on the march, all right, although not across the White House lawn. McKinley's fault was that he was unaware of it, incapable of perceiving it, certainly incapable of halting it; White would have done better to compare him, not

[5] The device was the Federal Reserve note, based, not on gold, but on economic goods actually in existence. As the goods were consumed, the notes were canceled, to be issued again when more goods were produced. Thus the currency automatically expanded and contracted as the volume of business rose and fell. This device is associated with the name of Carter Glass, the Representative who framed the bill and guided it through Congress, although he would have been the last to claim that it was his invention.

to a bronze statue, for there is a certain richness in bronze, but to a cast-iron statue, such as decorated the front yards of Canton, Ohio, in the semblance of dogs and stags, ornaments as harmless, as charmless, and as useless as the chief citizen of Canton and President of the United States.

Imperialism lurked in the minds of some young and ebullient politicians, notably the Republican candidate for Vice President in 1900, but that political imperialism was frank, aboveboard, and not very dangerous. The imperialism that made headway was the economic imperialism of men of a very different type. There was nothing stolid or inept about the elder Rockefeller, satrap of oil, Harriman of railroads, Baer of coal, Duke of tobacco, or about Morgan and his associates, the financiers. These men were imperial in every fiber and some of them, notably Duke and Morgan, even in appearance; their heads were Romanesque, reminding one of a bust of some ancient Caesar, while Rockefeller had a suggestion of lean Octavian about him.

They had all perceived the reality of economic power and had gathered it into their hands to an appalling extent. Bryan knew it, and he knew that in some instances they had achieved their ends by manipulating and perverting the power of the law, political power; so he decided that the way to halt them was to prevent the erection of a political empire. Unfortunately for his theory, political imperialism was by no means indispensable to the creation of industrial cartels, shipping agreements and banking associations. Most of the economic imperialists, indeed, had little liking for political imperialism. It imposed too many annoying responsibilities upon the imperial power.

So once more Bryan had the answer to the problem, but had it by the wrong end. He wasted his time boxing the cast-iron statue, and got nothing out of it but ruined hands; in 1908 he was unable to knock out even the obese Taft.

But all this became clear only after many years. When the

century began Bryan was the Voice that spoke the heart's desire of the common man, the ancient desire that has driven him since history began, the aspiration toward freedom from want and freedom from fear. Its latest manifestation in this country had taken the form of a movement called Populism, derived from the name of a third party, the People's party, which, although badly organized and worse led, had made formidable inroads, especially in the West and South.

At the Democratic National Convention in Chicago, in 1896, Bryan had adroitly seized the moment to stampede the Democratic party into accepting the more important demands of the Populists. He achieved it by an extraordinary oratorical effort that went down in history as "the Cross of Gold speech"[6] and that established him at once as the greatest master of the platform in American politics. But it did more. It made him also the leader of the disinherited—the discontented, the disappointed, and the mentally incompetent, too, but mainly those who had lost through no fault of their own. He knew the problems that harassed millions, and persuaded them that he knew the answers too, so for twenty years he was politically indestructible.

"It is simple," said the Voice. "Righteousness is the answer to all questions in this world of black-and-white. I know. Just leave it to me."

It is possible that this is an idiotic platform, but anyone who assumes that it is ineffective simply has not studied the political history of the American people, or, for that matter, the history of any other government in which the masses of the people participate. It is one of the greatest of platforms, and for an opposition leader, who never has to make its words good, it is probably the greatest without qualification.

---

[6] His peroration, after describing the woes that would be inflicted upon the poor by adherence to the gold standard, went, "You shall not press down upon the brow of labor this crown of thorns, you shall not crucify mankind upon a cross of gold."

3. The Teeth

BUT there is another nearly as good and in some circumstances better. Pugnacity is a human trait, too. The politician who can sing mellifluously of freedom from want and freedom from fear is able to attract a great following; but so is the one who sings not at all, but dances and yells, "Eat 'em raw! Eat 'em alive!" The fact that his rage may be synthetic does not necessarily matter, provided it is impressive.

Theodore Roosevelt died in 1919, and after thirty years it is evident that not his career only but his whole public character was as carefully fabricated as any in our national history. This is by no means an assertion that it was phony, unless one is prepared to charge Lawrence Olivier with fraud because in *Henry V* he persuades the audience momentarily that he really is a medieval knight, or Maurice Evans because on one evening he is the very essence of a melancholy Dane and on another a romantic Italian, whereas one knows that he is actually a twentieth-century Englishman all the time.

Theodore Roosevelt is impressive evidence to support the theory that statecraft is not a science, but a branch of the art of dramaturgy. He was an actor of genius, but his first audience was himself. He put on his show primarily to satisfy Theodore Roosevelt, and the fact that it also satisfied millions of others was no more than corroborative testimony that it was good. He despised what he was—weak, lapped in luxury, gently bred—so he deliberately set out to be what he was not, strong, hardy, rough. Of course he couldn't do it, and the effort killed him at sixty-one; but he put up a performance so magnificent that he has come down in history as the Rough Rider, and his contemporaries never doubted that he was the toughest of the tough. Indeed, as far as the history of his own times is concerned, he was just that, for the country responded to the impression he made upon it; and now that he has become as a tale that is told, the impression is the man.

As a child he was afflicted with asthma and to fight it undertook a physical regimen that would stagger a modern doctor. Why it didn't kill him outright is beyond the power of medical science to determine; but it didn't, and maintained persistently through many years it gave him a frame so sturdy that, although he was rather below medium height, he appeared to be larger. His head was almost spherical. He wore eyeglasses and a piratical mustache; but what fascinated the country was his wide, orator's mouth, equipped with teeth notable for their size and whiteness; when he grinned, as he did frequently, the dental display was almost as startling as it is when a crocodile opens his mouth. When he snarled, as he also did frequently, the effect was not merely startling, but formidable.

Roosevelt came bouncing onto the political stage much in the manner of that Chocolate Soldier that Shaw insists was never his. The brush with Spain in 1898 looks like a comic-opera war to a generation that has seen the real thing twice, but to a nation that had not fought for thirty-three years it was prodigious. In the action at San Juan Hill Roosevelt, as a cavalry colonel, displayed irreproachable physical courage, however dubiously one may regard his tactical dispositions; so to a country that definitely needed a hero, he was satisfactory

Even at the time there were some who accepted him with tongue in cheek. When his memoirs of the campaign were published, F. P. Dunne's fictional saloon-keeper, Mr. Dooley, remarked that the volume should have been entitled, *Alone in Cubia*, but in the main the country hailed him with wild acclaim. After thirty-three years the Civil War heroes were for the most part dead, and those surviving were pretty badly shopworn; there was little disposition to examine too closely a fresh and shiny one.

Nor were the voters' expectations disappointed, for Roosevelt put on the grandest show staged by any President since Andrew Jackson. From the histrionic standpoint, indeed, he was greater than Jackson, for in keeping the country stirred he had no such outside assistance as was furnished Jackson by Nullification, the Bank of the United States and the French crisis. Roosevelt's crises he usually cooked up for himself. He was a genius with the wind machine and blank cartridges; no other President has been able to raise such a terrific clamor over the trivial, not even Van Buren when he bought gold spoons for the White House, or Truman when he put a back porch on it.

The country was enjoying a moment of rare serenity when an assassin's bullet struck down McKinley and made Roosevelt President. The currency stringency that furnished Bryan his motive power in 1896 had been relieved by the discovery of considerable deposits of gold in the Yukon Valley and tremendous ones in South Africa. The international tensions that were building up to the explosion of 1914 were as yet imperceptible to the average American. Jobs were plentiful and wages on the rise. There was a collision in the Orient between Japan and Russia, but Roosevelt's only participation in that was as a peacemaker (which, incidentally, won him the Nobel Prize). He started the Panama Canal, which was an accomplishment of real size, even if his manner of doing it did store up trouble for the next twenty-five years.

But in general real frets and fevers were singularly lacking in the last fifteen years of the *Pax Britannica*, so the President proceeded to stir up a series of manufactured ones, and they were magnificent. He threw the country into a dither by calling a celebrated naturalist "a nature-faker," and when some of the savant's colleagues rose to his defense, he dumped the whole group into an "Ananias Club." He discharged a terrific oration against the theory of birth control, dubbing it "race suicide." When a rash young editorial writer on the New York *World* called him a liar, he launched a criminal prosecution—not an ordinary libel suit—against old Joe Pulitzer, the publisher, who happened to be on his yacht at the time, and harried that ancient up and down the world for months. He hurled firecrackers into cathedrals, chapter-houses, love-nests, and seances, into any place where a hushed and somnolent atmosphere prevailed, and while he did little material damage, he provoked such a bedlam of shrieks and curses as has rarely been heard in this land—and the country loved it.

He rose to his most tremendous climax—and, incidentally, brought upon himself his most terrific beating—when, without consultation with any adviser, he ordered the motto "In God We Trust" removed from the coins. A pious Congress, shocked into momentary forgetfulness of partisanship, rose in a majestic mingling of Democrats and Republicans to sweep this dastardly deed into limbo. No such smashing defeat was inflicted on any other President until, a generation later, the second Roosevelt tried to change the date of Thanksgiving.

One reason why Roosevelt was so extraordinarily effective was the fact that his was the first lively and inquisitive mind that had been in the White House since the Civil War. Johnson, Grant, Hayes, Garfield, Arthur, Cleveland, Harrison and Mc-Kinley were not all nonentities, and Cleveland remains a monumental figure; but it cannot be denied that they were a stodgy crew. As far as the arts, the sciences and letters were concerned, the White House had been for many years a mausoleum of dead ideas, but Roosevelt made it a center of lively conversation. If a man of any eminence, whether a pugilist, a poet, a broncobuster, or a philosopher, showed up in Washington, he was entertained at the White House, and the master of the house could usually ask the visitor intelligent questions. So Roosevelt acquired a following of such diverse elements as never was seen before. He was idolized by cowpunchers and by scholars of international fame, and his reputation for being interested in every type of man did much to reduce the force of the shock when he breached the color line by entertaining an eminent Negro, Dr. Booker T. Washington.

All this went to build up the legend of the wild man, the iconoclast, the scorner of all taboos, the uproarious character spoiling for a fight, the toughie who would eat 'em raw, eat 'em alive. As a matter of fact, he was among the most conservative of Presidents, a stout upholder, as he said himself, of "the old moralities," and an equally stout upholder, although he did not say so, of the old privileges. He called the privileged "malefactors of great wealth," but he did little to deprive them of their wealth, or to discourage their malefactions. He made noisy assaults on the trusts, but when the dust settled it usually appeared that the trusts were undamaged. He was known as the trust-buster but, as has been frequently pointed out since, the only one he busted finally and irrevocably, the Northern Securities Company, was probably the only one that truly operated in the public interest, the only good trust in the group.

But he was the perfect foil for Bryan, the ideal man of action as Bryan was the ideal philosopher for the time. For it was a time not much disposed toward real action or real philosophy. A voice and a set of teeth suited it perfectly, and it had both.

With the passage of time all this has become clear to the rising generation and with it has come a disposition to assume that because the philosophy of the first decade of the century was shallow and its ideal of action adolescent, therefore it was essentially fraudulent and there was no health in it. But the assumption is rash. Ignorance and adolescence are conditions, not maladies; experience usually corrects one and time always corrects the other; neither has anything to do with health.

The average American of fifty years ago had no acquaintance whatever with the political and social problems of the Armenians and the Burmese. He was unaware of the existence of Yalta and Tehran—if he had seen the latter name in Maury's *Manual of Geography* when he was a schoolboy, he spelled it "Teheran." If he encountered the word "Balts" in his reading he would probably have taken it to mean a variety of fish related to smelts. The Balkan Question did impinge slightly upon his consciousness; it was a matter of disposing of the Sick Man of Europe, the Unspeakable Turk, but the American felt not the slightest responsibility for settling it.

But if his ignorance of Europe and Asia was startling, he had certain information about this country that seems to have slipped from the grasp of the modern generation. He was keenly aware that the democratic system of government had never been perfected in the United States. He knew that it had been hammered into a tolerable form of government only by a century and a quarter of incessant trial and error, made possible by the free interplay of ideas; and he believed that continuance of the battle of ideas was essential to further improvement.

He had a firm grasp of the concept of moral order. He doubted the existence of absolute evil no more than he doubted the existence of gravitation, and confrontation with certain apparent exceptions to both did not shake his faith in the principle. In his opinion, crime did not pay, and the fact that an occasional Senator got into that august body by stealing a railroad and purchasing his seat with the proceeds was not enough to disprove the theory. He understood the statistical principle—if four thieves out of five were punished severely, then the generalization that theft did not pay was sound, regardless of the successful twenty per cent.

But the most spectacular of his attributes was a superb freedom from fear in the international realm. He had never a doubt that the United States was capable of whipping any military force that could be brought against it, therefore he saw no reason for deviating a hairbreadth from what the United States considered right and just in international dealings. For this he has been ridiculed unmercifully within the last few years. In a way, it was absurd. The American of 1900 had no real grounds for any such belief, because the collision with Spain had proved nothing; the Spanish empire of that date was so rotten within that it fell at a touch.

The only thing to be said for his belief is that it happened to be true. Twice since that date formidable coalitions have hurled against us all the military power that could be assembled, and the net result has been the destruction of five great empires, German, Austrian, Russian, Turkish and Japanese. But after the belief had been tested by experiment twice and proved to be sound, a new generation rejected it and as the century came to the halfway mark Americans were among the most nervous, apprehensive peoples in the world. Now which is the greater absurdity—to believe what has not been proved, or to disbelieve what has been proved by the most rigorous possible test, and that twice in one generation?

At the turn of the century it was the belief of the common man in the United States that by maintaining the widest freedom of thought and freedom of speech he had worked out a system of government that was definitely good, and capable of great improvement through the same processes; that he had worked it out in a moral universe subject to moral forces as orderly in their operation as the forces that control the movement of the planets, the errata observable in both being negligible and probably due to errors in calculation anyhow; and that he was undoubtedly strong enough to proceed along the path that had brought him thus far.

This was, if true, a considerable body of wisdom. If true, this is important enough to counterbalance many failings, perhaps to outweigh even a somewhat ignorant philosophy and a somewhat juvenile course of action. If true, the loss of this wisdom by a subsequent generation would be a material loss, to be prevented if possible.

Then where is the proof that it was false? Since 1900 it has been denied with violence by many nations, some of them among the most powerful in the world. They have denied it by philosophy, by law, and by the sword. They have staked their very existence on the denial, and where are they now? With a single exception they all lie in the Potter's Field of dead empires. The one survivor exists because in a moment of crisis it temporarily suppressed its denial and struck hands with us and with those who believe as we do.

Those who have risen up against us within the last fifty years have not disproved the faith of 1900. The calamitous end of our foes has tended, on the contrary, to prove it. But this, of course, does not end the matter, for those who march against us are rarely those most to be feared. Micah remarked twenty-five centuries ago that "a man's enemies are the men of his own house." Fathers of the Church may cry, *"Credo quia impossible,"* but to ordinary, commonplace people what is impossible is just not true; and through this gap in our defenses sneaks in the enemy who might destroy the faith that emperors and dictators could not shake.

It takes a brave man to be a freeman. This austere truth sets a condition upon all our theorizing. What is the One True Faith to a man of courage may be so utterly beyond the reach of the coward that to him it is as false as stairs of sand. For this reason the faith of 1900, although it was tried and tested in the furnace heats of an incandescent century, is not necessarily true of the men of 1950; for its truth can be proved only by those with the courage to try it, and the existence of such courage is itself no more than a hypothesis.

Still, it is at least a working hypothesis, or there would be no purpose to be served by this book.

4. *Unidentified Thought*

DURING the first decade of the century forces were gathering under the surface that were to blow the world of 1900 out of existence, but they were hidden from the average American. In 1950 students of public affairs ask with a kind of desperation, How could we have been so blind?

The answer is, Why not? What good would it have done us to see? There was absolutely nothing we could have done about it had we been gifted with the prophetic vision of Cassandra, for we had no authority, political, moral, or intellectual. The trouble was brewing on the Continent of Europe, and on that Continent the American as a political entity was regarded then not as a civilized man but as a half-witted child.

Of course there were Europeans who did not fall into this error, but they comprised a small group of exceptionally well-informed people of exceptionally good judgment. They were not numerous enough nor influential enough to direct the course of events. Over the whole Continent the weight of opinion inclined to the view that the American was not to be taken seriously except as a technician. It was widely known that we produced superb mechanics, probably the best in the world except the Germans, but as for political ideas, it was preposterous to suppose that Americans had any.

This was a serious mistake—as the event proved, a fatal one—on the part of Europe, but it was perfectly natural, for men in the mass never consider anything that is not thrust upon their attention, and America had not intruded into European affairs to an appreciable extent. Our isolation was more than geographical; it was an isolation of mind and purpose, as well as habitation. Fate had set the former British colonies in North America a specific problem in human relations with which they had been struggling since 1776 with no more than a qualified success; and the struggle had absorbed their energies and their attention almost to the exclusion of any effective interest in what the rest of the world was doing.

In the British Isles there was a somewhat better understanding of the situation on this side of the Atlantic, partly because British interest had twice been stung by armed collision with the American idea, but mainly because the British themselves were seeking, by a different approach, a solution of the same problem —that of liberty under law. Yet even in Britain the approach was different, and the British attitude was one of tolerant interest rather than serious and intense study.

Even when the problem was stated a few years later in plain and simple terms it did not register effectively. When an American statesman announced as the central purpose of all his work "to release the generous energies of our people," the phrase was taken for a bit of political rhetoric. As a matter of fact, it was parochial, in that the reference was to "our" people, which definitely did not include Europeans. Yet to release the "generous"

energies of Americans without at the same time releasing un-
generous and malign energies had been the central problem of
government since the foundation of the Republic.

Our success had been none too complete. For the first five
years we had tried the system of loose alliance, which failed
because it bottled up energy instead of releasing it. Then, under
the Articles, we had tried the system of confederation, which
proved to be little, if any, better. Finally we had turned to a
Federal Republic which in the course of time had developed—
or degenerated, if you prefer—into straight nationalism.

In the matter of releasing energies this had proved wildly
successful, and some of them were indubitably generous, but a
great many were not. At times it appeared that we had released
half the devils in the Calvinistic hell, and the side of the angels
was frequently hard pressed. Especially in the generation following the great internal convulsion of the Civil War it seemed
for a time that the "association powerful, wise, and happy" that
Jefferson said we had established was destined to end as a greasy
plutocracy, stifling in its own fat.

If we had escaped that fate, we had not escaped it far enough
to impress the world with our success; nor were our own people
by any means assured that we had escaped it finally. The more
blatant rapacities of the last third of the nineteenth century had
been suppressed, but plenty remained. If Europe continued po-
litely skeptical, it is no cause for wonder.

The chief barrier to understanding, however, was the simple
fact that Americans and Europeans were thinking of government
in different terms and when people think in different terms,
neither side is likely to believe that the other is thinking at all.
Jefferson's concept that talent, including the capacity to rule,
while it is always and everywhere scarce, is diffused in a fairly
even proportion through all classes of society, was certainly not
unknown to European philosophers and statesmen. Plato had

preached it and had insisted that the chief task of government is to discover and develop this talent.

Jefferson, scornful of Plato as he was, nevertheless followed him up to the last verb. He would have said that the task of government is to "release" rather than "develop" talent. His scheme of public education, with its careful screening at each successive level, shows his conviction that the natural buoyancy of talent will inevitably bring it to the top in the absence of artificial restrictions; and his idea of democracy was simply the removal of such restrictions.

This may seem to be a trivial and superficial difference, but in truth it plunges to the very center of things. The Russian Communists go right along with Jefferson to this point; but they have no confidence in the adequacy of mere release of the brains and character to be found in the masses. The talented proletarian is not merely to be educated in the sense of being taught how to exercise and strengthen his mental powers; he is to be indoctrinated, carefully, constantly, and by any means that may prove to be effective. It is not enough for him to think; he must think along authorized lines. This is the point at which Communism surrenders to the worst form of tyranny, "tyranny over the mind of man," and what it regards as democracy is instantly transformed into the very antithesis of what Jefferson believed in.

But Communism did not originate this idea of the necessity of directing the thinking of the common people. It permeated the political philosophy of all Europe—attenuated in France, and the Low Countries, even more so in Great Britain, but strong through the rest of the Continent. It lay at the very basis of the average man's political belief; so the fact that the Americans did not accept it at all deprived the European of any fixed point of reference by which he could measure American political thought. From that it was easy to assume that it was not, properly speaking, thought at all. Oh, there had been an occasional Crèvecourt or Bryce to discover and proclaim something far from nebulous in this system, but their voices were heard only by a relatively small circle of the intellectually alert, not by the European masses.

The truth is that the incessant clash of conflicting ideas by means of which American democratic doctrine was slowly being framed was largely ignored by Europeans as merely the gabble of contentious politicians, disputing points of no significance. For what content could there be in a so-called political philosophy which ignored the basis of all political philosophy, namely, indoctrination?

Europe up to 1914 was as little interested in our disputations as the average American is today in the differences between the Zhdanov school of thought and the Malenkov school in Russia. Is it conceivable that we, in our turn, may now be missing a similar bet?

Doubtless the men of 1900 to 1914 in the United States were concerned too exclusively with American affairs, and would have been well advised to study the undersurface European forces that were surging up to catastrophe; but it is hard to believe that they could have done anything effective toward controlling those forces, no matter how much they studied them. Europe was too contemptuous of American political ability to give weight to our opinion.

Why, indeed, should Europe, considering its prevailing mode of thought, have been impressed? We had erected a state of enormous size and unprecedented wealth, it is true; but as far as Europe could see it was a state without purpose, without direction, other than the multiplication of material comforts and luxuries. Not since the Gettysburg Address had there been a statement of American ideals clear enough to catch the attention of any mind not already fully conversant with those ideals; and even "government of the people, by the people, for the people" may have seemed rather aimless to a mind that had never been crossed by Jefferson's belief that such a government if perfected would inevitably be productive of everything desirable. To the European it meant simply the dictatorship of the proletariat, which filled him with a horror that the Russian experiment has served only to deepen and intensify. If it be assumed that the common people have no generous energies except such as may be instilled by an élite, then a program to release them becomes mere empty verbiage, unworthy of the attention of an intelligent man.

In any event, the American of 1900 to 1914 went about his lawful occasions ignoring, and in most cases ignorant of, the subterranean rumblings in Europe. This made him, in important respects, a different man from the American of 1950, who is alert to a tremor in Azerbaijan and definitely alarmed if there is a political explosion in Bangkok or Nairobi. This does not mean, of course, that he was a better man, or a wiser man, or a happier man, merely that he was different in that his nerves were unshaken. He could turn upon the problems that were his immediate concern a clearer and a steadier eye; so while his opinions on international affairs are worthless today, it is by no means so certain that his ideas regarding domestic affairs, especially the central problem of the maintenance and development of democracy, are equally obsolete. After all, he had been able to concentrate on that to an extent impossible to the next generation, and it is imaginable that he understood it better than we understand it now.

One of his attitudes, at least, is worth the careful attention of his successors; this was his violent antipathy to what he was accustomed to call Invisible Government. To his mind it meant the influence exercised by property interests that never came out into the open, but he was very certain that the poisonous element in that control was its secrecy. He would have been just as violently opposed to any other kind of invisible government. Such remnants of his generation as still participate in public affairs are opposed to it, whether the invisible influence is wielded by property interests, or religious interests, or racial interests, or caste interests, particularly the military caste.

Throughout the last quarter of the nineteenth century and the first decade of the twentieth the battle in the field of public affairs had been largely a struggle against secrecy. It was accompanied, of course, by the usual swarm of small and dirty clashes among individual politicians trying to snatch personal power from each other, and these frequently served to confuse the larger issue. But among the handful of leaders who sometimes put statecraft above politics the endeavor to make sure that power should rest in responsible hands monopolized the larger share of public attention.

Bryan's anti-imperialism campaign in 1900 is a case in point. Bryan was above all else pietistic. It is inconceivable that he was opposed to any program designed to bring the "benefits" of Evangelical Protestantism and popular self-government to the Filipinos. What he feared was that American occupation of the Islands would bring them under the control, not of sound Presbyterians and deserving Democrats, but of the Invisible Government, dominated by financial interests that never came to view and therefore could not be held accountable.

Nor was he altogether wrong, as the event proved. The American occupation was characterized by a forty years' battle to prevent the Islands from being taken over for exploitation by American commercial interests, notably sugar, tobacco and soap, none of which had any public representative among the governing officials. There were times when that battle was almost lost, nor is it possible to assert with confidence that it ever was completely won.

But while this profound distrust of the unidentified permeated the political thinking of the American people, the effort to express it clearly, to give it point and direction, had been confused, uncertain, badly organized. There had been an effort in the eighties by certain honest, elegant, but pretty ineffective gentlemen who constituted the Mugwump movement. They did prevent the election of Blaine, undoubtedly an agent of Invisible Government, but the unimaginative Cleveland was not the man to give sharpness and permanence to the movement. There had been efforts by extremists in the Socialist party and in the Populist party; but while some of their leaders, for instance, Debs, Weaver and Bryan, were imaginative enough, they were without exception woefully bad thinkers. There was what appeared to be an effort led by the brilliant Theodore Roosevelt, but as time passed it became evident that despite the noise not much was being done to unhorse the Cossacks of the invisible power.

Then came Wilson.

5. The Player Who Pulled a Gun

WHAT the man Thomas Woodrow Wilson actually was, that is, how he appeared in the sight of God, has been the subject of acrimonious debate for forty years, and doubtless will continue to be disputed throughout the predictable future. We don't know, we can't know, we never shall know short of Judgment Day, and the debate about it is as purely a form of intellectual gymnastics as is the invention of new varieties of non-Euclidean geometry.

This is not to disparage the effort, which has engaged and no doubt will continue to engage some of the century's most brilliant minds. It is designed merely to emphasize the fact that, as far as this discussion is concerned, it makes not the slightest difference what he was; all that counts here is what he appeared to be in the sight of common, ordinary American citizens. For it was to what he seemed that they responded, and it was their response that affected profoundly their own destiny and that of the world.

He came upon the stage of national affairs as a triple novelty, in that he was a Democrat, an intellectual, and a thinker. Let no one assume that the second and third terms were repetitious, in the eyes of the average man. In 1910, when most Americans first heard of Woodrow Wilson, the country swarmed with intellectuals who, in the estimation of the ordinary citizen, had never had a thought in their lives, but who only thought they thought. Wilson was not one of that type; when he expressed a thought you could understand it, or at least part of it, with no effort. In fact, you couldn't help understanding part of what he said, and it opened new vistas to most of us.

He was a Democrat who seemed to know the trick of getting elected. In 1912 it had been exactly twenty years since a Democrat had exhibited that facility on the national stage, and this enormously stimulated the curiosity about him.

Then he had been a college president, therefore he was assumed to be formidable. Here was a point that the politicians somehow missed. Democratic leaders were fearful that Wilson's austere bearing might affect the voters adversely; they overlooked the fact that it was precisely what the average man expected in a former college president. To faculty, trustees, and presidents of alumni associations a college president may be, like Burns' field mouse, a "wee, sleekit, cow'rin', tim'rous beastie," but to the innocent commonalty who cast the votes he is an awesome figure, a very Moses descending from the Mount bearing the Tables of the Law. If he were anything other than grave, dignified, even a bit acidulous, the average man would suspect him of being a fraud. Therefore to the crowds Wilson's somewhat granitic front was no more than evidence that he really had been a college president, and probably a good one. Instead of being affronted, the crowds accepted it as quite in order and proceeded to the consideration of other matters.

There was much to consider. Wilson brought to the discussion of public affairs a new and fascinating technique, the best that the country had seen since Lincoln's—which is to say, the best that the country of 1912 had ever seen, for those who had known Lincoln were almost all dead or in retirement forty-seven years after Lincoln's death. It was the trick of speaking in language of great simplicity and clarity, yet seriously.

Simple, clear and serious English is startlingly effective anywhere at any time; but in the year 1912 in the United States of America it was doubly effective, because it had not been heard from the White House in many years. For sheer dustiness of their English style nine of the ten gentlemen who followed Lincoln would be hard to match anywhere; while the one exception, Theodore Roosevelt, had never been taken quite seriously by a large segment of the country, and after the Bull Moose campaign, in which he led a revolt against his own party, he was not taken seriously by the majority.

This is not to be construed as an assertion that the nine were nonentities. On the contrary, all were men of some force of character, and at least two, Cleveland and Taft, were men of exceptional strength and ability. But none wrote well, and Cleveland, ablest of them all, had developed a style so fabulously bad that one of his phrases became immortal—"after twenty years

of almost innocuous desuetude these laws are brought forth."
Even Theodore Roosevelt flashed and gleamed in campaign
speeches and impromptu deliverances rather than in his more
important state papers, which were usually pretty dull.

To a man born as late as 1912 it is almost impossible to convey
any idea of the attitude of the country toward the White House
when Wilson became President, but he may gain some hint of it
if he will stop to consider that it was regarded as a sensational
break with the past when Wilson announced his determination
to be not merely the President, but the leader of the Democratic
party, as well. Ever since Andrew Johnson the President had
been regarded as a man above party, at least in theory; and as
a matter of practice he was, for at least four-fifths of the time, a
man below party. Cleveland and Theodore Roosevelt alone had
been dominant; the others were dominated.

The White House was not regarded as a source of ideas, certainly not of ideas relating to the structure of the government.
To the modern generation, this may be downright incredible,
but it is the fact. All of Theodore Roosevelt's unconventional
notions had to do with matters that could not by any possibility
lead to an appreciable modification of our system; even his prosecution of Joseph Pulitzer had a precedent in the cases brought
under the Alien and Sedition Laws of John Adams' time. The
White House was immensely respected by the average man, but
it was fusty, rusty, dusty, and he usually supposed that it must
always be so.

True enough, the events of the summer of 1912 had forecast
a change of attitude. There had been more portentous summers,
no doubt—that of 1860, for example—but for a breath-taking,
dazzling, super-colossal political circus its like had never been
seen before. It began in Chicago with the Republican National
Convention, where William H. Taft, one of the Presidents
below party, had been renominated over the violent objection of

Theodore Roosevelt, one of the contestants for real leadership of the Republicans. The fight, as a matter of fact, was not between Roosevelt and Taft; it was between Roosevelt and the group of conservative leaders who were backing Taft and who had pretty well controlled his administration. The conservatives won, but Roosevelt and his friends were so infuriated that it was plain that they would not support the ticket.

Then the scene shifted to Baltimore, where the Democratic National Convention met a week later. A precisely similar battle was raging in that party. Half a dozen candidates were in the field, but the real fight was between the conservative and liberal groups, each led by a man who was not himself a candidate, Charles F. Murphy, leader of Tammany Hall, in New York, and William J. Bryan, thrice-defeated nominee and recognized leader of the liberals.

It had been hot in Chicago that June, but the heat of the sun had been far more than matched by the heat of the convention. It was hotter in Baltimore, but again the weather proved to be insignificant by comparison with the emotional temperature generated in the Fifth Regiment Armory, where the sessions were held.

Bryan, as a member of the Nebraska delegation, had come to the convention pledged to the candidacy of the Speaker of the House of Representatives (the Democrats had captured Congress in 1910, so the Speaker was a Democrat), who had been christened James Beauchamp Clark, but early in life had shortened his given name to Champ. He was regarded as something of a liberal, but first of all as a sound party man, representing the regular organization of Missouri, and the more ardent liberals, especially in the East, preferred Woodrow Wilson, formerly President of Princeton University, but in 1910, to the general astonishment, elected Governor of New Jersey.

Bryan, however, stuck to his commitment for fourteen ballots.

But then it became apparent that Murphy was going to swing his votes to Clark, whereupon Bryan rose and, in one of the most remarkable speeches in the history of American politics, declared that any so-called liberal who would make a deal with Tammany was not worthy of the support of real liberals, and would not get his support. He switched to Wilson.

The remarkable quality of Bryan's Baltimore speech was not in what he said, but in the defiance of the accepted rules of politics that it embodied. The rules of the game required Bryan to continue his support of Clark. Clark's record as a liberal was at least passably good, and his record as a party man was irreproachable. Bryan was a liberal and had been three times the nominee of the party which, according to the rules, committed him to respect for good party men. Clark was from Missouri and Bryan was a Westerner, while the territory beyond the Mississippi had never had a President. Clark had always supported Bryan, while Wilson had once said that Bryan ought to be knocked into a cocked hat for the good of the country. Clark was unquestionably the favorite of Nebraska Democrats and the delegation had been pledged to him without any question of fraud. There was, in fact, nothing against Clark except widespread doubts as to the sincerity of his liberalism, doubts that solidified into certainty when it became apparent that his managers had made a deal with Tammany. But the rules of the game made no provision for that.

So when Bryan at Baltimore heaved the rules overboard and deserted his own man merely because he no longer believed in him, the shock was perfectly genuine. There were two thousand delegates and alternates in the hall and eight or ten thousand spectators. Among them were many whose political careers were involved, and many more whose emotions were involved. The sentiments of the Clark people were precisely those of a poker player who has just filled a royal straight flush and looks up to find that his opponent has pulled a gun. The pandemonium that exploded when it became clear what Bryan was going to say—they didn't wait for him to complete his announcement—is indescribable. Hard-bitten, veteran reporters at the press table between the speaker and the crowd slid low in their chairs and prepared to dive under the table, fast, when the rush started:[7] for there was murder in the air. But Bryan, complete with alpaca coat and palm-leaf fan, simply faced the mob, ponderous, immovable, as little shaken as the granite walls of the armory itself, until some sort of order was restored and he could finish what he had determined to say.

At that moment the American party system began to come of age. From that moment it was no longer entirely a game of make-believe, for an element of deadly seriousness had entered it which has remained and has tended to spread. Of course, there are still avid players who see nothing in it but a game. There is still plenty of dealing and dickering. Gentlemen still make private agreements among themselves, and candidates sometimes are still nominated in a smoke-filled hotel room at two o'clock in the morning. But it cannot be done with the old assurance. Since Bryan dragged reality into the business that day in Baltimore, the game has been played with the uneasy knowledge that a six-shooter beats any hand in the deck and that somebody may pull one—either to overturn the table, as the Ku Klux did in the Democratic convention of 1924, or to take the pot, as Willkie did in the Republican convention of 1940.

After the Bryan speech Clark was finished. He died game. The convention dragged on through sixty-nine ballots, but from Charlie Murphy's standpoint it was a losing fight, for Bryan's

[7] One of them was John W. Owens who, twenty years later when he had become editor-in-chief of the Baltimore *Sun*, used to describe that moment as the tensest in a career that had carried him into many hot spots in half the countries of the world.

torpedo had sprung every plate in the conservative ship and it was only a matter of time until it went down.

Nor was there much doubt about the election. The disgruntled Roosevelt organized a new party, called "Progressive,"[8] which actually won more popular votes than were given to Taft, the Regular Republican; but there is good reason to believe that most of the Roosevelt votes were drawn from Wilson, rather than from Taft. Had there been no Progressive party in the race, Wilson's electoral majority might have been even larger.

But the campaign was half over before Americans in general began to realize that they had not in fact nominated Bryan's man. The election itself was over before some of them realized that Bryan was Wilson's man. But before the President-elect moved into the White House the whole country knew it, and some even hoped that Bryan, his usefulness ended, would be tossed aside. That was, however, too extreme, even for a precedent-breaking President. Bryan received his due recognition. Not only was he appointed Secretary of State, but he was able to place the campaign director of publicity and his long-time supporter, Josephus Daniels, in the post of Secretary of the Navy. Nevertheless, it was the Wilson Administration, and no one was in any doubt about it.

[8] Strictly an official name, hardly heard during the campaign or since. Shortly after the convention the candidate, still the darling of the newspaper reporters, in reply to a question as to how he felt, answered, "Strong as a bull moose," and from that moment his movement became the Bull Moose party in popular parlance. Relatively few Americans knew it had any other name.

6. Enter the Twentieth Century

YET the magnitude of what had happened was unsuspected by the average American even on March 4, 1913. It is easy to believe that it was unsuspected not only by the people, but also by the man who took the oath of office that day. Changes he certainly intended to bring about, but they were comprised in a series of relatively mild reforms, which he proceeded to urge upon a Congress thoroughly in sympathy with the program. The Wilsonian idea, in the beginning, was nothing more than an intelligent adaptation of existing institutions to modern conditions. Basically, it was a conservative program, because its aim was the conservation of the existing system by strengthening it against new shocks; it most certainly did not envisage reconstruction of American political philosophy from the ground up.

But the twentieth century entered the White House with Woodrow Wilson, the grim, the bloody, the humorless century, in which no nation could survive with a small boy at its helm, and in which one, Germany, was to be twice destroyed for suffering puerility to exercise authority.

The man Wilson puzzled the intellectuals among his contemporaries. Only the common people understood him. The intellectuals endeavored to follow the sinuosities of an alert and vigorous intelligence at grips with a Protean world situation that assumed new shapes and new forms with bewildering speed. Few of the intellectuals could think as fast as Wilson under any circumstances; none could follow his thought successfully without the advantage of his information. No man in the country, perhaps none in the world, has a tenth of the precise and accurate information that is laid before the President of the United States every day. The Secretary of Agriculture may be better informed about crops, the Secretary of Commerce about industry, the Secretary of the Treasury about finance, the Secretary of State about foreign relations; but they all lay the gist of their information before the President, who alone sees the picture as a whole. Then if the President is highly intelligent to begin with, and trained to think fast, as a university president must be, it is hopeless for anyone else to try to keep pace with his mental processes.

The intellectuals could not do it, and from the early days many of them were puzzled, suspicious and angry. But the common man felt no obligation to try to keep up, and being at ease he perceived what escaped the observation of the highly educated, to wit, that whatever else this man might be he was unquestionably adult. He had faults, and serious ones, but they were the faults of a grown man, not those of an adolescent or a perpetual sophomore.

Wilson was not playing a game. Wilson did not regard statecraft as primarily a matter of scoring a point for our side while preventing the opposition from scoring a point for theirs. He would have heard with Olympian scorn the ineffable remark of one of his successors, "The business of America is business," but in a certain sense he acted on that principle; at least he was fully convinced that the business of a party leader is business, not play-acting.

The program of legislation driven through Congress in the first two years of the Wilson administration stands unrivaled to this day in the annals of American lawmaking. Its volume was astonishing, but still more astonishing is the fact that not one important item in the list was ever repealed. Much of it was

extended later, and part of it had to be suspended when all civilian activities were held up by the necessities of war, but none
of it had to be undone.

Far more sensational things were done during the famous
Hundred Days that inaugurated the New Deal, but many of
them were done so badly, in the haste and clamor of the time,
that they soon had to be done over again. The Wilson legislation stood, and by the time he left office was so thoroughly embedded in American tradition that the question of repealing it
was not seriously considered.

Fairly typical of the whole program was the creation of the
Federal Reserve System. It illustrates both the Wilsonian approach and the response of the country more clearly than they
are illustrated by any other legislation of the period. The Secretary of the Treasury was William G. McAdoo, a financier; the
ablest Congressional authority on banking and currency laws was
Carter Glass, a Representative from Virginia. Both were essentially conservative, but both were intelligent. Taking the information supplied by McAdoo's experts and drawing on his own
knowledge of politics, Glass wrote and rammed through Congress an act that transferred ultimate control of the monetary
system from private bankers to the government. Viewed in the
perspective of more than thirty-five years it was plainly the sensible thing to do, indeed, the inevitable thing; yet the anguished
screams of bankers resounded from end to end of the Republic
and persuaded timid souls that full-grown Socialism was just
around the corner.

The same attitude was taken toward the setting up of Land
Banks for the benefit of agriculture, toward all the labor legislation, although it was in fact very mild by comparison with
modern labor laws, and even to the strengthening of the anti-
trust laws.

Yet in fairness to the bankers it should be pointed out that there was in all this legislation, and conspicuously in the Federal Reserve Bank Act, a principle diametrically opposed to the tendency of American government since Andrew Jackson's day. This was its challenge to the spirit of *laissez faire*.

Disregarding Lincoln, who was driven by a military crisis along many paths he would not have followed voluntarily, Jackson was the last President who had regarded government as an instrument to be used by the people to promote the general welfare. Only one repudiated that idea flatly, and Theodore Roosevelt gave it some lip service; but since Jackson no President had applied it boldly and vigorously.

It is an ironical circumstance that the one President who repudiated it was the last Democratic President before Wilson, Grover Cleveland. With characteristic boldness, he put into words the principle on which all the others acted without committing themselves publicly. Cleveland said:

The lessons of paternalism ought to be unlearned and the better lesson taught that while the people should patriotically and cheerfully support their Government, its functions do not include the support of the people.[9]

Cleveland not only preached this doctrine, but in the crisis of 1893 applied it with such rigor that at the next election he was thrown out of control and his party adopted Bryan as its leader. But the lesson was ineffective because the astute political general, Mark Hanna, doubly aided by a tremendous slush fund and a business revival, managed to defeat Bryan. For twenty years longer the Cleveland thesis was to prevail and politicians in power held that the government's responsibility for the general welfare was strictly limited to the preservation of public order and defense of territorial integrity.

But the doctrine of limited responsibility has ever been more

[9] Second inaugural, March 4, 1893.

convenient to politicians than attractive to the people. It saves the politician in office from a great deal of painful labor and even more painful thinking, so it has been elaborated and expounded by the best elaborators and expounders in public life. The contrary doctrine has received no such careful attention except from theorists who almost invariably ran into nonsensical extremism and ended as Socialists or Communists. But it has always been latent in the thinking of the plain American, even though it might take no more definite form than the vague inquiry, "What do we pay taxes for?"

As an American doctrine it is far older than Jackson, older than the Constitution. It was already old when the Declaration of Independence asserted the right of the people at any time to "alter or abolish" the existing government "and to institute new government, laying its foundation on such principles and organizing its powers in such form, as to them shall seem most likely to effect their Safety and Happiness." Even then the happiness of the people, as well as their safety, was regarded as a legitimate charge upon government.

Long before that the travelers in the *Mayflower*, intoning, "In the name of God, Amen," invoked Divine sanction of their purpose to enact and enforce laws such "as shall be thought most meete and convenient for the generall good of the Colonie." A year before that, down in Virginia they had permanently altered, and temporarily abolished, the existing system of government by a London-appointed representative and had substituted control by representative burgesses, not in pursuance of any theory of statecraft, but in order that government might better support the people. Ten years before the burgesses assembled, heavy-handed Captain John Smith, constituting himself the government without reference to king or law, had used the governmental power to drive gentlemen to hoe in the cornfield on the theory that no vested interest takes precedence over the community's need. In short, the idea had been familiar to the minds of the people at least as long as the English had been in North America.

Its philosophical implications meant nothing to the common man. Philosophical implications rarely do, as theorists are incessantly discovering anew and always to their horrified surprise. In 1913 it was easy to prove by irrefutable logic that to deprive bankers of part of their power over the monetary system was a step in the direction of Socialism. But the common man's theory was charmingly innocent of logic, irrefutable or other, and based on no discernible principle whatever. It was (and is) simply this: whatever is necessary isn't radical.

In a civilized society to suppress blatant injustice and flaunted inequity—both the reformers and the common people usually said iniquity—was necessary. Therefore the legislation passed to effect that reform was not radical. Socialistic? Maybe. Maybe it was also antinomian, as some critics averred, or merely logomachic, as others contended. Nobody understood exactly what any of those words meant, so what of it? Private control of the public money had been proved by experience to be a nuisance and a danger, so its elimination was necessary; and being necessary, it wasn't radical, no matter what or how many polysyllables were used to describe it.

So it was with the rest of the Wilson legislative program. The attack upon political, social and economic ills of long standing was skillful, vigorous and practical. Therefore the country— that is to say, the great mass of the voters—was not shocked because it included some ideas that had long been advocated by the Socialists. The Schoolmaster seemed to know what he was about; therefore the common man, without feeling any great enthusiasm for him personally, relied on him.

It is a curious thing that the theorists, that is, those persons who thought that the country should have been shocked into revolt by the mere word "socialism," and who were stunned when the voters insisted upon applying the pragmatic test, regardless of labels, were yet the people who insisted that Wilson was an "impractical idealist." They were themselves the romantics; they were the people who believed that there was, or should be, some magic power in the mere word, some abracadabra that was a sufficient answer to all inquiry, while Wilson was the realist who based his program on a careful study of cause and effect, with no regard to mere words. But the opposition was highly vocal. It controlled most of the media of publicity—the radio did not count as yet—and through the press, in particular, it established a widespread impression that Wilson was the dreamer and they were the hard-bitten realists.

However, as against the record of definite accomplishment, this argument was not effective. In the mid-term elections of 1914, the Democrats maintained their control of Congress.

7. An Adult for President

UP TO this moment Woodrow Wilson was, at most, an exceptionally able President of the United States. On the record of his first two years in office there was reason to believe that he might take rank with Grover Cleveland and Theodore Roosevelt. He differed from both in temperament and training, but in sheer ability he was plainly their equal; that, however, was as much as the ordinary man saw. No doubt close students of public affairs and especially those who were close to the

President perceived more, but the man who knew nothing except what he read in the newspapers had, in the beginning of 1914, no convincing evidence that Wilson would rank higher than somewhere toward the bottom of the list of the ten best Presidents. In the fervid oratory of the party speakers, of course, he was already being ranked with Washington, Jefferson and Lincoln; but no man of sense took party oratory at face value. In the spring of 1914 Woodrow Wilson, in the estimation of the average American, was pretty good, better than Taft, possibly better than T.R., but hardly of the stature of old Andrew Jackson, while as for Jefferson, or Lincoln—bosh!

It is possible that the average man was right, at that. The most ardent exponent of the Great Man theory of history cannot deny that the times have something to do with the making of the man. If Wilson had been permitted to continue his work of reconstructing the American national system of government he would certainly have attained a respectable place in history, possibly as high a place as his hero, William E. Gladstone, attained in England; but he would never have loomed as a portentous figure in the history of Western civilization, and the common man who saw him would never have had occasion to speak of the event in the tones of a French peasant of an earlier day when he said, "I once saw the Emperor pass by."

The explosion in Europe in 1914 was a revelation to all the world of the vast incompetence of government as it is practiced among men. The response of the American people to the event is incomprehensible unless one bears in mind that the dominant, overwhelmingly dominant, emotion of the time was complete astonishment. The American—meaning, of course, the man in the street, not diplomatists, statesmen, and trained observers of international affairs—was accustomed then, as now, to project his own thinking upon the rest of the world; and the rest of the world was not accustomed to thinking of America at all in relation to the balance of power. It was a profound shock to us to discover that we had Europe on our hands; and doubtless a more profound shock to Europe to discover that it had America on its hands.

The initial reaction was utter disbelief, and this was not confined to the uninstructed crowd. Nobody was more incredulous than the great lords of commerce, industry and especially finance. Even after hostilities had begun prominent American bankers assured the world that the conflict could not possibly last more than ninety days, because at the end of three months every nation in Europe would be bankrupt. The fact that bankruptcy is merely a word and a word, as Falstaff observed centuries ago, is a mouthful of wind, was a concept incomprehensible to men whose whole world was built upon a foundation of stocks, bonds, debentures and promissory notes.

Nor did the man in the White House entirely escape involvement in the general misconception. Even then the President of the United States was far and away the best-informed man in the country; more of the facts were before Wilson than were in possession of any other individual. Yet every newspaper reader was in possession of the essential fact, namely, that they were fighting in Europe; all the rest was merely corroborative detail. Wilson disbelieved what was before his own eyes, not for the same reason, but for the same kind of reason that the crowds and the bankers disbelieved. Wilson was as firmly convinced of the power of reason as the bankers were of the power of finance; war was obviously senseless, therefore sensible men would not long continue to fight.

So it was his faith in intelligence that led him into making the only completely idiotic utterance of his career. Incidentally, it was one of the most popular of all his utterances. He called upon the country to preserve strict neutrality, not in deed only but in word and thought as well.

In August, 1914—Great Britain declared war on August 4—
Americans were united to a degree rarely attained in the history
of the country. Even Theodore Roosevelt and Senator Lodge,
of Massachusetts, approved the declaration of neutrality when
it was issued. With the exception of a few partisans of the Allies,
on the one hand, or the Triple Alliance, on the other—people
whose partisanship was stronger than their Americanism, therefore people who were in, but not of, the country—all Americans
were agreed upon one point, to wit, the essential unreality of
the war. The common man knew that he didn't want to fight,
therefore he believed that nobody wanted to fight. The banker
knew that he couldn't afford a war, therefore he believed that
nobody could afford a war. The President knew that the war
violated every dictate of reason, therefore he believed that all
intelligent men would regard it as contrary to reason. The
common man believed in good will, the banker in good business,
the President in good sense, as the ultimate, dominant force in
human affairs. None of these beliefs was consistent with the
belief that the war would be long and catastrophic, so none
believed it.[10]

Here began the first operation of that rending process by
which the twentieth century was to strip the American of the
many-layered shell of optimism that protected him from the
realities of world politics; and that was to impose upon Europe
a realization that the terror lurking in the West, thitherto
ignored, was potent indeed.

Needless to say, the unity of August, 1914, was momentary.
The falsehood of his basic assumption became plain to Wilson
very soon; but the magnitude of his own error gave him a
measure of the aberration of the country at large, and imposed

[10] The prediction of the British army commander, Lord Kitchener, that the
war would last three years was regarded by Americans in the summer of
1914 as an example of the characteristic infatuation of the military mind.

upon him a caution that more ardent spirits soon found excessive. On May 7, 1915, the great passenger liner *Lusitania* was torpedoed by a German submarine, and a hundred and twenty-four Americans were among the eleven hundred and ninety-eight of the ship's company that drowned. This was plain notice that the old concept of "civilized warfare," far from being an immutable principle of international law, had no more validity than any of the other grandiose dreams of nineteenth-century statesmen.

But Americans in the mass were still unwilling to believe it. Too much of their intellectual and emotional capital was invested in the theories of statecraft that had been developed in the long period of comparative peace since Waterloo. It was a psychological impossibility for them to give up rapidly all the prejudices that they had been cultivating for a hundred years. Many never could give them up; and millions who abandoned them temporarily under the compulsion of events resumed them promptly when opportunity offered.

Some of these prejudices—that in favor of the concept of civilized warfare, for example—attested to a high level of civilization in the population generally. Others—as the perennial suspicion of Britain dating back to the Revolution and the War of 1812—were mere survivals of obscurantism, while others—the German and Irish antipathy for Britain, for example—had been imported during the high tide of immigration. But they were all real enough, and none could be discarded without an effort covering a considerable period.

The skill with which Wilson held a course that would allow these prejudices to subside, or to cancel each other, is worth the close scrutiny of every student of politics, but to describe it as an element of the man's greatness is to tread on dubious ground. It attested the adroitness of the politician and in a democracy a man who attains the rank of a great statesman must be a consummate politician; but political adroitness is an avenue to great achievement, rather than the thing itself. If Wilson had been merely adroit he would rank today with David Lloyd George, rather than among the masters of his age.

It was his perception of the one valid excuse for waging war that set him apart. We would fight, he said, "to make the world safe for democracy."

It was a phrase too simple to be understood. With a single exception it consisted of words of one syllable, and the exception, "democracy," was a term that by 1917 was as familiar to charwomen and plow hands as to doctors of philosophy. Had the statement come from a streetcar motorman its meaning could not have been mistaken; but coming from a politician, it gave rise to endless bitter debate.

For politicians are not given to stating exactly what they mean, all that they mean, and no more than they mean in words of one syllable. When an American politician gives tongue the judicious hearer takes the statement, adds somewhat thereto, or subtracts somewhat therefrom as circumstances influence his judgment, and by this process arrives at an approximation of the idea the politician intended to convey.

But "to make the world safe for democracy" is incapable of such treatment. Add anything to it, or substract anything from it, and you reduce it to incoherence; if somewhat must be added or subtracted, then the thing becomes a mystery. To make sense at all, it must be taken as it stands, and with Americans, especially American intellectuals, it was an article of faith that no politician's utterance is to be taken as it stands. Applying that principle to this utterance they arrived at a state of utter confusion.

Two misconstructions were especially widespread. One was that of the simple, nonintellectual party worker. He read it, "to make the world safe for the Democrats" and approved heartily, assuming that it meant indefinite tenure of office for himself and his friends.

The other was that of the highly sophisticated. Starting with the assumption that no President could say what he meant and no more, they studied the phrase in the light of their knowledge of Wilson's character. One of the flaws in that character was a broad streak of intellectual arrogance, and they fell into the logical fallacy of assuming that arrogance of any kind, even intellectual arrogance, is incompatible with a belief in democracy. Then democracy was the key word in which the assumed ambiguity must be found. Wilson was at least the titular leader of American democracy, and it was that for which the world was to be made safe; in other words, it was to be made safe for his leadership. His own job was to be expanded indefinitely and fortified. He aspired to be King of the World. There, then, was the true rendition of the mysterious phrase; it meant, "to make the world safe for autocracy."

This nonsense was actually propounded in earnest by men who claimed to be among the heavy thinkers of the time, notably by the Hon. Henry Cabot Lodge, Senator from Massachusetts, who had accepted without demur the label of "the scholar in politics" until, to his annoyance, it was transferred to Wilson. It is a curious illustration of the way in which the intellectual can hang himself with his own logical chain when he insists upon converting simplicity into subtlety.

But millions of plain men, neither bitterly partisan nor oversophisticated, had no trouble with the phrase at all. To them it was a summation of the more intelligent form of isolationism. In their opinion the United States had neither the right nor the desire to make democrats (or Democrats) of the Bulgarians, the Magyars and the Turks. All we aspired to was to run our own affairs as we saw fit with no risk of having our ships sunk, our business throttled, and our citizens abused by some such puerile caricature of a potentate as the Kaiser Wilhelm II. If that safety was to be achieved only by fighting, then we would fight. If we couldn't live unmolested as long as Prussian militarism flourished, why, that was sufficient reason for destroying Prussian militarism. To make the world safe—not democratic, but safe for democracy, was an ambition that seemed to the common man strictly within our rights and not in any sense encroaching upon the rights of others.

Without doubt, the common man was oversimplifying the case. He was leaving out of consideration one of the most important factors, the characteristic ability, still little understood, of democratic power to affect autocratic power adversely merely by existing. But since he was blissfully ignorant of the existence of that factor, he was untroubled by any doubts that he understood what Wilson meant, and that it was a reasonable statement of our position.

Wilson himself, in 1917, was probably just beginning to realize how democracy, by the very nature of its being, builds up a sort of osmotic pressure against any other system to which it happens to be close neighbor, a pressure that increases most in an era of peace and prosperity and that in time is certain to become intolerable. But Wilson's own state of mind is irrelevant to this discussion; our study is confined to his effect upon the great mass of the American people and, through them, upon the world.

The impression of those first two years was one of great reasonableness. In view of Wilson's subsequent reputation for being utterly unreasonable, this is worthy of note. It is easily substantiated, however, by examination of the current newspapers and especially the magazines that strove to avoid a rankly partisan attitude. The people saw in Wilson a President who respected no shibboleths, but based his decisions on intelligent consideration of the facts as they existed. He was playing no game. He was working at a serious, complicated job and, as the voters saw it, doing remarkably well. "A brainy guy," was the verdict of the man in the street.

This worried the professional politicians who managed the affairs of the Democratic party. It was obvious that Wilson was not a popular hero in the style of Theodore Roosevelt, or Lincoln, or Jackson, that is to say, a man who commanded not only the allegiance, but the jovial affection of the masses. Most of the professionals had forgotten, if they had ever known, that there could be any other kind of popular hero. Nobody could turn Wilson into "Woody," as Roosevelt had been "Teddy" and as the earlier heroes had been "Abe" and "Andy."

The professionals might have worried less if they had stopped to consider that the President who dominated the imagination of the country more completely for a longer time than any other had always been "Mr. Jefferson" to his friends. The opposition called him "Mad Tom," but that was an epithet, not a tribute. His supporters gave him respect, rather than affection, but they gave it to him without stint and for half a century. Wilson seemed to be acquiring, during his first two years in the White House, the same sort of hold upon the electorate; and there is no reason to suppose that it would have been less effective in the twentieth century than it had been in the early years of the nineteenth.

But before he could establish his position his work was interrupted.

8. *The Voter Thought*

YET two years proved to have been enough to enable the President to establish his influence sufficiently to maintain a position of dominance after the storm burst. He was greatly assisted by the extremism of the contending factions, one pro-Ally, the other pro-German, but both violently anti-Wilson. The common man, observing that the vituperation with which Theodore Roosevelt, one of the most articulate leaders of the pro-Ally faction, lashed at the President was exceeded only by the vituperation that George Sylvester Viereck, spokesman for the pro-German faction, poured out, naturally enough decided that a man so detested by both contestants was probably right.

Silently, doggedly, stubbornly, the masses stuck to Wilson. In 1916 they re-elected him. Unthinking Democratic orators had coined the slogan, "He kept us out of war," and rang the changes on it in spite of Wilson's repeated objection. Perhaps the people re-elected him because of that slogan; perhaps they re-elected him in spite of it; at any rate, they re-elected him, and then, in 1917 when he led them into war, they followed him just as faithfully.

At that, the election was a very close thing. The Republicans had nominated the best possible candidate to oppose Wilson. Charles Evans Hughes, then an Associate Justice of the United States Supreme Court, was as free of any suspicion of childishness as Wilson himself. In the popular estimation Hughes was also a man of great erudition and one whose personal integrity was above the reach of calumny. He, too, was somewhat austere, but the people consider a certain austerity correct in a judge as it is in a college president.

For once we had an election in which neither candidate was playing a game and in which the issues were not the old, familiar party stuff, largely fraudulent, but completely and appallingly real. The emotions aroused were correspondingly real, and found vent in a campaign foul beyond precedent even for American politics. The candidates themselves, of course, were impeccable. Neither was capable of stooping to scurrility, but on the lower levels scavenger politicians exceeded all bounds, especially in their attacks on the President. Mr. Hughes had nothing to do with this, and there is no reason to doubt that the "whispering campaign" filled him with disgust and chagrin.

The verminous element took its cue from the fact that Wilson had remarried a year after the death of his first wife in 1914. At any rate, the unspeakables developed the curious notion that they could convince the country that he was a lecher, and that it would destroy him. They were certainly wrong on the first count, and perhaps on the second. They convinced nobody of intelligence, and it is by no means certain that all the unintelligent, who may have credited the slanders, voted against Wilson on that account. American politics was growing up; the voters were realizing more clearly every day that the qualifications of a man fit to deal with an international crisis are not necessarily the qualifications of a Sunday-school superintendent. Nevertheless, the effort to besmirch the President's private character was one of the most reckless, most persistent, and filthiest in the history of American politics. Not since Jefferson had a President suffered as much from that type of slander.

The people studied the merits of the candidates carefully, so carefully that the result was in doubt for more than twelve hours—or, rather, for twelve hours it was assumed that Hughes had won, and not until the returns from the remote country precincts of California came in was it certain that Wilson had been elected. The narrowness of the margin makes it impossible to assign any one factor as the determining cause. It has been the fashion to assert that Wilson won on the slogan, "He kept us out of war," and therefore won by fraud. But this overlooks the fact that while some people undoubtedly voted for him under the mistaken impression that the slogan was true, others, and a great many, voted for Hughes because they mistakenly thought that Wilson had kept us out of war when every consideration of decency required us to go in. In 1916 the pro-German element in this country was very noisy, but the pro-Ally element was very angry and very determined. "He kept us out of war" gained some votes for Wilson; but it also cost him some, and it is entirely possible that it cost more than it gained.

But if what happened to Wilson and Hughes is still debatable, there is no doubt about what happened to the average man in that election. He thought. The assertion is not to be taken as universal, of course. Undoubtedly there were some who went to the polls in the same old mood that had characterized them in other elections, a mood remarkably similar to that of the crowds at the races, or at football games. But the deciding votes were cast by men who thought carefully, and many of whom prayed powerfully, before they marked their ballots. It was no holiday event in 1916; it was desperately serious business.

For the old world of illusion was going up in flames like a wood-and-canvas stage set and the naked brick and steel of the real world were showing through. Horrified, bewildered, unbelieving, the American had to make a decision on the spot, and he had to be right the first time. Under such circumstances men and nations mature with great speed. The political development of the United States leaped forward twenty years on election day, not because Wilson was the choice, but because the people voted soberly with a mind to things that mattered dreadfully, and not with their heads full of the claptrap of ordinary political campaigns.

It was nerve-racking, but it was probably salutary. The time had to come when the American, as a political entity, could no longer be suffered to devote his attention exclusively to the development of his own municipal system, for the simple reason that that system, by its sheer weight and power, was beginning to affect all other systems to an extent that could no longer be ignored. We did not realize it. Europe realized it imperfectly and confusedly. But an adjustment of some sort was inevitable, and the man elected to the Presidency of the United States in 1916 was commissioned to make it.

It was not a mandate issued to him by the voters. The voters had their choice of the man, but the mandate was none of their doing. It was issued by fate, destiny, the march of events, the development of history, or by the Lord God—give it what name you please, it was a force far beyond and above the control of the American voter. As a rule, he suspected dimly if at all that the mandate was issued; he knew only that the times were critical, and hesitantly he decided that the Schoolmaster was the best choice to act for him in the circumstances.

It is possible that it was an error. Hughes might have been better. But it is possible that Knox might have won the Revolution sooner than Washington did. It is possible that if McClellan had been sustained he might have closed out the Civil War earlier. It is possible that if Tilden had been inaugurated in 1877, the whole history of the United States might have been different; the First World War might have begun at Tangier in 1905, or it might not have been fought at all. There is no limit to speculation on what might have happened if at any critical angle history had taken another turn; all that is relevant today is what did happen.

What did happen in this case was that Wilson was elected and that he met the crisis in a way that rocked the world.

Naturally, it was a way totally unexpected by the majority of his countrymen when they went to the polls in 1916. Any method of meeting the crisis would have been unexpected, because they had not expected the crisis itself; but to assert that it was a method disapproved by the majority is nonsense. The majority had no opinion on the subject. The majority looked to its leaders for suggestions. The method advanced by Wilson appealed to American common sense. More than that, it had been inspected and sharply revised by such Republican leaders as William H. Taft and Elihu Root, and had been indorsed in principle by almost every politician in both parties—certainly by all whose opinion carried much weight. In any event, it was a solution of sorts, and at the end of the war it was the only solution available. The average voter did not understand all its implications, but for that matter, neither did Woodrow Wilson, or Georges Clemenceau, or David Lloyd George, supposed to be the best-informed statesmen in the world. He who understood all its implications would have been a philosopher, prophet and sage wise beyond all records of human wisdom.

The point is that the Wilsonian formula was acceptable to the common man. A minor Republican leader, but a shrewd one,[11] admitted privately that eighty per cent of the people were for it and expected Congress to adopt it. The opposition did not originate in the masses, but in certain special groups, including those disgruntled by the outcome of the war, extreme radicals, intellectuals incapable of accepting reality, and, most potent of all, the political opposition eager to seize any means

[11] James E. Watson, a Senator from Indiana, forgotten now but in his time admittedly one of the smartest political tricksters in the country and a man with an uncanny knowledge of public opinion. He was a violent opponent of Wilson for strictly partisan reasons.

of discrediting the administration and bringing their own party back into power.

All these groups combined were not numerous and would have been impotent against any really militant public opinion. But the average man, although he accepted the Wilsonian formula, accepted it passively. In the field of international relations he was inexperienced and frankly uncertain, therefore exceptionally vulnerable to shrewd *ex parte* pleading, the thing that the modern world inexactly terms propaganda.

But all this was three years in the future when Wilson stood before Congress on April 2, 1917, and called the country to arms. He knew what he was doing. He was aware that war meant the abandonment of all and the reversal of much that he had been trying to do for the past four years. At one o'clock in the morning he said to a friendly newspaper man,[12] "Once lead this people into war, and they'll forget there ever was such a thing as tolerance. To fight you must be brutal and ruthless, and the spirit of ruthless brutality will enter into the very fiber of our national life, infecting Congress, the courts, the policeman on the beat, the man in the street."

At noon he said to Congress, "The day has come when America is privileged to spend her blood and her might for the principles that gave her birth and happiness and the peace which she has treasured. God helping her, she can do no other."

[12] Frank Cobb, editor of the New York *World*. Quoted by John L. Heaton in *Cobb of "The World."* New York: E. P. Dutton & Co., 1924.

9. *The Lilting Dance of Death*

SO AMERICA'S part of the world went up in flames, along with the rest. This is not a figure of speech, but a plain statement of fact. Cities flamed in Europe, ships flamed on the sea. For the most part, the houses in America stood, only an occasional factory, or warehouse, or wharf going up in flames at the touch of the saboteur. But on the battle front sparks flashed from millions of rifles and machine guns, great streaks of flame leaped from the muzzles of thousands of cannon, and every spark, every streak burned up something of the labor of American workers, something of the savings of the American people, something of the natural resources that should have been the heritage of generations to come.

To feed the munitions plants and create the battle fleets the iron mountains of the Mesabi range melted away. To build the vast, sprawling cantonments the forests of Oregon and Florida went down faster than wheat before a mower's scythe. To feed the battlers and the workers supporting them the cornfields of Iowa, the potato fields of Idaho and Maine, the cattle ranges of Texas, were ruthlessly pillaged. All passed through the fires of the new Moloch and of a hundred billions of our national inheritance left nothing but cinders and shards and fumes.

Fifty thousand of the nation's sons were consumed in the holocaust and six times as many suffered hurts.

"The spirit of ruthless brutality" entered "into the very fiber of our national life." The average American, the kindly, hopeful American, who had disbelieved in the reality of war, who had been nauseated a dozen years before when forty-seven Jews were massacred at Kishinev, went about this business to the strains of a lilting tune,

> Send the word, send the word over there
> That the Yanks are coming, the Yanks are coming,

and read with grim satisfaction that the German dead choked the stream at Chateau-Thierry, that the guns had made rubble of the entire St. Mihiel salient, that the enemy was sending division after division to ruin in Belleau Wood and the Meuse-Argonne.

> We're going over,
> We're going over,

screamed the brasses and the woodwinds, and if we couldn't go over we could at least harry some poor devil at home for being named Schmidt, or for playing the Magic Fire Music on his phonograph, or for printing "sauerkraut" on his restaurant menu instead of "liberty cabbage." Some spies and saboteurs went to jail, but it is to be feared that for every criminal put behind the bars at least four landed there for no crime other than being noisily offensive to their nerve-strained neighbors; and thousands not actually arrested were hounded and persecuted for mere unpopularity.

Two months before the Armistice Eugene V. Debs was indicted and four months after the cessation of hostilities he was given ten years in the Federal penitentiary at Atlanta. For this the government of the time has been bitterly criticized, because there was not a bishop in America more completely void of criminality than the aging leader of the small Socialist party; but as a matter of fact there was nothing else to do with Debs. He had been roaring his dissent up and down the land ever since the declaration of war; and even at his trial he baldly asserted his moral right to obstruct the measures of the government in time of war. There is every reason to believe that he stirred up some foolish young fellows to resist the draft and so brought pains and penalties on them with a "ruthless brutality" of his own. In short, he shared the prevailing spirit of the times, although unwittingly; and the spirit of the times was to release Barabbas and crucify the Nazarene.

Fortunately for Debs, however, this was in the early days of the twentieth century, when our education in the ethics of force was barely beginning. Twenty-five years later no man of any perceptible stature was imprudent enough to imitate Debs' blatant defiance. If one had been, there is little reason to doubt that he would have been dealt with as were the saboteurs landed from a German submarine—he would have been taken into custody and the next news of him would have been a terse official announcement, "The sentence of the court-martial has been carried out." As it was, in 1920 Debs in the penitentiary got almost a million votes for President, a larger vote than any Socialist candidate ever polled before or since; and being released a year later lived undisturbed for five years more and died at the age of seventy-one.

In 1950 it is hard to believe that one who deliberately taunted the government in time of war would live out the Psalmist's span, seeing that one who taunts it in time of peace is in grave danger of landing in a prison cell.

At that, we acquired the psychology of total war very rapidly in 1917 and 1918.

> The drums rum-tumming everywhere,

sang the crowds, and made certain that the sound of the Long Roll was not out of anyone's ears, anywhere, at any time, not even in the sanctuary. In fact, the men in uniform were frequently a good deal more temperate in speech than the men in editorial offices and even the men in holy orders. The German occupation forces in Belgium and France had been stupid in attempting to maintain order by terror; they shot not merely guerillas taken with arms, but mayors and burgomasters, lavishly; they shot an English army nurse for helping prisoners of war to escape, and thereby gave the British a martyr hardly less valuable to their cause than the St. Joan the English had given the French centuries earlier; they penned civilians, especially Belgians, in concentration camps, where many died under shocking treatment.

All this was as manna from heaven to those ingenious Britons whose job it was to whip up the war spirit in this country as well as in Great Britain. Using the atrocities that actually had been perpetrated as a base—and there were some, although few to compare with Malmédy, not to mention Lidice and still less the extermination camps of a quarter of a century later—they skillfully erected upon them a structure of horrors that would stir some emotion even in the present hardened generation and that drove Americans unacquainted with modern war into a frenzy of excitement. People believed in all sincerity that the Imperial German army rolling across Europe in its manner of making war was indistinguishable from the Mongol Horde, and that it might be said of Ludendorff as it was of Genghis Khan, that where his horse's hooves trod the grass never grew again.

This gave the clergy an excuse to revert to the Old Testament and the commination of the Hebrew prophets which they imitated with marked success. The walls of American churches shook to thunders of denunciation that might have made Ezekiel and Jeremiah turn pale. Nor was it at Sunday worship only that the average man was spurred to greater excitement; he could not attend a theater, or a movie, or any other place of public assembly without being confronted by a Four-Minute Man, that is, a speaker who was supposed to confine his address to four minutes, but who was expected to cram into it all the hell-fire and damnation that two hundred and forty seconds could hold.

So among the people at home the war rapidly took on the aspect of a *jehad*. They called it a crusade, but the Crusades were fought, at least in theory, for the recovery of the Holy Sepulcher, whereas the Mohammedan Holy War was frankly an expedition aimed at the extermination of the infidels. Ours of 1917-18 was perhaps less crusade or even Holy War, than an expedition like those of the ancient Israelites, certain that they had the orders of Jehovah himself to smite with the edge of the sword every living creature. Through all America the swelling chant resounded,

> And we won't come back till it's over,
> Over there!

It is one of the most ironical ditties ever sung, for as a matter of fact we came back when it was barely beginning over there; but we didn't know that until years had passed.

10. *What Price Glory?*

FOUR million young men poured into the army camps to learn the techniques of ruthless brutality, and two million were transported overseas to apply them. For the first time since 1865 military thinking became familiar to large masses of the American population.

Even in 1865 the effect was probably less profound, for the Civil War began as one of the most informal of conflicts and to the very end the true professional soldier played a rather subordinate role. As for the skirmish with Spain, in 1898, it is sufficiently characterized by the fact that both Theodore Roosevelt and William J. Bryan were colonels. Even in 1917 it was assumed at first that the amateur would play a prominent part. Many people thought that Leonard Wood, originally a doctor of medicine, should command the army, and it was almost universally assumed that Theodore Roosevelt would lead a brigade, probably a division.

But the Commander-in-Chief was the President, and the President was an adult. The war to him was no adventure. He went into it, as some critic observed shortly afterward, not in the spirit of a knight entering the lists, but in that of a policeman entering a barroom brawl. He was there to break it up, not to afford opportunity for warriors to win glory; and to break it up with all possible speed, skill was more important than enthusiasm.

With that purpose dominant he selected for the job a stony-faced product of West Point and the regular army, one John Joseph Pershing, a soldier to begin with, a soldier to end with, a soldier all the way through. A year or two earlier this officer had been given an impossible assignment; with a heavy column of all arms he had been sent in pursuit of a highly mobile force of mounted Mexican bandits that had raided a border town in our side of the line. He had everything against him. His force was badly equipped for the task. He was delayed for weeks in a tangle of bureaucratic red tape. He operated in almost impossible country, hot, arid and empty. He was faced with an explosive political situation in which the slightest failure of discipline among his own men might easily have precipitated a long, costly and exasperating war. He was knifed in the back by jealousy in Washington. If ever an American officer had cause for bitter complaint it was Pershing in Mexico but, as far as the public was aware, he never opened his mouth. He didn't catch the bandits, but he did not precipitate a war either; he obeyed orders, he held his men under iron control, and he kept his tongue even better disciplined than his men.

To a harried President, under heavy political fire from all sides, this loyal subordination was grateful in the extreme, and he rewarded it with the command of the American Expeditionary Force in Europe. The choice was not popular, but it was good. It was a war of position and by the time Pershing arrived in force the enemy was approaching exhaustion. The situation therefore called for no brilliant strategy, but for steady, relentless pressure, steadily increasing; this is largely a matter of discipline and supply, and discipline and supply are precisely the fields in which the amateur is usually weakest and the professional soldier is at his best.

Two million young Americans therefore learned the grim business of war under one of the most business-like warriors outside the German General Staff. They did not like it, but they learned beyond peradventure that modern war is not a task to be entrusted to enthusiastic boys. The riflemen should be young, to be sure, in order to stand the physical strain, but the commanders should be full-grown, hard-headed, imperturbable. In a war of position, especially, a Rupert, a Murat, a J. E. B. Stuart, are likely to be as dangerous to their own commander as to the enemy.

This meant a sudden and radical psychological readjustment to young men brought up on traditions of Stonewall Jackson and Sheridan. But it meant an increasing maturity in their attitude toward war. Most of them came into contact with harsh reality long before they reached the front, for only now and then, when there was some breakdown in the vast replacement system, were wholly untrained men flung into battle as they had been constantly during the Civil War. In the camps the young men learned that war is a matter of study, careful calculation and the movement of heavy weights over long distances, far more than a matter of wild charges and brilliant forays. The glamour, the dazzle went out of it, and "blood, toil, sweat and tears" came in.

All this was doubly reinforced in France. They didn't sing "Over There" within sound of the guns. They didn't go in for lilting braggadocio of any kind; from the battle-worn British they picked up the cynicism of troops on active service—

> Two German officers crossed the Rhine,
> Parlez-vous—

and developed a cynicism of their own, livelier, perhaps, but no less biting—

> Ashes to ashes, and dust to dust—
> If the Camels don't get you the Fatimas must—

but most of all they sang of anything and everything that did not remind them of the stinking compost heaps in French farm-yards, of the endless miles and the chalk dust of the *Routes Nationales*, of rain and mud and cooties and the long, olive-drab hospital trains dragging their somber way back from the front—

> Ho! for the coonyac, ho! for the wine,
> Ho! for the mam'selles, every one is fine,
> Ho! for the hard tack, bully beef and beans—
> To hell with the Kaiser and the goddam Marines!

They regarded Europe, and were not favorably impressed, but they had to admit it was there. To the overwhelming majority of them Europe had been hitherto a word, a more or less bookish concept, utterly separated from their own lives and with which they had expected never to come in contact. But here it was, for the moment their only world and for many of them destined to be the end of the world. They chose no part of it, but what choice had they? Northern France, into which they were dumped, was especially hateful. It was a natural reaction, for northern France had been battered by four years of war and was left hideous beyond all description. Relatively few of the soldiers escaped into the unscarred areas of the Republic, to see something of France as it had been. France was to most merely ruins, mud, stenches, and a population made hard and grasping by four bitter years.

Yet it was a maturing process, even if warped and one-sided. Two million young Americans had Europe thrust upon them, violently and unforgettably. For years it might be something to run from, but it was something. Hitherto, it had been nothing. The American who slogged through the ruined villages and over the endless hills might emerge from the experience a more violent isolationist than he had ever been before, but he also had an awareness that he had never had before. His world was no longer bounded by his county lines. He was growing up, rapidly.

Filthy, gloomy, angry and unutterably weary, the average doughboy received as his dominant impression of the First World War that of its fantastic abnormality. Soldiering under Black Jack Pershing was not a good school in which to develop militarists. It was too matter-of-fact, too directly purposeful; the idea was to finish up the job in the shortest possible time and get the hell out of there; and out of there meant, to the over-whelming majority, out of uniform; the war did not last long enough for many to become too inured to the idea of military service as a way of life. As Dr. Samuel Johnson regarded being in a ship as being in jail with a chance of being drowned, so the doughboy usually regarded being in the army as being on the chain gang with an excellent chance of being shot, even though you did not make a break. So his thoughts seldom dwelt upon glory; if he attained glory, it would be because it was thrust upon him. But he sincerely desired to go away from there and he couldn't go while the German army survived as a fighting force; wherefore he developed a high efficiency at eliminating Germans. To the end the Germans denied that the Americans were real soldiers, but the casuality list showed that they developed into exceedingly practical killers. Occasionally an American unit was trapped and slaughtered, but in no major engagement did the enemy inflict losses appreciably heavier than those he suffered, and the Americans had tremendous reserves while the enemy's were used up. The end was inevitable.

But the exultation that it brought to the rank and file was merely the exultation of being through with a dirty and disagreeable job. They lifted the roofs of the *estaminets* with the roaring chorus,

> K-k-katy,
> My beautiful Katy,
> You're the only, only girl that I adore,

but it was not with the idea of returning to Katy mounted upon a white charger and glittering with ribbons and stars, that they sang. Their ambition was more modest. They had small desire to pose as military heroes—that was to come years later at American Legion conventions. In France it was only to get home alive and to sink swiftly into civilian life again;

> And when the moon shines
> Over the cowshed,
> I'll be waiting at the k-k-kitchen door!

So the army came marching home, greatly matured in many respects, but still cherishing the infantile delusion that it had finished the job over there, and little inclined to resume, in the field of politics, the fighting that it thought had been definitely ended in the field of war. The army was swiftly demobilized in more senses than one; it was dispersed as a fighting force no more completely than it was dispersed as a political force in the longer and sterner battles that lay ahead.

11. *The Hatchet Men Assemble*

TOYNBEE expresses the opinion that Alexander of Macedon established his best claim to be called "the Great" in his vision of *Homonoia*, or Concord, which was essentially the vision of One World in which men of all nations should live as brothers.[13] But Alexander had on his hands an army desperately fatigued, although victorious, and a civilian population without the faintest conception of what he had in mind. His vision, therefore, remained no more than a vision; nevertheless, in the judgment of the historian, it raised him to a level of true greatness that all his conquests were unable to attain.

At the close of the year 1918 this same vision possessed the

[13] Even the historian's colder judgment will single out, as the greatest of all men of action, those oecumenical rulers—a Cyrus, an Alexander, an Augustus—who have been touched with pity for the sufferings of their fellow men and, having caught the vision of the unity of Mankind, have devoted their personal genius and their political power to the noble enterprise of translating this dearly bought ideal into a humane reality.—Arnold J. Toynbee, *A Study of History*, London: Oxford University Press, 1939, vol. vi, page 6.

official leader of the American people. He, too, had on his hands a weary army and an uncomprehending populace; and he, too, failed to translate the dream into reality. But if the mere effort lifted the Macedonian from the ranks of the mighty into the ranks of the great, why deny its power to do as much for the American?

In the midst of the clamor of warfare the President seemed to the average man to be, first of all a spokesman with a command of language almost unparalleled in the history of the Presidency. Wilson's ability to say the right thing in the right way aroused the admiring astonishment of the country from the beginning; but after the outbreak of war that admiration rose to an extraordinary fervor. In act and bearing he might have been austere, but in words his sense of the dramatic was unerring and a finer ear for the balanced rhythm of English prose has seldom been known.

This was rightly considered by the average American part of the armament of the leader of a nation in arms. Wilson's speeches were missiles striking joints in the enemy's armor that our steel could not reach. His bitterest enemies admitted that he was a great orator, and the yells of wrathful denial that each successive speech extorted from the German press were proof enough that his oratory was striking home.

Yet only a few understood the source of the effectiveness of his speaking. Most of us were content with the superficial explanation, that they presented their ideas with crystal clarity yet dressed in musical, memorable prose. We overlooked the fact that this explanation was insufficient when the speeches were translated into German, French, Italian, by hard-worked, indifferently educated and certainly uninspired military and press translators; yet they remained effective. Clarity and eloquence could not account for that, for both were frequently lost in translation, but the power was not lost. It lay in something above and beyond the skill of the rhetorician.

Of course we did not miss it altogether, not even the unlettered man. We had a word for it. Wilson, said the street crowds and the subtle doctors alike, is an idealist. It was a true word, made grossly false by the way we uttered it. We said, Wilson is an idealist, as we might have said, Wilson is one-eyed, or, Wilson has a wooden leg. We meant, Wilson is an idealist—and what a pity! For we were not yet politically mature enough to understand either the might of idealism in an adult mind, or its appalling danger as a weapon in the hands of a nation still afflicted with political infantilism.

It quite escaped most of us that the word "idealist" in its original meaning describes a man who holds to one set of philosophical hypotheses, rather than another set. Originally, it had no more ethical significance than any other group designation—that is, it disclosed no more about a man's character than is disclosed when one says that Jones is a Rotarian and Smith is a Kiwanian. An idealist, in the beginning, was simply a man who held that the determining force in the world is the idea rather than the material substance.

But by the year 1917 the word "idealist" retained its original meaning only in histories of philosophy and classroom lectures. The ordinary man said "idealist" when what he meant was "romantic," a man with more faith in fantasy than in fact. The truth was that the average man himself was the romantic, because he could not realize how profoundly the world had changed since 1776, and Wilson was the stern realist, seeking to adapt American theory to the facts of life.

Yet it is incontestably true that in one phase of his thinking, and that a vital phase, he did substitute fantasy for fact. He misjudged badly the level of political maturity in the American people and especially in their leaders.

It was an understandable error, for in one phase of politics these men had attained a maturity surpassing that of any similar group in the world. The men in Congress and the Cabinet, leaders in private life, Taft, Roosevelt, Root, as well as the counselors of politicians such as President Butler of Columbia, and President Lowell of Harvard, did understand the mechanics of a democratic polity better than they had been understood anywhere else.

Why not? They and their predecessors had been studying the problem of the operation of democracy in a capitalist economy for a century and a half. For five generations their attention had been centered on that single problem in the field of statecraft without even one important distraction. The Civil War was not a distraction; it was merely a period of intense concentration on one phase of the general problem. If in so long a period of such intensive study the American politician had learned nothing about how to make democracy work, he must have been subnormal. As a matter of fact, he had learned much. In the business of keeping the machinery of democracy operating smoothly he had become expert. To call him immature in that respect would be fatuous.

His immaturity is revealed by the fact that, since his attention had not been diverted from his particular problem for a hundred and fifty years, he assumed that it never need be diverted, and, in fact, should not be diverted. Wilson himself fell into this psychological trap at the beginning of the war; his plea for neutrality was based on the notion that America should maintain her preoccupation with her particular problem, assuming that the world would mistake preoccupation for judicial impartiality and so turn to her as an umpire.

But the world made no such mistake and Wilson, much more rapidly than his countrymen, realized the absurdity of expecting it. In the opinion of mankind there is no neutral ground between right and wrong, and a man or a nation that professes to have no preference between them has no opinion on anything that the world is bound to respect. If there were an authority beyond good and evil, that authority, instead of being the best, would be an impossible umpire of a dispute involving good and evil.

What the President failed to appreciate was his own unique position as the best-informed man. Disregarding his great intellectual endowment, his possession of better information would have enabled him to think faster than party leaders less well informed; add a native ability to think rapidly, plus lifelong training as a historian in the accurate assessment of evidence, and it became inevitable that he should be a long stride ahead of his colleagues, not to mention the leaders of the opposition who had relatively little access to many of the most important facts. In truth, he was miles ahead of most of them, and his fatal error was in not realizing it and making greater efforts to bring them up to date.

This weakness in his position he would have endeavored to correct had he realized its importance, but there was another, and a more important one, with which he was not the man to deal. There was in Woodrow Wilson all the moral arrogance of a dyed-in-the-wool Calvinist. With ignorance he could be patient; but with what he regarded as swinishness he was incapable of dealing tactfully and effectively. When he came to the sty, he pinched his ultra-righteous nose between thumb and forefinger and passed by on the other side; and this attitude helped to destroy him.

In the course of a century the two-party system had proved its value in American politics so conclusively that it had attained a considerable measure of sanctity even in the eyes of the common man, and decidedly in the eyes of political leaders. Accordingly, party loyalty acquired an identification with moral excellence that in some men went to absurd lengths. There is reason to believe that Theodore Roosevelt, although he had led a bolt in 1912 and never uttered any public peccavi, had moments when he was troubled by fears that he had done something morally wrong. In any event, from 1913 on, his desperate anxiety to restore the Republican party to power, which the outbreak of war did little to subdue, strikingly resembled the excessive piety of a returned prodigal.

With less brilliant leaders of his party the emotion was simpler, but quite as intense. In their opinion, the Republican party had a moral right to the White House. In the fifty years after Lincoln only one Democrat had occupied it, and he got there because the Republican party made blatant mistakes—the first time in nominating a worse than dubious character, the second time in nominating a stuffed shirt. These errors had to be admitted; but the small-time politicians felt that when the Republicans nominated a good man, they had a right to the Presidency and any other was an interloper. Hughes was a good man; therefore when Wilson won anyhow, the small fry felt that it was all wrong. He was a Democrat living in a Republican's house, eating at a Republican's table, sleeping in a Republican's bed. It was intolerable, and the first duty of all good party men was to get him out of there. It was a duty that overrode all other considerations.

To Wilson this was simply swinish. In his academic years he had studied party government, he had written on the subject, he had come to be regarded as an authority. He had perceived the value of party loyalty and had emphasized that value not once but repeatedly. Following his election he had proclaimed his purpose to be a party leader as long as he was in office.

But all this was in time of peace. With the world going through such agony as the war had inflicted upon it, with the whole fabric of democracy under heavy assault, and with the future of the Republic itself in peril, it seemed to him that concern over what party label was borne by the man in the White House was worse than unworthy, it was subhuman, it was porcine. His disdain made him incompetent to deal with it; for to deal with it effectively he would have had to admit that this revolting vice was in fact simply a misplaced virtue which the men addicted to it did not know was misplaced. He mistook stupidity for crime, and the mistake contributed to his undoing.

The first great break came in the summer of 1918 when, with the war obviously roaring to its climax, Wilson called for the election of a Democratic Congress to help him make the peace. Lincoln had done the same thing in 1862 and it was generally regarded as natural and reasonable; but at that time the Democratic party was smeared with the suspicion of secessionism, while in 1918 no such taint lay upon the Republicans. As for making the peace, many eminent Republicans, notably Taft and Root, were on record as supporting Wilson's ideas. What more did he want?

To the common man it appeared that Wilson was the one more interested in partisanship than in the great issues at stake. Naturally, the Republicans instantly seized upon that impression and rushed to strengthen it with every propaganda device that ingenuity could present. They fanned the misconception into a flame of resentment and the result was that the people administered a sharp rebuke to Wilson at the polls. They delivered control of Congress to the Republicans, very largely because they resented the President's supposed unreasonable partisanship in a moment of crisis.

So the common man in 1918 defeated his own aspirations. He granted power to the rankest of partisans under the impression that he was rebuking partisanship.

How rank this partisanship was came to light years afterward, when historians began to probe into one of the most significant interviews in American political history. Two weeks after Wilson had sailed for Paris, but before the Peace Conference had formally opened, therefore many months before the treaty was drafted, Theodore Roosevelt, then on his deathbed, was visited by Senator Lodge, of Massachusetts. Of the talk that followed Lodge said later, "The draft of the treaty was not then before us, but we fully discussed the League of Nations in all its bearings. We were in entire agreement. The position that I have taken, and now take, had his full approval. The line I have followed in the Senate and elsewhere is the one he wished to have followed."

The sick man's sister, Mrs. Corinne Roosevelt Robinson, was present, and later she corroborated the Senator. "I do not mean that definite clauses in the League were definitely discussed, but many contingencies in the document, contingencies which later took the form of definite clauses, *were* discussed, and the future attitude toward such contingencies more or less mapped out."

In other words, even before the Peace Conference assembled, these two had laid plans to defeat any possible treaty that Wilson might bring back from Paris.

If Wilson had known of this interview at the time, he would have called it flat treason. For the line to be followed, and which Lodge did follow, was not to oppose ratification flatly and frankly, but to obstruct it by reservations supported by endless debate. If the reservations were accepted, Lodge was prepared to introduce others—he told a supporter that he had at least thirty in reserve if the ten he presented should be accepted —until the treaty should be so completely rewritten that it should be his treaty, not Wilson's. If they were not accepted, there would be no treaty.

If the common man had been aware of this scheme, he, too, might have called it treason. But the gravamen of any crime is in the intent. It is nonsensical to suppose that Theodore Roosevelt consciously harbored any desire to work hurt to his own country; on the contrary, it was certainly his desire at this time, as it had always been, to secure its future safety and happiness.

But in the realm of politics his was a far from mature mind; he had ever been the joyous player of the game, convinced that to score a point while preventing your opponent from scoring is not merely legitimate but the very aim and end of politics. He believed, as he believed in Holy Writ, that rule by the Democratic party was bad for the country. He believed that the writing of a successful peace treaty would score a tremendous number of points for the party that achieved it. He thought that if the Democrats did it, they would score so many points that they would remain in power for twenty years. Therefore, to prevent their scoring, by any means whatever, seemed to him distinctly a service to the country. With a perfectly clear conscience he planned to hobble and humble Wilson before he had any knowledge of what Wilson was going to do, and before Wilson knew what he could do.

It was not treason. It was simply the incapacity of a politically immature mind to see the whole picture and to understand the distant aim. Such insight had not been necessary to an American leader during Roosevelt's active career, so he had never been driven to develop it. But lacking it, he pulled down the temple on all our heads.

Nor is there any good reason to doubt that Lodge, his echo and mirror, shared his sentiments, his sincerity and his blindness.

12. *The Doomed Man Sallies Out*

WOODROW WILSON may have been, merely as a man, no better than Theodore Roosevelt. In at least one respect, indeed, he was obviously a worse man, for there was an acerbity about him from which Roosevelt was free. Toward a friend who had failed him, or who he thought had failed him—Hibben of Princeton, House, Tumulty, all too many others—he was capable of acting with a hatefulness that would have been disgraceful in the sourest, most disappointed old maid in the land. There is no point in mincing words; it was a blemish upon his character fairly comparable to Alexander's drunkenness, Caesar's lechery, Napoleon's crass vulgarity.

But in 1917 Wilson, unlike Roosevelt, was in a position of responsibility, and he had to learn. His greatness lay not in the fact that he was high, holy, and all-wise from the beginning, for he was nothing of the sort, but in the fact that he set himself to learn, and having learned, did not shrink, trembling and appalled, from the Herculean labor that was thrust upon him, but rose to meet it, grappled with it, flung health, strength, life itself into the struggle and went down, defeated indeed, but unsubdued.

Even the common man was well aware that the President was revolted by the war, but he did not understand clearly the basis of his repugnance. Some thought that Wilson was chickenhearted, tending to swoon at the effusion of blood; some thought that the sheer costliness of the thing harrowed up his Scottish soul; some, remembering his pious upbringing, decided that the fear of hell gat hold upon him.

No doubt all these explanations have some color of truth. The man was sensitive, quickly moved by human suffering; he did deplore waste; and he had no doubt whatever that the God of the Presbyterians in the end will balance every man's account with direful exactness. But there was another consideration that sickened him probably more than all these combined. He perceived then what everyone could see twenty-five years later, namely, the utter irrationality of the whole business.

Wilson, be it remembered, was a scholar, which is to say a man who had dedicated his whole life to the thesis that intelligence is the supreme force in the universe, leaving the supernatural out of consideration. A scholar is committed by the nature of his calling to the theory that any genuine improvement in man's lot is achieved by reason alone. But war is a flat denial of all this. War is the repudiation of everything that Wilson had believed in and stood for and worked at since he came to manhood. A scholar who goes to war has denied, if not his God, at least his sovereign; for scholarship is acknowledgement of the sovereignty of the mind. Wilson directing the most powerful war machine on earth was in the very nature of things an apostate, unless he could find a sufficient extenuation for his course.

But to be sufficient it had to be good, very good, better than the extenuation offered by any war leader before him. He knew it, and the knowledge jarred his very soul.

His just claim to greatness is the fact that he could find it and having found it could urge it upon the world with all his intellectual power, all his political power, all his moral power until they, and his physical strength with them, were exhausted.

That extenuation he embodied in a phrase not too happily chosen because it was open to the ridicule of skeptics—"a war to end war." In this country the common people accepted it without demur, but without any great enthusiasm, at first. In 1917 the common people had no objection to a war to end war, but they would have been satisfied with a war to end the Kaiser. Not until the expenses began to pile up formidably—costs in money, in material, and, above all, in men—did they begin to appreciate the vast implications of the phrase. An ordinary man, harassed by growing shortages in everything and staggering under an increasing tax burden, saw more and more to be said for Wilson's idea; but it was those dreaded telegrams beginning, "The War Department regrets . . . ," that made the thing clear. That scattering of anguish and despair through homes all up and down the land—sown lightly in 1917 and 1918 by comparison with the sixfold heavier sowing a quarter of a century later—convinced the plain man that Wilson had found the only excuse for war that a rational human being could accept.

In December, 1918, he went to Paris to attend the Peace Conference in person. It was another violation of the rules of the game, and one that he could not explain, because it was grounded in complete distrust of the leaders of our allies, and it would have been ruinous to proclaim that distrust. Wilson had taken the measure of Georges Clemenceau, of France, David Lloyd George, of Great Britain, and Vittorio Emanuele Orlando, of Italy. He did not hold them in light esteem. He knew them for able men, formidable men, but statesmen of the old school, skeptical of his thought, skeptical of American thought—or, perhaps, less skeptical than incredulous of the existence of anything properly describable as political thought in America.

To such men the existence of war was a primary fact in international relations, and they had no more intention of trying to abolish it than they had of trying to abolish the law of gravitation. They were perfectly aware of its irrationality; but they were not, like Wilson, committed to the scholar's faith that the affairs of men can be and must be subjected to the rule of reason. They were not, like every American, committed to government by the people for the people. Lloyd George and Orlando represented monarchies, and Clemenceau was skeptical of everything, including democracy.

To rely upon these men to translate into reality the dream of a warless society of nations would have been fatuous. To have any chance of success that dream must be supported by a representative as powerful as any of the three, indeed, as powerful as all of them combined. There was no such man available. Wilson was under no illusions as to his own power to outgeneral the shrewdest diplomats in Europe, but he did have one resource that none of them possessed. That was the effect of his wartime oratory on the common people of Europe.

It had been stronger there than at home in measure as the common people had suffered more in Europe than at home. But Wilson alone represented to those people the chance of escaping future war—not any other American, still less any European. Everything depended upon what was written into the peace treaty, for the common people were aroused and the moment would not come again. Provision for rational settlement of international disputes must be written into the peace treaty, for it could not possibly be arranged later. This was not true of any other detail of the settlement. Debts could be scaled down or abolished through ordinary diplomatic procedure at any time. Boundaries could be rearranged through the medium of conferences called at pleasure. But the definite repudiation of war as an instrument of national policy must be made at the moment when the people were at white heat against war; for politicians would never repudiate it except under severe pressure. It was too convenient as a trump card in their game.

So Wilson went to Paris.

It became the fashion in later years to say that in so doing he

sealed his doom, but it is nonsense. His doom was sealed anyhow. It was sealed even before Lodge sat at Theodore Roosevelt's bedside and concocted schemes to kill any possible treaty
that Wilson might negotiate. It was sealed at the moment when
he devoted himself heart and soul to an idea too vast to be com-
prehended by a nation not yet sufficiently disciplined to look a
generation ahead. All such men are doomed; but if the idea
proves to be true, then the cup of hemlock, the cross, the stake,
the paralysis and death that surely await them turn out to be not
the colophon at the end of the tale, but merely an incident in
a story that goes on and on, acquiring a splendor in later years
that it never had while the hero lived.

13. *"Not Wilson, but Humanity"*

SO IT was with Wilson. In Paris he did battle with the
Ancient Three for six exhausting months while the world
looked on amazed, largely uncomprehending, yet, as far as the
common people of America were concerned, convinced that in
the main Wilson was right. He lost on many points, for the old
system was too strong to be completely defeated; but he won
on the main point, which was the embodiment in the treaty of a
system for substituting reason for war in international relations.
Grudgingly, the Three Old Men—old not so much in years
as in their representation of the old idea, the old mode of
thought, what theologians call the Old Adam—set their signa-
tures to the Covenant of the League of Nations. Much in the

Treaty of Versailles was wrong and more was foolish; but it was Wilson's belief that with war eliminated, wrong and folly could be corrected by reason without perpetrating a worse wrong and a greater folly in the senseless destruction of war. But in this he had rushed far ahead of his time and put a strain upon the maturity of American thought that it was unable to bear.

For although we understood democracy better than any other people and in that respect had attained an advanced maturity, we did not understand the application of its principles beyond the field of our own municipal law. Above all, we had had little effective instruction for many years in the theory of government as an instrumentality for promoting the general welfare. Therefore Wilson returned to ask indorsement of his work by a people confused and uncertain. In general they approved. They were ready enough to beat down any frontal assault on the whole system; but they were not prepared to cope with an underground attack, mounted by sappers and miners of devilish skill.

But this is the sort of attack that was made. The record of the fight for ratification of the Treaty is a document of the utmost value to the student of politics, and especially to the analyst of propaganda. Not a single item of popular mythology was overlooked. Every ancient prejudice afflicting the American people was pressed into service—prejudice against Britain, prejudice against all foreigners, prejudice against novelty. Every newly-spawned prejudice was worked to the limit—prejudice against France, prejudice in favor of Germany, above all prejudice against military service and the military mind. Every moth-eaten illusion was dragged out—the illusion that Washington had advised isolationism, the illusion that Southerners (Wilson was a native of Virginia) would like to betray the Union, the illusion that the British were secretly working to destroy the

Republic, the illusion that "international bankers" had been responsible for the war. With uncanny skill they played upon every trace of infantilism lingering in the mind of the ordinary American—suspicion of the new, suspicion of the intellectual, suspicion of the scientific method.

Against all this there was only one effective battler, Wilson himself. The ablest men in the country in both parties supported him; but the ablest were not always the cleverest, and only Wilson had sufficient prestige with the masses to accomplish much. He made progress. His tour of the country, beginning rather coldly, became so successful that the opposition, alarmed, detached some of its smartest propagandists to follow him, trying to undo his work.

But fate intervened in a manner so striking that one is tempted to paraphrase Hugo's remark about Napoleon and suggest that God became bored with the American people. At any rate, on September 25, 1919, Wilson collapsed. He was brought back to Washington completely incapacitated, and made only a slow and partial recovery.

That was the end of the chapter, but not of the book. The fight dragged on for months that stretched into years, but only one outcome was possible after the leader fell. The common American was betrayed with almost unparalleled cynicism, but, after all, primarily he betrayed himself. In international affairs he was still a simpleton, or he could not have been betrayed. He listened to the confidence men and bought the gold brick. In 1920 he repudiated Wilson, repudiated the League of Nations, repudiated common decency, and put the government in the hands of a corrupt and conscienceless gang who robbed the common man, betrayed him, debauched his government, and held him up to the ridicule of the civilized world.

Yet there had been a moment. Through the dust and smoke of battle, through the foul miasmas of rotten politics, through clouds of ignorance and prejudice, we had caught a gleam of something shining. It seemed far away and the vision did not last, but for a moment we saw it, and we did not forget. Twenty-five years later we remembered and, with our blood and tears flowing, wondered what might have been had we had a little more courage, a little more steadfastness, a little more of a rational, adult attitude in 1920. The memory was bitter, yet not without its touch of pride; for there was a moment when we had almost been great.

Remembering, we heard the ring of truth in the words of that strange, little old man in South Africa. Smuts said, and we knew he was right, "Not Wilson, but humanity failed at Paris."

II
Lenin Passes

1. *Theogony*

HESIOD, a poet who died so long ago that we are not sure to which century he should be assigned, is supposed to have written the last word on the designing and fabrication of gods; and when Hesiod wrote the actual operation was already so far in the past that his thesis had to be pieced together out of shreds and scraps of information in traditions not written but handed down orally. No contemporary professed to know anything about it.

Later scholars who have delved into this ghostly subject, even Sir James Frazer, who wrote twelve volumes on it, have merely explained and elaborated Hesiod's work, recording the appearance of essentially the same phenomena among primitives in every part of the world. Not even Frazer goes beyond Hesiod, and anthropologists have assumed unanimously that the manufacture of gods is an activity characteristic of none but the earliest periods of a people's history, while it usually is confined to prehistory. Certainly there was a time when every Roman emperor became *divus* immediately after his election, but that was as purely formalistic and as empty of real piety as is the American custom of making every college president a Doctor of Laws immediately after his inauguration.

Our generation is the first in many centuries that has been in position to add a chapter to the *Theogony* of Hesiod; for a god has been created before our eyes, and not any two-for-a-nickel tribal deity, but a very great god, worshipped over millions of square miles by scores of millions of devotees, and even now warring bitterly and powerfully against all the older gods, including Buddha, Christ and Mahomet.

Theological affirmation of this is, of course, denied, vehemently. But theological affirmation never was necessary to the establishment or disestablishment of any faith; the real god is not the one the priests proclaim, but the one the people worship. When the walls of Russian schoolrooms bear framed mottoes, reading, "Remember, even when you are alone, Lenin sees you. Lenin is everywhere," there is no doubt that Lenin is a god, and what the priests may say on the subject is irrelevant.

Of course the average American had no idea of what was going on at the time. In the first place, he was very much absorbed in the Wilsonian drama at home; but apart from that, the Russian drama was too far removed for him to see it clearly —far removed in space, but still further in spirit, in custom, in tradition. If the First World War was incredible, the creation of a new major cult was still harder to believe; even a full generation after the beginning many Americans still do not believe it.

Perhaps the Americans least able to credit it were the intellectuals, especially those who had made a study of comparative religion. Their very familiarity with the examples of deification in history unfitted them to accept this example, for they were not ready with a psychological explanation. They could understand how a conqueror-king, Alexander the Great for example, came to be deified by the nations he had subjugated. They could understand how a great mystic, such as Gautama Buddha, came to be deified by millions impressed by his spiritual power. They could understand how a great popular leader and triumphant warrior, such as Mahomet, came to be deified against his express command, by the people whom he had spurred from lethargy into dazzling world conquest. But none of these, nor any other historical example, had prepared them to see any nation make a god out of a corporation lawyer. They didn't believe it could happen. To this day many of them don't believe it did happen, although the evidence has been before their eyes for twenty-five years.

Nevertheless in the heart of a city that is indubitably the second, and aspires to be the first, among the world's great capitals lies the mummy of a certain Vladimir Illich Ulyanov, who began the practice of law in Samara in 1892 and continued it in St. Petersburg until 1895; and the cadaver is the object of daily adoration exceeding that given the relics of any of the saints, Christian, Buddhist, or Moslem. On all solemn festivals the great officers of state, attended by the finest troops of the mightiest army in the world, repair to the tomb in exactly the spirit in which Islam's faithful repair to the Kaaba, and on that holy spot pronounce harangues that are in everything but form prayers to the spirit of the dead lawyer. At other times the common people approach as near as the ever-vigilant guards will permit, clearly moved by the same impulse that sends pilgrims to the Holy Sepulcher at Jerusalem. Throughout a vast empire youth are instructed and adults are adjured to conduct themselves in a manner that would meet with his approval; and the small fry are assured that he has his eye on them. Of course he is a god, and, as far as mundane influence is concerned, one of the greatest.

Because this happened in our time, it must be accounted among the most important of the forces that have bent and twisted and hammered the American into the shape he holds today. The fact that he took little note of it at the time, and understood only a tithe of what he observed, has nothing to do with the result. Regardless of what we saw or did not see, felt or did not feel, Lenin is one of the Four who will make us the subject of incredible tales to posterity.

But the attitude of the ordinary American toward this phenomenon was affected, indeed, was determined, by this lack of comprehension of its real nature. In this, however, the common man was at one with the uncommon men of the time; leaders and led were afflicted by the same blank incomprehension. If John Doe, farmer, or plumber, or grocer, missed the point, so did Woodrow Wilson, Warren G. Harding and Calvin Coolidge, all Presidents of the United States; and as late as Hoover and the second Roosevelt we were still fumbling, although understanding was beginning to dawn.

Perhaps this error may be attributed in some degree to the long and singularly thorough education in the practical aspects of democracy to which the masses of the American people had been subjected. It may seem ridiculous to assert that superior education may lead to gross mistakes, but as a matter of fact nothing is more common; a doctor of philosophy is always assuming that people with whom he talks are better informed than they really are. Why should not a people, schooled for nearly two hundred years in the ways of democracy, be utterly unable to comprehend the ignorance of other peoples on that subject? Yet if no proper allowance is made for the ignorance of the other party to a discussion, mistakes are inevitable.

The wonder is not that the American people took the wrong

line in dealing with Russia. The wonder is rather that we got ourselves involved in military hostilities against the Russians only briefly, in 1920 and 1921, and since then have managed to escape physical collision.

For in 1917, at the time of the Bolshevik Revolution, it was the very definite opinion of the plain American that politicians, all of them, are distinctly less than superhuman. Even Wilson, although most of us regarded him as a great man, was certainly no more than a man; while as for the ordinary run of political office-holders and aspirants to office, the man in the street held that to describe them as men was to give them the benefit of the doubt.

It was accordingly utterly inconceivable to the masses in the United States that any twentieth-century nation could take, in all sincerity, the attitude that the Russians took toward Lenin. We had great difficulty in understanding the German attitude toward the Kaiser and were slightly puzzled even by the British attitude toward the House that had precipitately changed its name to Windsor when the war broke out. The Russian attitude was far beyond us.

So we rejected it, flatly. We estimated the fierce urgency of Russian political oratory at the value we were accustomed to give political oratory in this country, never dreaming that any population would accept such stuff at face value. This skepticism of course played into the hands of the Bolsheviki, who portrayed it to the Russian people, not as a considered opinion based on reason, however erroneous, but as the characteristic obduracy of the heathen confronted by the True Faith. It was, in their eyes, like the hardening of Pharaoh's heart six times, after six successive wonders; it was no doubt regrettable, but nothing could be done about it. The Chosen People had no alternative; they must disregard it and go ahead.

It was an error on both sides, but that it was an avoidable error

is not so certain. Had the ordinary American been better informed regarding the history of Russia, and especially regarding
the history of radicalism, he might have been somewhat less
bewildered, but probably not much; for it must be borne in mind
that Lenin himself had no idea of the effect he was to produce
on the masses of his countrymen. The last thing he desired was
to become a god. "Religion is the opiate of the people" he had
maintained for years. He was no sectarian. Perhaps what he had
in mind primarily was the Russian state church, the form of
religion with which he was most familiar; but his dictum applied
to any and all. It may be that he would have been appalled had
he realized how what he regarded as his statecraft was rapidly
being transformed into a new theology. There is hardly a doubt
that he would have been scandalized had he known that his
embalmed body was to be laid out as an object of worship, and
his sepulcher to become the holy place of an empire.

If he did not expect any such development, why should it
have been expected by an honest, but far from intellectual, dry-
goods merchant in Indiana, or tobacco warehouseman in Georgia,
or shoe manufacturer in Massachusetts, or lemon grower in
California? Not many of us could define the word "theogony,"
and if we could, we supposed that the generation of gods had
ended with the childhood of the race, had been definitely of the
past when Hesiod wrote. Naturally, we were not prepared to see
the creation of a new god. Naturally, we did not recognize what
was happening when we did see it. Naturally, we made mistakes
in dealing with the phenomenon—not merely the man in the
street, but the wisest of our national leaders, too. Woodrow
Wilson was deceived, Charles E. Hughes was deceived. The
immensely learned Dr. Nicholas Murray Butler, President of
Columbia, and the immensely superior Dr. A. Lawrence Lowell,
President of Harvard, were hardly better informed with regard
to what was really happening in Russia than any streetcar motor-

man or asphalt spreader in the street. All alike, we were convinced that the creation of a new religion was not to be looked for in our times; so we were caught napping.

At the moment—that is to say, until after the death of Lenin in 1924—the effect of this apparition upon the average American was inconsiderable. It caused him some annoyance and perturbation, to be sure, but he had been annoyed and perturbed by many things, so that was not in any sense a new experience. It was only years later, when the truth about what he had seen began to percolate into his mind, that his credulity was subjected to a strain greater than the strain to which his physical stamina had been subjected by the First World War. But when he did realize the truth, the basis of many of his assumptions was loosened, and he acquired a new and far from reassuring view of the world he lived in.

2. *The Silken Curtain*

WHEN Nikolai Lenin strode across the stage of world events our view of him was doubly obscured. In the first place, he was upstage, and we were intent upon the tragedy of Woodrow Wilson, being played just behind the footlights. In the second place, the stage was divided by something like those curtains of transparent gauze that theater managers drop before a scene to give an effect of fantasy, of unreality, a dreamlike quality.

This curtain was the whole complex of experience, tradition

and environment that makes it virtually impossible for the average American to understand the arguments of European radicals, and especially the central theme of *Das Kapital*. It is not a language difficulty. The books have been translated adequately, sometimes brilliantly. Any reasonably literate American knows the meaning of the words and is familiar with the grammatical structure of the sentences. But he misses the force of the argument because it does not jibe with his own habits of thought.

In part this is probably due to the fact that our own struggle to subdue a wilderness is so recent that memory of it still persists in millions. Karl Marx held that class warfare is an inevitable condition of social advance. But it is obvious that in order to have class warfare, you must first have classes so definite and so rigid that they are capable of waging war. Under frontier conditions, however, classes are impossible, because the wilderness presents a clear and present danger to every human being in the community, a danger so great that the combined efforts of all are no more than sufficient to cope with it. We discovered this as early as 1608, when tough John Smith drove the gentlemen of Jamestown to labor in the cornfields lest all, gentlemen and commoners alike, die of starvation. We had practical experience of it as late as 1893, the date of the official closing of the last frontier; and in reality our experience has continued down to the present, because there are more frontiers than the official one, and every American community has found a combined effort necessary to overcome difficulties not imposed by any king or baron but inherent in the situation—public education, public health, public safety in America have been opposed, not by the privileged primarily, but by the absence of the necessary facilities. At times the privileged have opposed public services of all kinds, but not often enough nor consistently enough to constitute themselves the main obstacle.

The American, therefore, while he is opposed to privilege in principle, is not conditioned to understand Marx's vehement conviction that it is the one great enemy of humanity and that relentless war upon it is the first duty of man. The first duty of man, as the American has seen it, is to subdue the physical environment rather than the ruling class, to control the forces of nature rather than to control an aristocracy whose very existence he does not admit, to compel the earth to produce rather than to compel the rich to disgorge.

This attitude no doubt is changing and is destined to change further as the physical exploitation of the continent becomes more complete. But in the years immediately after the first great war, when Lenin was making Marxism a word familiar to all American ears, it was held by the vast majority of the people of this Republic; and it served to give the argument in *Das Kapital* an aura of theatricality that killed its effectiveness as a guide in the practical affairs of everyday life. Even those Americans who admitted that Marx put on a good show, held that it was, after all, only a show, deliberately exaggerated for dramatic effect and not to be taken very seriously.

So through the veil of his own lack of imagination the ordinary American watched Lenin pass, not quite sure he was there —or, more precisely, not quite sure that he was seeing what he thought he saw. It was dramatic enough, but from the American's point of view somewhat wavery and uncertain and very far away.

Even the man's physical appearance contributed to strengthen this impression. Lean and cadaverous was Lenin, slightly reminiscent of Christ as portrayed by those pietistic artists who insist on depriving Him of all strong humanity, still more resembling medieval portrayals of Satan as the tempter, but most strongly of all suggesting to Americans the character of Ichabod Crane, the skinny and ridiculous schoolmaster of Washington Irving's tale. Emphatically, there was no hint in his appearance of Jupiter

the Thunderer, or of Apollo, Ruler of Light. His very beard
was thin and scraggly, his look—as pictured, for almost none of
us saw him except in pictures—that of an arid personality. At
first, we mistook him for one of the odd bits of flotsam thrown
up by the turbulence of a great war, and little to be regarded.

He was in Switzerland when the disturbances began in Russia
in 1917, and the Germans, with a much clearer perception of his
quality than we had, allowed him, although he was an enemy
alien, to cross their territory in a railroad coach set aside for his
use, in order that he might reach Petrograd, lately St. Petersburg and soon to be Leningrad. The German idea was simply to
complicate things for the Russians, and it worked, magnificently.
At that, it might not have worked without able assistance from
the Allies. The empire had collapsed and the Czar had abdicated, but a fair degree of order had been restored under the
liberal leader, Kerensky. The first Communist effort to upset
the regime was a disastrous failure. Lenin, making contact with
the sometime American newspaper reporter, Leon Trotsky,
launched a revolt which was smashed so promptly and completely that Trotsky took to the cellars and Lenin fled to Finland. With a little intelligent support from the Allies and the
United States, Kerensky might have kept things in hand.

But the Allies were in no condition to act intelligently. The
collapse of the Eastern Front meant to them that the whole
remaining power of Germany and Austria would soon be hurled
against them, and the prospect frightened them into lunacy.
They drove Kerensky into undertaking a last offensive, although
the Russian army was already beaten and an offensive could
only result, as it did, in a massacre. After that, Kerensky was
finished, and the Bolsheviki took over. This was the famous
November Revolution, which was won by default, for the
Kerensky government was incapable of striking a real blow.

The news of this came through to the American people in

the vaguest and most uncertain way. The real state of the Russian army had been carefully kept from them by military leaders obsessed by the characteristic military delusion that friendly populations must always be kept in ignorance of the true magnitude of difficulties; therefore the average American could see nothing blameworthy in that last effort, and when the Russians turned savagely upon the Kerensky government for making it, most of us attributed their wrath to their moral and political obtuseness, not to our own folly in demanding of them more than flesh and blood could bear. It was tragic, but what else could have happened?

But there was vastly more than military censorship between us and the Russians in those clamorous years when Russia turned definitely toward the blood bath. There was in addition the double veil suspended between us by our experience and theirs. The average American regarded himself as a pretty smart fellow when it came to understanding human foibles. Had he not been seethed in the melting pot of all nations and all races? Had he not been accustomed, all his life, to rub elbows with aboriginals, Orientals and Africans, as well as with representatives of every European country? Who, then, could be better trained to understand and make proper allowance for the foreignness of any foreign nation? The Englishman and the Frenchman might be excused for lack of comprehension of anything alien, considering how homogeneous were their own countries; but the United States was a composite of all nations, therefore the American could observe them all clearly.

What we forgot was our own Americanism. Certainly we had learned how to get along with Ah Sin, Rain-in-the-Face, and Uncle Tom, but we could not realize that all three were, in fact, American types, far from representative of Chinese, Indian and African culture. All we had learned to understand was American types, slanted somewhat by race, religion and national origin, but very distinctly American, therefore radically modified from the human types of China, Africa and pre-Columbian America. Lenin's first great colleague, Leon Trotsky, had himself picked up a thin patina of Americanism during a couple of years' residence in this country, and that may be one reason why we found him more comprehensible than his leader.

But Lenin was emphatically not an American type. In many respects he bore an odd resemblance to Wilson, but few of us perceived it, or were willing to admit it if we did see it. It was plain enough that the man, like the college president was an intellectual, like the Presbyterian was somewhat ascetic, like the leader of the Democratic party was a powerful orator, and like the Princetonian had developed a marked intellectual arrogance, yet we assured ourselves that he was not in the least like Wilson.

Fundamentally, we were perfectly right. Wilson was an American, Lenin a Russian, and that profound difference canceled out all superficial resemblances. Neither could see the other without a distortion that falsified the whole picture; nor were the followers of either better able to penetrate the veil that different experiences of life had hung between them. Worst of all, neither could perceive the veil. Military censorship we could recognize and allow for; but the refraction caused by life-long habits of act and thought escaped our notice, not merely in the early twenties, but for a long time afterward.

Vladimir Ulyanov had had an older brother, Alexander, brilliant, idealistic, and apparently a man of unusual personal charm. In any event, the younger boy seems to have developed the sort of hero-worship that is common enough in every race and every country to be easily understood anywhere in the world. Possibly Alexander Ulyanov was an ambitious man, but Vladimir did not see him in any such light; at seventeen he saw his elder brother as a selfless patriot, interested only in winning relief for the oppressed.

But his first mild efforts brought savage retaliation from the officers of the law, whereupon he turned to desperate measures, conspired to overthrow the government by force and violence, was detected, and in 1886 was hanged in Stüsselberg prison.

The effect might have been predicted by a man who has never looked inside a textbook on psychology, but who has known young boys. Vladimir developed a cold, hard, bitter hatred of the institution that had, as he believed, murdered his hero; but he also perceived the titanic strength of that institution and realized that it could be attacked successfully only by cunning. From that day on, to omit nothing he might do toward destruction of the empire became not merely his ambition and his pleasure, but his high and sacred duty.

If Woodrow Wilson had been injected with such poison at seventeen, it is imaginable that he might have become just such a man. Wilson was descended from the Scotch Covenanters, and the world has seen few more persistent haters and few harder fanatics. They, too, were inspired by the butchery of their heroes and they gave the empire they opposed a vast amount of trouble through many years. Any man endowed with brains and character who becomes embittered in early adolescence is a dangerous man; and if his bitterness against the existing powers is reinforced by a conviction that they are too powerful to be attacked successfully except by cunning stealth, he is a fearfully dangerous man. This is true regardless of his nationality; had Wilson been driven by circumstances to employ his extraordinary intellectual endowment implacably and furtively against the government, he might have been more fearful than Lenin.

But of this the average American had no inkling in the early twenties. Peering through the silken curtain but not realizing that it existed, what he observed was a monstrosity, apparently an avowed enemy of the human race, an apparition as incomprehensible as it was appalling. It stood to reason that this thing must be put down, by any means that happened to be handy.

Unfortunately, the means at hand were very questionable indeed. Nevertheless, the American cheerfully used them, in all good conscience. He proceeded to back every military adventurer who boasted of his power to exterminate the Bolsheviki—Denikin, Kolchak, Wrangel, half a dozen others, were furnished with money and weapons. Some of these soldiers of fortune turned out to be thorough-paced villains themselves, and some who were fairly decent personally collected armies consisting of the scurviest rascals in Europe, contemptuous of all discipline and looking upon the war merely as an excuse for raving of every type, including the foulest. In the end, they were flung out of the country, one and all, but not until they had subjected Russia to three years of horror the like of which the average American had never imagined.

So the common man in Russia, peering through the curtain from his side, saw a picture of something that did not exist. He saw the decent, well-meaning, essentially kindly American as the supporter and backer of such hordes of cutthroats as had seldom been released upon a helpless population. He assumed that the American must be doing this for something more than mere amusement, and the only other motive that could account for it was profit; which made of us the jackal prowling in the wake of the fiercer beasts of prey, hoping to pick up his share of carrion.

So hatred spread and hardened on both sides. The tragedy was that there existed no force strong enough to rip away the gauze. True, there were exceptional men who did not take the ordinary view, but they commanded little confidence, either here or in Russia. Here they fell into two classes. One was that of the romantics, to whose eyes the angle of refraction was even greater than that to the eyes of the average man, but who saw everything in Russia through a rose-tinted haze. Many of these hurried to Russia and a handful stayed there, but the great majority soon returned disillusioned and more violently anti-Russian than the rankest reactionary who had stayed at home. These had little effect on public opinion for the sufficient reason that the average man knew that they had never had any sense about anything else, so could hardly be expected to have any about Russia.

The other consisted of a handful of genuine scholars and philosophers, men whom study reinforced by a broad culture had endowed with historical perspective. Such men, aware of the existence of the curtain, could make a reasonably accurate allowance for its effect and arrive at an approximation of the truth. But they were all scholars and most of them were intellectually somewhat cloistered. None was highly articulate in the language of the street, so none was heard with attention. When they were heard at all they seemed to the common man to be persons who breathed a rarefied atmosphere, doubtless extremely pure, but hardly able to sustain life in the lower orders; so they enjoyed respect but little influence.

Thus the gossamer curtain entangled the flies so lightly, so gently that they rarely realized that they were entangled.

3. Descent Upon Trebizond

WILSON, the leader of men, died at Pueblo, Colorado, September 25, 1919. Wilson, the individual, lingered for five years longer, a hopeless cripple, defiant to the last, but powerless to control, or even greatly to modify, the course of events. His last five years are wonderful material for study by philoso-

phers, poets and dramatists, but for the purpose of this discussion
they may be ignored. What he was to do toward shaping the
American he had done by the time he collapsed; the remainder
was the drama of an individual, not of a nation.

Like Cyrus the Younger, Wilson fell leaving his army in far
Babylonia, and the subsequent retreat furnishes a tale not less
startling, in its very different way, than the march of the Ten
Thousand Greeks from Cunaxa until they poured over the
mountain barrier and down upon unsuspecting Trebizond.

The American Expeditionary Force came home early—unfortunately, some have said indecently, early—but the army re-
ferred to here is not the AEF, but the army of liberal political
thought, which Wilson had led into a region vastly more remote
than Germany, and which, when he fell, was left not merely
without a leader but, as the rank and file supposed, also without
a cause. We had penetrated uncounted parasangs into the realm
of internationalism—like Babylonia in the eyes of the Greeks,
an enormously rich and fertile country, but also enormously
complicated, enormously bewildering, enormously far removed
from our experience, enormously far from home.

The "flight from freedom" that characterized America in the
period immediately following the First World War engaged
the puzzled attention of psychologists for some years—up until
the moment when the flight from freedom after the Second
World War came upon them and obscured it. Its causes are,
indeed, undetermined, but its characteristic phenomena have
been repeated often enough to form a recognizable pattern.
Americans who are usually hardened into greater resolution by
disaster—Long Island, Bull Run, Pearl Harbor—show a curious
tendency to be appalled by victory and to shrink from its con-
sequences. Having fought the Revolution to establish the people's right to overthrow by force and violence a government
they found intolerable, and having won, we promptly enacted

the Alien and Sedition laws to prevent anyone's so much as criticizing the government. Having fought the Civil War to prove that a State cannot quit the Union, we promptly decided that eleven Southern States had, in fact, quit the Union and were become conquered alien territory. Having fought the First World War to make the world safe for democracy, we promptly set to work to make America utterly unsafe for democracy by violent persecution of unpopular minorities. Thirty years later we repeated both operations with increased gusto.

But the flight in 1920 is easier to understand than any other except the flight in 1865. In both instances a great leader had fallen suddenly, Lincoln by the hand of an assassin, Wilson by the hand of God, and had left no successor capable of controlling the situation. In such cases the leader is always blamed for not having trained a man to take his place, and the blame is usually nonsensical. Lincoln and Wilson, like Cyrus the Younger, were making conquests in the vast unknown. Cyrus was conquering geographical areas, and the others penetrating regions of thought, but the sense of strangeness, the necessity for prompt decision and rapid improvisation, and the prevailing terror of the unfamiliar were the same. The leaders had enough to do to train themselves; what they hardly understood they could not possibly have imparted to others.

Wilson went to Paris feeling that his task was not to end the war against Germany, but to justify the war against Germany by making such conflicts unnecessary in the future. He was aware that his conviction on this point was much more intense than that of any other man of sufficient weight to head the delegation, so he headed it himself. The others were pretty well persuaded that the war was already justified; the European delegates were utterly certain that it was so. Wilson, almost alone, regarded victory, territorial readjustments, and the destruction of Prussian militarism as wholly inadequate excuses for having fought. If the conference did no more than merely end the war against Germany it would be a failure in his eyes; only if it made provisions that would end war as an instrument of national policy would it be a success in any real sense.

The average American agreed in principle, but it was all new ground and he had to rely on some guide to find his way across it. He was content to follow Wilson, even in unexplored territory, but he had no such confidence in any other leader.

More than that, it soon became plain that not even Wilson had measured all the difficulties. The conference at Paris proved to be more difficult than the President himself had expected— so difficult that he won only after a long and desperate battle in which his losses were terrific. He started for Paris backed by the famous Fourteen Points, each the psychological equivalent of a division, since they had broken the German will to resist; but in the diplomatic struggle he lost point after point, until at least ten of the fourteen had been wrecked; but the main one, the establishment of an international organization with the authority to settle international disputes by law and not by war, survived, and that he deemed well worth the loss of the rest.

Unfortunately, the leader himself had received a mortal blow. It did not become apparent until later, and if the struggle had ended at Paris he might have recovered; but the collapse at Pueblo was certainly precipitated by the exhausting effect of the fight at Paris. He went down; and down with him went what confidence the average American had felt in the whole enterprise. Our first adventure in world politics, after a campaign not less brilliantly successful than the march of Cyrus into Asia, had ended in a comparable disaster, and the impulse of the rank and file was to get out of there by whatever means seemed practicable.

The savage attack of the "little group of willful men" inspired by Lodge and Theodore Roosevelt is usually blamed for the defeat of the League of Nations, and it was the proximate cause of that defeat. But while we may apply to them the Scriptural commination, "Woe to that man by whom the offence cometh," for the larger view it is essential to bear in mind the preceding phrase, "It must needs be that offences come." Lodge, Borah, Johnson, Fall, Brandegee, Knox and the rest may not be exonerated for what they did, but the essential failure went deeper and spread further; it was the incapacity of the common, ordinary American to rise to the occasion. Smuts hit it—in the United States as at Paris, it was not so much that stupid men triumphed as that humanity failed.

At the same time there was no justification for the black despair that overwhelmed some liberals so completely that they wrote the average American off as incapable of self-government. It was a defeat and a bad one, so bad that we paid the first large installment of its price between 1941 and 1945, are still paying, and will continue to pay for some generations; but it was far from being unique, or even exceptional. If we collapsed, so did the rest of the world and especially the new power that was forming in the obscurity of the dust and smoke. Lenin was most certainly no help to Wilson at the critical moment.

He had a valid excuse. At the moment when the fight was staged in Washington, Lenin was fighting for his own life against, among others, American troops. But later events showed conclusively that if he had had opportunity he had not the will to support the sort of project that Wilson had in mind. Lenin was an exceptionally intelligent and well-educated man. If he had no faith in the ideal of a pacification based on agreement instead of conquest, what hope to find it in the Russian masses?

All the circumstances considered—and the most important circumstances were their own confusion, inexperience and lack of competent leadership—the Americans were in a hopeless position. With the advantage of hindsight, we can see all sorts of brilliant things they might have done. The power of Artaxerxes was shattered. Babylon lay wide open. A short, resolute advance in 1920 might have carried us into a position of security from which we could never have been dislodged and the horrors and losses of the Second World War might have been spared. But so might the Ten Thousand Greeks have Hellenized the world two generations ahead of Alexander the Great had they had the advantage of brilliant and inspiring leadership.

But confusion and inexperience are realities—intangible, but not less real than an army with banners. Any theoretical program that fails to take them into account is as fantastic as would be a projected line of march that should fail to take into account the fact that Caucasus lies across the path. The truth is that once Wilson collapsed, American internationalism was done for, and a retreat was inevitable.

A dreadful march it was, too, through frozen mountain wildernesses infested with *banditti* of countless varieties. As the Greeks soon left the Persians behind, but had to contend against unknown and uncivilized races almost every step of the way, we soon lost track of Europe and its problems and had to spend our time fighting off raiders who were enemies, not merely of world order, but of the human race itself—the witch-hunts of A. Mitchell Palmer, with thousands of prosecutions and whole trainloads of deportees rolling across the Continent; the savagery of a rising hysteria culminating in the martyrdom of Sacco and Vanzetti; the stealings of the Ohio gang debauching public office up to the Cabinet; prohibition with its attendant reign of the hoodlums; the sudden breaking out from the depths of bigotry and obscurantism spearheaded by the Ku Klux Klan, frank hater not merely of learning but of common decency; the resurgence of commercial greed bent upon the reduction of labor to serfdom, if not to chattel slavery.

Entangled in the mountains of Armenia the Greeks seemed to

have lost, not merely the conquest of the world, but even such contact with civilization as they had established through their long, laborious history. So the retreat from Paris carried our generation of Americans into wild gorges and gloomy defiles where strange creatures lurked in ambush, not merely less than Americans, but sometimes apparently less than civilized men— robbers, murderers, witch-hunters and idolaters, practitioners of barbarous rites and adherents of unclean creeds. Strange and wild indeed were our adventures in the mountains of Armenia as one looks back upon them now, fit subject for many an incredible tale ere we broke over the last high ridge and looked down upon Trebizond and the sea.

For the common man had lost more than a leader, something more important than a leader. There were times when he seemed to have lost life, liberty and the pursuit of happiness, for all that they were called "unalienable rights." There were times when he seemed to have suffered the last, fatal loss, loss of his confidence in himself and in his capacity to control his destiny.

There were times when it seemed that he had no rights that anyone was bound to respect. He could be kicked with impunity by the high, the middle-class and the low. Whether in Massachusetts, where to soothe the nerves of the commonwealth a cobbler and a fish peddler went to death assisted on their way by learning, represented by Harvard, science, represented by the Massachusetts Institute of Technology, and literature, represented by an author-judge; or in North Carolina, where Ella May Wiggins lay dead on the highway, shot down for making ballads against the textile barons; or in Louisiana, where masked terrorists executed their enemies by putting them under a steam roller equipped with cleats; or in Chicago, where the reigning lord of crime cut down his enemies seven in a row; or at Herrin, Illinois, where twenty-six died for claiming the right to work; everywhere it seemed that the plain American had no defense as against the aristocratic, the rich, the vicious, or the criminal. An incredible tale, indeed, and an incredible fate for him who had lately aspired to establish the rule of justice under law from pole to pole.

But it is sustained by the records. It is thoroughly documented. It happened.

4. The Diadochi

THE emptiness of American statecraft after Wilson fell was a source of great satisfaction to some, and of acute distress to others, but it was felt by everyone. The common man, distrustful of his own judgment, and distracted by the contradictory clamors of his would-be leaders, knew only that there was nobody in sight comparable to the man he had followed through eight epochal years. Harding and Coolidge, Cox and McAdoo were all well enough in their way, no doubt, but at most they were Antigonus and Seleucus after Alexander. Indeed, they were hardly that, for the generals who divided the empire after the Conqueror, and whom history contemptuously lumps together as the Diadochi, the Successors, were at least formidable to those whom they held in subjection, and from 1920 to 1924 it was the unanimous endeavor of American statesmen not to overawe, but to soothe. Even the young Roosevelt who ran for Vice President with Cox on the Democratic ticket in 1920, and who was soundly beaten, gave nobody the slightest alarm. To the minority who knew he was there at all, he appeared to be much more of a cream puff than the benevolent Ohio editor who headed the ticket.

As for the liberals who had marched on the great adventure, they split like Xenophon's Greeks. Some turned into reactionaries of the most extreme type, some went off into various radical movements, some degenerated into slick politicians, limber enough to serve any war lord who offered good pay and a chance of loot. Only a small, devoted band maintained their discipline and burnished their arms; and they were regarded humorously by the rest of the world. A Newton D. Baker could deliver one of the finest orations of modern times to a Democratic National Convention without evoking any other response than a shrug.

The average man might regard all this with a vague discomfort, but what could he do about it? For the moment, the answer was, nothing at all. He was not yet sufficiently sure of himself in the realm of high politics to formulate, much less to enforce, his own demands. But they deceived themselves who thought that he had learned nothing from the great and disastrous years. He had learned at least that the world beyond his own borders is vastly more complicated than he had supposed and that modern war is more dreadful than he had imagined. Regarding the new power forming in the East he knew little, but that little included one clear and firm conviction—he did not want to fight it. For thirteen years after 1920 we officially ignored the existence of the Communist State, but at no time during those years was there any possibility of instigating the American people to make war against it.

The presence of Harding and Coolidge, those complete vacuities, in the White House was quite satisfactory to the great lords of business and politics, whose opinions the common man has always respected—too readily for his own good many times. We had taken an interest in world affairs once, ran the common talk, and what had we got out of it? A debt and a headache, both prodigious. In the name of common sense, then, let us hereafter cultivate our garden.

This was all very well, except that it was the common sense of Candide and of Dr. Pangloss, those triumphant evaders of reality. The fact that the world was taking, must take, and must continue to take an ominous interest in us was not mentioned by his leaders and not perceived by the common man. The gentry who were intent on getting "back to normalcy," who declared that "the business of America is business" fascinated us by their talk so completely that we failed to note that they were making "normalcy" unattainable and conducting a travesty of business in neglecting to move heaven and earth to repair the ravages of the war before economic disaster overtook us.

For the accumulated capital of centuries had been so completely incinerated by the war that normal trade was impossible until the ravages had been remedied, at least in great measure. Capitalism by definition presupposes the existence of capital, not merely in one spot but distributed throughout the system. At the war's end a disproportionately large proportion of all the liquid capital left in the world was concentrated in the United States—so large a proportion as to make impossible the movement of international trade on the traditional capitalistic basis.

A restoration of the balance should have been the first concern of businessmen interested in the resumption of normal business; and private business did undertake it, to the extent of some ten billions of American capital sent abroad in the first few years after the war. But ten billions were not nearly enough. Five or ten times that sum would have been necessary and any such financial operation was far beyond the strength of private business; only the government could have managed it, and the government would have been strained. A leader of extraordinary vision coupled with extraordinary powers of persuasion might just possibly have succeeded in mastering the difficulty; but a

Coolidge might as soon have been expected to carry off the Washington Monument on his narrow shoulders.

As far as the public was aware it never entered the mind of the vacuous little man in the White House that he was under any obligation to give serious attention to restoration of the economy of the Western World. If it had been suggested to him he would have rejected the idea instantly. Coolidge had a genius for evading responsibility. When the system of currency exchange broke down completely under the overload of war debts, his only comment was the pettish question, "They hired the money, didn't they?" and he refused to trouble himself further.

The disheartening factor in the situation was that this puerility passed for shrewdness with millions of Americans. Had it been a domestic situation that was obviously deteriorating with appalling speed, a President who put his feet on his desk and napped for an hour or so each afternoon would have been bitterly condemned. But the domestic situation was not yet alarming; and our education in international statecraft was not far enough advanced to enable us to perceive the duty of a President of the United States to act promptly and decisively to protect the country against economic as well as military threats from without. The depressing truth is that we all drowsed with Coolidge while opportunity slipped away.

But it fitted neatly enough into the picture of the world that was being offered to the Russian people by the intellectual founder of the Communist system. Drowsiness is not always the signal of approaching death, but it looks like it. An observer, persuaded beforehand that death is approaching, and who observes the patient falling into a stupor with alarm bells clanging on every side, is pretty sure to be confirmed in his opinion. Lenin had been persuaded by Marx that capitalism not only had within it the seeds of its own decay—a truism applicable to every system —but that those seeds had already sprung up and were about to bear fruit. Nothing he perceived in the United States during the last five years of his life was inconsistent with that theory; on the contrary, the apathy with which this country looked on at the progressive ruin of capitalism in Europe strongly confirmed the theory. Perhaps it never occurred to Lenin that any twentieth-century people could be so naïve as to assume that the collapse of capitalism in Europe might be regarded with comparative indifference by the very center and fount of capitalism.

In any event, he took vigorous and fruitful advantage of the situation. It was during these years that the canon of the Soviet system was fixed and implanted in the minds of the Russian people. The feebleness of American action in the face of the mounting crisis was text enough for any doctrinaire; a propagandist far less skillful than Nikolai Lenin would have found it easy to cite the American course as proof of everything that Marx had said. As it was, within those five years it became—and it remains to this day—an article of faith with the Russians that the United States is not the refutation, but the conclusive demonstration of Marx's belief that capitalism is inherently so stupid that it must work its own downfall and that right speedily.

It was not that we were completely inert, except for the President. If Coolidge did nothing to encourage, neither did he do anything to discourage, the efforts of more alert people with some comprehension of the danger. Dozens of heavy thinkers thought heavily throughout the period. Diplomatists negotiated incessantly. Premiers and finance ministers came and went. Conference followed conference. Young Plans followed Dawes Plans, treaty was piled upon treaty, final, definitive solutions were proclaimed over and over again. It was all very technical, very complicated, very impressive, and completely idiotic. The election of 1928 came and Coolidge was finally translated to Nirvana with nothing done, and by that time it was too late. For they had called in experts, fiscal experts, industrial experts, legal experts, experts of every imaginable kind, by platoons, by battalions, by regiments; but they had never called in the only man who could take effective action. That man was the plain, nonexpert voter and taxpayer.

With all the devising, nobody devised anything like the Marshall Plan. Nobody dared. For the aim of everyone in public life at the time was to soothe, not to exacerbate, the public and the Marshall Plan is brutal and harsh—as brutal as fact, as harsh as one of Woodrow Wilson's appeals from drunken statutes to sober conscience. The Marshall Plan roughly and unmistakably calls on the average American to pay—partly in cold cash, partly in stepping aside to let the other fellow make a dollar now and then, partly in lending American brains to help competitors get on their feet. True enough, it promises a return, and a handsome one, but not for a long time; at the moment it only orders the plain American to shell out, to come across, to stand and deliver; and between 1920 and 1924 nobody believed he could be persuaded to do it.

Perhaps he couldn't, at the time, but nobody knows, because nobody had the courage to try. It would have taken sublime faith in democracy to make the effort a quarter of a century ago, and nobody had such faith. For a quarter of a century nobody screwed up courage enough to take the chance, and then only because the situation had grown so desperate that sublime faith in democracy offered the only possible way out. But when it was tried it turned out that the average American was quite capable of seeing the point. The intricacies of exchange balances and the complexities of multilateral international trade may be beyond his comprehension, but he is perfectly capable of understanding that when the accumulated property of the whole world has been blown to bits, everybody has to pay; and it does not seem to him unreasonable that he should pay his part.

Perhaps the real trouble with the Successors was that secretly they agreed with Lenin's low estimate of capitalism under a democratic political system. In the matter of the war debts, for example, they dodged and squirmed for years after it had become plain to the dullest that payment in gold was impossible, and payment in goods would be ruinous in the existing state of our economy; therefore payment must be relinquished. They did not believe that the people could understand, which is to say, they had no sustaining faith in democracy. So they refused to call in the only man who could have saved the situation, the ordinary American. They chose to rely on experts, with the result that the situation got away from them and the eventual losses became stupendous.

5. *Variation on a Familiar Theme*

IN LATER years it became the fashion among writers, especially the more censorious, to assume that when Lenin was laying the intellectual foundation of the Soviet system his work went unobserved because the American was too drunk to take accurate note of what was going on around him. Among the very young the impression prevails that the so-called Jazz Age was marked by a collapse of morals, public and private, unparalleled since the Restoration period in England.

It is a titivating bit of mythology, but mythology it is, as far as the subject of this discourse, the ordinary American, is concerned. It is true that the enactment of prohibition had the unexpected, but logical, effect of converting public drunkenness from a disgrace into a distinction. Obviously, a man couldn't get tight unless he knew how to get it, and enough people didn't know how to make the one who did seem to be an energetic and knowing fellow. It is true also that the operations of the Ohio Gang debauched the public service on the highest levels to the point at which we saw a former officer of the Cabinet in a prison cell for taking bribes while in office—a disgrace that had never befallen the United States up to that time. It is true that fashion hiked women's skirts up to such an altitude that the lingerie shops were filled with knickers meant to be admired by the public. It is true that popular novelists began to write out plainly details of amorous experience that they had thitherto modestly —and obscenely—indicated by a row of asterisks.

But such incidents, when and where they have any relation to morals at all, are of slight importance. They might excite the clergy, the politicians, literary circles, and Bright Young Things, but all these together constitute a very small percentage of the whole population. The masses went about their lawful occasions in their usual way, indulging, perhaps, in appreciably more head-shaking and more scandalized talk about the pass things were coming to, but otherwise not much affected.

What did reach down nearer to the foundations of national morality was the average man's too ready acceptance of political soothing-syrup, dispensed lavishly by titular leaders who had not the slightest intention of leading, but were bent on preventing the people from starting somewhere and compelling them to follow. This was, indeed, profoundly immoral in that it repudiated that basic tenet of morality, "whatsoever a man soweth, that shall he also reap," and if he soweth the seeds of catastrophe, calamity shall be his harvest. By indifference, inertness, denial of any responsibility for the state of the world, the American was sowing the seed of catastrophe throughout Europe; and he reaped a bumper crop.

"The League of Nations is dead," said Harding shortly after

his election. Yet he had been elected in part on the promise of some of his most eminent supporters, Root, W. H. Taft, Hughes, and many others, that his election was the one way of saving the life of the League. Nevertheless, the repudiation went unrebuked by the American public; and by its acquiescence the public incurred a share of responsibility for the repudiation. This was immoral. By comparison with this, the gaudy carnalities against which press and pulpit thundered uselessly were trivialities unworthy of notice.

But, as is usually the case, the genuine immorality was loudly acclaimed as the virtue of a sturdy, uncorrupted people, not by politicians only, but by all the self-appointed Catos in the country. Neither press nor pulpit is overzealous in denouncing those sins that the tithing congregation is inclined to.

Greed came in for some belaboring, especially after greed overreached itself in 1929 and was ridiculously exposed, but evidence is not at hand that the average American was conspicuously more greedy in the Jazz Age than he was before or later. Perhaps greed was a trifle more naked and unashamed, especially during the great boom in the stock market, than it is ordinarily; but it is a fairly constant factor in the human equation. It contributes to every disaster, but it is not clear that it contributed more than its usual quota to bringing on the woes that befell us ten years after the end of the First World War.

As far as the average American, the ordinary man who held no public office, appeared on no stage, wrote no books, brawled in no speakeasies, and was unknown to readers of the tabloid newspapers, was concerned, the great sin of the Jazz Age was not drunkenness, nor lechery, nor plunder, but a vast, a criminal irresponsibility. The plain man was disposed to let Coolidge do it; and if Coolidge was obviously doing nothing, that was his responsibility, for which the average man could not be held to account.

Unfortunately, he was held to account. As for Coolidge, he

napped happily through five and a half years in the White House, then for four years more watched without comment the misery of his successor and eventually was gathered into Abraham's bosom before the full power of the calamity he had done nothing to avert burst upon the country. If he was held to account it was not before any human tribunal and not in this world; which may be a closer approximation to justice than it would seem to be at first glance. For in the last analysis the President of the United States acts, not on his own account, but as agent. The principal is the sovereign voter, that is to say, the ordinary American—the extraordinary one, too, but the ordinary one is the one who counts, since by force of numbers he holds the power. It is a sound maxim of law that the principal is accountable for the acts of his agent and also for failure of the agent to act at all. It seems to be also a principle of the logic of events; for it is a matter of common knowledge that nonfeasance does bring trouble in its train.

So if it was the average American who paid the cost of a do-nothing policy in these years, why not? He hired Coolidge, didn't he? He kept Coolidge in office for an additional term after it was demonstrated that he was an empty barrel. Why, then, lay all the blame on the agent for a policy accepted, if not dictated, by his principal?

It is certainly true that Coolidge was assisted, and possibly true that he was saved, in 1924 by a quarrel in the Democratic party. The election of that year was therefore only in part a public indorsement of the Coolidge record, for the President profited greatly by resentments among his opponents. Some people who did not like him voted for him out of sheer disgust with his opponents; and a great many who did not like him refused to vote at all which was, of course, to his profit.

Mischief-makers had for some time been busily fanning the embers of the ancient Protestant-Catholic quarrel, and by 1924 they were so successful that the long-smoldering fire burst into a conflagration in the Democratic National Convention, where William G. McAdoo, a Scotch Protestant, was opposed for the nomination by Alfred E. Smith, an Irish Catholic, and the contest was so long, so stubborn, and so bitter, that when both were retired and the nomination given to John W. Davis, eminently respectable, but a corporation lawyer, that is to say, belonging to a breed none suspects of having too much religion of any kind, the contestants on both sides were too angry to give him more than fainthearted support, and he lost the election.

This affair administered a pretty severe shock to thoughtful Americans, as, indeed, it should. It revealed the fact that religious tolerance, which most of us were accustomed to regard as built into the very fabric of the American system, is, instead, an alarmingly thin veneer on the surface. If it had had any connection with intense piety, something might be said for it, but every rational observer knew that what was involved was not religion, but clericalism; it revealed, not a strong religious spirit in the American people, but a disposition to employ the religious spirit to further political schemes, which has been uniformly disastrous throughout the history of Western civilization.

The guilt was evenly distributed. If Tammany Hall grasped at the Presidency with the aid of the priests, the Ku Klux Klan grasped at it with the aid of the presbyters. There is some consolation in remembering that neither got it; but the escape was bought at a high price when the consideration was the choice of such a *roi fainéant* as Coolidge.

But the shock to the thoughtful was by no means as profound as it should have been. To see American politics degenerate into a squabble between priest and parson was enough to make the judicious grieve; but to sink into such puerility at that particular moment was a folly of vastly greater magnitude than it seemed to be at the time. For it meant that as our attention was absorbed by this dreary farce, it was distracted from events of immeasurably greater importance. Coolidge died in 1933, McAdoo in 1941, Smith in 1944. All of them outlived Lenin, Coolidge by nine years, McAdoo by seventeen, Smith by twenty; yet the influence of the three politicians on the lives and destinies of men in 1950 is hardly more perceptible than that of the father of Melchizedek, who was nonexistent, while that of Lenin is more formidable today than it was on the day that he died.

The fact that we did not see him, or seeing, did not observe, is the glaring error of the Jazz Age. The average man took a holiday from thinking. Since 1913, when the inauguration of Woodrow Wilson brought sharply into his mind the concept of the use of government as an instrument to promote the general welfare, through the period of the First World War and the extension of that idea in the League of Nations, the plain man had been thinking hard. To be sure, his concentration was not that of a mathematical physicist, but for him it really was hard thinking. The problem of government had been rasping and fretting his frontal lobes more persistently than ever before. He was tired of it. Ardently he desired to turn his mind to other things; and if he turned it to such matters as the Pope in the White House, gin in the bathtub, and two chickens in every love-nest, the triviality of the things he considered was of small moment. What counted were the things he refused to consider.

For if there is even one bit of knowledge that the thunderous century has taught its victims with a certainty beyond dispute, it is that in a democracy the average man takes a holiday from thinking only at infinite peril and immeasurable cost. "There is no discharge in that war," for there is no possibility of delegating the voter's authority. He may only refuse to exercise it and acquiesce in its usurpation. In fact, he does, all too frequently; and that is why without cessation he bleeds, and pays, and groans.

To the ascetic type, for whom the whole moral law is summed up in the simple imperative, "Don't," it may seem fantastic and outrageous to dismiss as trivial the swilling, and wenching, and swindling, and general blackguardism of the Jazz Age, and to insist that its real immorality lay, not in what it did, but in what it refused to do. Nevertheless, it is incontestably true that all the stealing of the Ohio Gang did not bankrupt us or even embarrass us seriously; that women have let their skirts down again and monogamy is still widely practiced; that the Pope did not take over the White House and the Anti-Saloon League can no longer make Congress squat whenever it cracks the whip; that all the evil activities that so agitated the moralists are now merely as a tale that is told.

But because we failed to study the man Lenin seriously and assiduously; because we failed to comprehend the power of his false doctrine and to counter it with more powerful truth; because we fell into the ancient error of believing that heresy may be killed with a sword of steel whereas it is vulnerable only to the sword of the spirit; because, in short, we played around with wretched toys instead of attending to our real business between 1919 and 1924—now we are in serious trouble. No man can see the end of it; but we have already paid plenty for our Jazz Age holiday from serious thinking; and assuredly we shall pay plenty more.

6. City of Brass

"I DO not know the method of drawing up an indictment
against an whole people," confessed Edmund Burke, who
nevertheless made a pretty good effort somewhat later, when
he came to consider the French Revolution. His confession,
though, is sounder than his effort. The indictment of a nation
never stands unless it is drawn with a clear understanding that
the limit of its accountability is that of *particeps criminis* and
that the other side shares the blame. The common man in the
United States during the Long Armistice cooked up a fine mess
of trouble for himself and the rest of the world, but to assume
that he was solely responsible for it would be fatuous to the
last degree. He perpetrated some injustices and many follies;
but he also suffered injustices and was the victim of countless
follies. If there were such a thing as a final balancing of the
books in history it might turn out that he was more often
victim than villain.

Our failure to comprehend the size, or even the nature, of the
mighty upheaval in Russia was tragic; but certainly we got
small assistance toward effective understanding from the other
side. The doctrinaire Lenin, for all his undeniable ability, was
in one respect the same sort of jackass that Sidney Smith had
been a hundred years earlier when he inquired, "Who reads an
American book?" Lenin's folly was less excusable because the
American experiment had been proceeding for an additional
century when he dismissed it and there was vastly more
material available than there had been in 1824.

Lenin was, of course, as much the creature of his environment as any other man, and his early environment was the medieval intellectual atmosphere of Czarist Russia. His world had never known the Renaissance and had hardly been touched by the Enlightenment of the eighteenth century—as far as the masses of the Russian people were concerned, it had not been touched at all. Dialectic still held a higher place, in his mind, than observation and experiment as a means of arriving at truth. The dialectic materialism of Marx required no confirmation, as he saw it, for it was pure reason, which supplies its own confirmation.

Once he was saddled with the responsibilities of power, this nonsense blew up, of course. His adoption of what he called a "New Economic Policy" was officially explained on the ground of expediency, but it was tantamount to an admission that what he mistook for pure reason was something less, for it did not work. But by that time it was far too late for him to readjust his whole philosophy.

To do him justice, he was forced to rely on dialectic since, in the political realm, the method of observation and experiment was not available to Russians. The stupid rigidity of Imperial Russia looked upon any application of that method as treason and punished it ferociously. Alexander Ulyanov died on the gallows for making some tentative motions in that direction; and Vladimir would have gone the same way if he had tried to imitate his brother. Argumentation was the only course open to him; but argumentation uncorrected by observation and experiment inevitably creates the closed mind; and a mind closed long enough can be opened by nothing short of dynamite.

Furthermore, in Switzerland Lenin found little more reason than he had found in Siberia to suppose that the American experiment deserved his careful consideration. Its material success was obvious, and he took note of that; but that it had attained any philosophical success was no more apparent to him than it was to other European observers. He lacked the deductive genius that filled Sherlock Holmes with excitement over the fact that the dog did nothing. To the negative fact that the United States had not exploded from internal pressure he gave much less than its true significance if he gave it any at all; but in the realm of politics this thing that had not happened was the most significant fact of the nineteenth century.

From the very special case of Russia Lenin built by argument a system that he applied to the whole world. Naturally, the world did not understand it, but this lack of comprehension was no disadvantage in the eyes of the creator of the system. For his dialectic taught him that others could wish to understand only in order the more quickly to undermine it. Interchange of ideas with the rest of the world was the last thing he desired, for his philosophical system was so perfect that the introduction of any new element could not enrich but could only contaminate it. Therefore, like the djinn in the Arabian Nights, he built a City of Brass whose walls were pierced by no gate.

He was driven to this course not only by the philosophical structure of Marxism, but also by circumstances. Lenin did his work in the midst of turmoil. The years from 1917 to 1924 were years of combat and hysteria, when most of the world had reverted to the primitive belief that "stranger" and "enemy" were synonyms; and this belief applied to alien ideas even more strongly than to alien persons. An unemotional, objective examination of any proposition, especially in the field of government, was well-nigh impossible; when much of the old world is falling down about men's ears their normal response to any suggestion of change is one of hostility. It is hardly to be denied that most of the world beyond the borders of Russia hated Lenin before it heard what he had to say.

But he was unperturbed by this, because it was what Marx had taught him to expect. That exile, imbued with the Hebraic doctrine of the Chosen as a small minority of humanity, and schooled in rationalistic German philosophy, believed that he could sit inclosed by the walls of the British Museum and create by reason an infallible political order. To Lenin, who had spent much of his own life in prison, in Siberia, and, later, in the intellectual prison that immures the conspirator even when he is physically free, this idea seemed rational enough. Because it is a bookish product, Marxism appeals to bookish men, who study man exclusively from his records and not from observation and experiment upon living specimens.

But history, as Gibbon, who can certainly qualify as an expert, remarked, "is little more than the register of the crimes, follies and misfortunes of mankind," and the man who has obtained his knowledge of the world exclusively from history knows little about it. Knowledge of history is valuable only for the illumination that it throws upon the events of today; the man whose knowledge of what is happening around him is deficient can make little use of historical learning.

It is incontestably true that Lenin's knowledge of events in certain fields was enormous; but there was at least one field in which it was practically nonexistent. That field was the development of democracy in the United States.

The reason for this gap in his learning is obvious. The written records of that development are scanty and unreliable. We have histories, essays and dissertations without number; but we have yet to produce an adequate study of the strangest development in our national history, the fact that the writ of the Supreme Court runs in Oregon, in Florida, in San Diego, California, and in Portland, Maine.

The legalistic side of it, of course, is thoroughly understood. We have detailed information about the settlement of the Oregon Question with Great Britain, about the acquisition of Florida from Spain, of California from Mexico, and about the erection of Maine into a separate state. But we have no more than a dim comprehension of the spiritual process that has led men of Spanish, Mexican, British origin—and for that matter, Chinese, French, Russian, German, Italian and every other nationality—to believe that they can rely on a fair measure of justice from a tribunal consisting of five Englishmen, one Scot, two Irishmen and a Jew, as of today, and which tomorrow may include, as it has included before, such names as Duval, Lamar, Shiras, Van Devanter and Cardozo.

The immediate—and inadequate—answer is that the experience of a century and three-quarters has shown that the Court does administer the law with a tolerable degree of fairness; and this experience has built around the institution a respect so tremendous that at times it threatens to run into blind worship. Nevertheless, the bench is occupied by fallible men. At times it has made unjust decisions. Some, indeed, have been so patently wrong that the Court itself, at a subsequent sitting, has reversed them; and others have been reversed by the action of Congress or of the States by constitutional amendment.

There is nothing in an appointment to the Supreme Court that sanctifies a man; yet this group for more than a hundred and fifty years has dealt out substantial justice so consistently that today throughout a continental domain the man who would defy its ruling would be regarded as insane. It is evident that there must be some extremely powerful force operating to hold it to the ideal of equal justice administered without fear or favor.

To explain that this force consists in respect for a great office and for the judicial oath is to beg the question. What made the office great and the oath sacred? Unquestionably, the honorable record of the Court in the past. In the early days of the Republic men frequently resigned from the Court for what would now be regarded as trivial reasons—to run for Governor of some State, or for the House of Representatives, or even to accept an appointment on a State bench. In our time a Justice lays himself open to criticism if he openly aspires even to the Presidency of the United States. The prestige of the Supreme Court did not exist from the beginning, but has been built up by its own record.

It would be pleasant to attribute this record solely to the quality of the men appointed to the bench, but it would be highly questionable. It is true that no Justice has ever been convicted of dishonesty, but more than a few have convicted themselves of smallness of spirit and lack of vision. Nevertheless, the Court as a whole has been great.

The reason is that it has been constantly subject to correction by the American people and has been corrected more than once when it deviated from what the people regard as substantial justice. It took a long and desperate war to overrule the Dred Scott decision, but it was overruled. It has taken constitutional amendments to overrule some others, but even that slow, complicated, and vexatious process has been adopted, when necessary. Only in a narrowly legal sense is it true that there is no appeal from the Supreme Court; one appeal does lie; it is the appeal from the Court to the sense of justice of the average American. It is slow and difficult, but it is possible, and the Court knows it. A decision that does not square with the conscience of the average man will not stand. It may be valid in law for many years, but eventually it will go down; and the Court's care to avoid subjecting itself to such reversals accounts for its record and its high honor.

It was not within the experience of Karl Marx that a people, left politically free, would or could develop a sense of justice sufficiently acute and strong to become an overriding influence upon judicial institutions. It was not within his experience because he had not seen it demonstrated. When he published the first volume of *Das Kapital* in 1867 the American experiment was in anything but an encouraging state. It had just been put to the test of the bloodiest war fought in Marx's lifetime and was left in such a condition of exhaustion that its survival was in question; and when he died, in 1883, this country was still negligible as an international influence. As a man of the library, he could not possibly have judged correctly what was going on here.

Lenin had more information, but he ignored it. For everything that had happened in America he had an explanation derived from the writings of Marx—an explanation as plausible, as ingenious, and as wide of the mark as the Greek philosophers' explanation of the solar system. There is no reason to doubt that Lenin was perfectly sincere in his opinion that the American was quite transparent and therefore not worth detailed study.

Nor was there any compelling reason, from his standpoint, why he should exert every effort to make his ideas comprehensible to Americans. According to the Marxian idea the United States was merely a late offshoot of the European capitalistic system—an exceptionally vigorous and flourishing offshoot, no doubt, but infected with the incurable malady of capitalism and therefore, as dialectic materialism taught, inevitably doomed. If there was nothing important, except technology, that Russia could learn from America, neither was it supremely important to cultivate the sympathetic understanding of adherents of a dying system.

Least of all was Lenin inclined to spend much time studying the psychological make-up of the ordinary American. The leaders might be worth examining, as they were pretty sure to be opponents in diplomatic and economic, possibly also in military, struggles, but in the Marxian ideology the common people were simply another proletariat, to be guided and governed by superior men, and incapable of making any important contribution to political philosophy on their own account.

Here was another historical equivalent of Alexander's drunkenness. It is a temptation to say that if he had escaped this error, Lenin might have accomplished a far greater work than he did; but it is a doubtful assumption for, lacking the arrogant certainty that betrayed him into this error, would he have been Lenin? Could anyone without arrogant certainty have set up the Communist system, or any system at all, in the chaos that was Russia in 1917?

But that is beside the point under consideration here, which is merely to remind the reader that if the ordinary American failed to understand the Russians in the early days of the USSR, one reason was that the Russians had no great desire to be understood.

7. *Sunday Punch*

BUT attempts to apportion praise and blame for what happened twenty-five years ago are as futile as the traditional inquiry into who hit Billy Patterson. Whatever the explanation, and whoever was to blame, the historical fact is that we did not gain any adequate comprehension of Lenin's work, nor estimate accurately its effect; and the failure was one of the most important influences in shaping the modern American.

For the man is only half educated who has had experience of the benevolent powers that work in his favor and none other. To follow a great leader is an illuminating experience; but no more so than it is to walk in dread of a great leader who threatens us. Following Wilson and dreading Lenin, the American was subjected to both experiences, and he learned, albeit slowly, from both.

They were both effective as releasers of energies. To the American, who has achieved his ends, as far as he has achieved them at all, by the approach of political liberty, it may seem absurd that any people should be filled with buoyant hope by a system that disregards political liberty. But the fact he cannot deny. Leninism did fill the Russians with an eager resolution such as they had never exhibited before. Perhaps it was not so much generous energy as demoniacal energy that Lenin released, but energy it was.

More than that, the mechanism that set it off was essentially the same trigger that detonated our own latent powers, to wit, the assertion that status is not ordained of God and forever immovable, but may be altered for the better by labor and thought. That is the driving power in Communism, precisely as it is the driving power in democracy. We know how mighty it has been in our own system, therefore we should have been prepared to find it powerful in another.

The fact that we did not is open to two explanations, both of which were undoubtedly operative to some extent. One was simply our abysmal ignorance of the real conditions of life among the masses in Imperial Russia and, for that matter, in the rest of Eastern Europe. The other was the fact that it had been so long since the legal fixation of status was abolished among us that we had forgotten the effect. The rights of the nobility are not even a memory to native Americans, they are only something he reads about in books, as he reads of Cinderella's pumpkin coach and of the exploits of Sinbad the Sailor. We could not imagine how new, strange, and inspiring it was to the Russians to find themselves released from the grim reality of those rights, even though our own forefathers had felt exactly the same way.

Charles Dickens died the year Lenin was born, 1870, but the Englishman all unwittingly wrote a fine description of Communist Russia in the years of the Long Armistice. Dickens misnamed it and misdated it, but it will serve. He called it, not Russia in 1930, but the United States in 1830, yet anyone who will read the American episode in *Martin Chuzzlewit* and compare it with the reports of travelers in Russia a hundred years later can hardly fail to be struck by the similarity. Manners and customs were different, certainly, but the spirit was identical— the exuberance running into braggadocio, the insane self-confidence, the incredible ignorance of the rest of the world and the lordly contempt for it, are exactly similar.

All this is partly deplorable and partly ridiculous, fair game for the satirist. But these surface extravagances covered and, unhappily, concealed something vastly more important that was neither deplorable nor absurd, namely, a tremendous release of energies. The comedians that Dickens portrayed mercilessly were building up the strength that was suddenly revealed at Gettysburg and those in Russia were building up toward Stalingrad.

Impossible as it was for us to perceive it at the time, this Lenin was a beacon of hope to hundreds of millions—their first hope and their only hope. To assume, as we did assume for seventeen years, that a system with this significance would collapse of its own weight was folly, and in a democratic people inexcusable folly. It is evidence of the extent to which our own democracy had become formalized and rigid. Our refusal to recognize Russia for seventeen years was a confession that our leaders relied on the strength of the system, not on the spirit of the people who had created the system. Coolidge once boasted, according to the secret service man who guarded him, that he would have to be called back because the Democrats know nothing about money. Coolidge did know about money, but he had not the remotest conception of value. Coolidge knew about votes. But what he had learned about liberty, he had learned by rote, and he had no more idea of its meaning than the average Presbyterian child has of the meaning of the Shorter Catechism, in which he may be letter-perfect. Unfortunately, in this Coolidge seems to have been fairly representative of the country.

The delusion that our system is our strength, and not the spirit that built the system, pervaded the whole country. Even after we had recognized Russia and been dealing with her on terms of formal equality for seven years, the delusion persisted. When Germany attacked, there was not a military man in the United States, and very few diplomatists, statesmen, or newspaper correspondents, who gave Russia more than three months. Many of them figured that it would be closer to three weeks. Russia obviously did not have our system, hence Russia could have no strength. The fact that Russia did have the spirit that animated this Republic in its early years was not observed, or if it was observed, was disregarded. We had come to rely on the framework, the mechanism, and so were completely deceived.

The perfect revelation of our attitude was the report of Charles A. Lindbergh, aptly described by J. P. Morgan as the "inspired mechanic," who saw something of both the German and the Russian war machines before they clashed. The German machine was plainly the better, so in Lindbergh's mind there was no possible doubt of the result. "God is always on the side of the heaviest battalions," Voltaire's cynicism, was accepted in essence by those who knew that the more efficient organization now represents the heavier battalion; and once again it turned out to be a delusion.

What, then, was the real reason for our failure to realize that Lenin, no matter how fantastic his economic theory, was releasing a gigantic force that was bound to sweep through a large part of the world? Was it, in fact, misapprehension of Lenin, or misapprehension of the sources of our own strength? If democracy is, after all, only a means to an end, then to make a fetish of democracy is to deny the end. We have written over the portal of the Supreme Court the legend, "Equal justice under law." If that is the end, then the success of any political system is to be measured by the closeness of its approach to the end, not by the avenue through which it makes that approach.

The failure of Leninism may be attributed to, but is not to be measured by, its repudiation of democracy. The measure of its failure is the distance by which it fails to attain the ideal of equal justice under law. Yet we persistently measured it by the fact that it had chosen dictatorship, rather than democracy, as the avenue of its approach. This is a clear indication that we had come to believe that democracy is the end and that equal justice under law is a secondary consideration.

The flat truth is that a good many of us had been doing—and are still doing—exactly that. The political faith with which the Republic began had become formalized, frozen into a ritual gabbled by everyone, but understood by all too few. Etymologists assert that "hocus-pocus," meaning fraudulent nonsense, is a debasement of *"Hoc est corpus,"* one of the most solemnly significant statements ever heard by man. Similarly "democracy" in the minds of many Americans had come to mean merely the process of counting noses. It might mean government of the people by the people, but it had lost all necessary connection with the key phrase, the vital phrase, for the people.

It is not to be denied that at the moment when Lenin died, in the year 1924, there was a large and influential section of opinion in America holding that as long as the people were governed by themselves, it was of small moment that they might be governed for the Standard Oil Company, and the Aluminum Corporation of America, and United States Steel and fifty-seven other great corporations. It was held quite consonant with democracy to govern for the classes, rather than the masses. If the people could be hoodwinked or terrorized into governing for wealth and privilege, rather than for themselves, it was regarded as quite democratic, as long as the governing was done by themselves. To "hear the blessed mutter of the mass" was sufficient; any comprehension of its significance was easily dispensable.

To the extent that the average American had forgotten the spiritual significance of his own history, he could hardly be expected to recognize a repetition of that significance in another, especially if that other repeated it in an unfamiliar and unfit form. He did not recognize it. The movement that Lenin headed did not take the direction, as regards its polity, that the movement headed by George Washington took; therefore the movement headed by Lenin was fraudulent and bound to collapse from its inner weakness. Sublimely confident of this outcome, we waited seventeen years for that collapse before we would admit officially that the thing existed.

Unfortunately for us, the supremacy of mind over matter is not complete. The fact that a man firmly and sincerely disbelieves the germ theory of disease doesn't immunize him against typhoid fever. The fact that the driver of a Ford coupé knows that he has the right of way doesn't prevent him from being translated to bliss eternal with great suddenness if the driver of a ten-ton truck knows that he has it. The fact that we were persuaded for seventeen years that Lenin was a political apparition composed mostly of mist and moonshine, didn't prevent contusions and brush-burns when we scraped against the cast-iron reality.

Of course the power that has jarred our eyeteeth in their sockets was not that of Vladimir Illich Ulyanov, the sometime lawyer of Samara. He was merely the trigger that released it. The power was the yearning for justice, equal justice under law, of a hundred and seventy-five million human beings. Nevertheless, the man who releases such power is a very great man and, above all, a formidable man. It is an absolute necessity for those who are to oppose him successfully to understand him, especially to understand the nature and source of his power, so that they may avoid coming into collision with it if that is at all possible. Gene Tunney explained long ago that he really beat Jack Dempsey sitting at the ringside, watching the champion fight other men; for it was there that he figured out a method of defense against the murder that was behind Jack's blows. He could never have escaped had he not known exactly where the power lay; but since he did know, it was but a matter of time.

Lenin would not have been easy for us, even if we had gauged the source of his strength correctly from the beginning. But we might have saved a great deal of time and escaped some nasty jarring, if we had been right. Yet how could we guess, when so many of us had forgotten where our own strength lay?

8. *Davus Sum, Non Oedipus*

TIME at last had its way with him and Lenin passed. Four years later Coolidge passed, and almost immediately thereafter the Jazz Age took just that one last drink which is fatally too many and passed out. The ordinary American found himself with Hoover and a hangover in the cold gray dawn.

Without doubt the most remorselessly educational experience of the half-century is that which the common man underwent in the years following the panic of 1929. Of all the layers of illusion in which time and circumstance had wrapped him, the thickest and most opaque was the illusion of the sapience and puissance of the American businessman in general and the American financier in particular. Even after the AEF returned, victorious, but nursing plenty of sprains and contusions and profanely skeptical of the old tradition that any free-born American can whip at least three of any other nationality whatsoever, we retained our faith in the American businessman as far superior to any competitor anywhere.

For at least a generation before the crash of 1929 one of the favorite themes of essayists, commencement speakers, editorial writers and other such back-seat drivers had been the vast improvement in the conduct of affairs that would be worked if only we had a businessman for President. It seemed to occur to none of the theorists that government itself is not a business, but very decidedly an art, requiring for its successful practice a natural aptitude as marked as that required for good landscape painting. Nobody thought of demanding a businessman for Chief Justice, or a businessman for Surgeon General of the Public Health Service, or a businessman for Presiding Bishop of the Episcopal Church. It was admitted that to hold these offices a man must first qualify as a lawyer, a doctor, or a clergyman; but the idea that nobody but a trained and talented politician knows how to be a successful President was regarded as heresy. Had not a man fresh from a university made one of the greatest of Presidents? That was true, but it was also irrelevant, for a university president who lasts ten years is always a pretty fair politician.

The illusion that a businessman for President would solve three-quarters of our public woes persisted until we got one; but sardonic fate thrust him into office at the moment when all American business was on the point of being exposed to a harsh northern light that would abolish in an instant every trace of the rosy haze through which we had been viewing it. A businessman had been President barely half a year when the stock market crashed and American business was suddenly revealed as impotent to prevent starvation in the midst of plenty.

Naturally, the businessman in the White House became the chief scapegoat. It was unjust, but not a whit more unjust than the treatment his predecessor had received; the difference was that it was reversed. Where Coolidge had been unjustly praised, Hoover was unjustly blamed. Injustice is an occupational risk inseparable from the Presidency; when things go well he will be lauded to the skies, and when they go ill he will be damned to the Pit, regardless of his responsibility for either the good or the evil.

Herbert Hoover was unquestionably as sincere a man, and as patriotic, as any of his predecessors. For industry and native ability he excelled two-thirds, perhaps three-quarters of them. But his talent was that of an administrator applying definite policies, clearly understood. Unfortunately, at the moment when he assumed office the definite, clearly understood policies the government had been following had led to ruin; new policies were urgently needed, but as they had not yet been formulated, how could they be defined or understood?

As a matter of fact, had Hoover been endowed with the genius for brilliant improvisation demonstrated by his successor it is doubtful that it would have done him much good. For to the average American in 1929 the panic was even more incredible than the First World War had been, fifteen years earlier. His feeling was that you just couldn't do that to American business; and not until it had been done, done over and over, through three sickening years, was he ready to admit that you could do it, and that his estimate of the power and wisdom of businessmen had been considerably too high. Then at last he was ready for experiment, but probably not before.

The lapse of twenty years has softened the asperities that

rasped the Hoover administration and already it is clear that his place in history is going to be materially higher than men thought it would be when he left office. Everyone above the level of the semiliterate knows now that the calamity was not of his making, and his incapacity to handle it is less remarkable today than the gallantry with which he struggled against hopeless odds.

For a shocked and bewildered nation insistently put to Hoover a question more difficult than the riddle of the Sphinx, and demanded an instant, categorical reply. Like a badgered witness under cross-examination, Hoover heard the voice of the people thundering at him, "Why is it, Mr. Hoover, that what goes up must come down? Answer me, yes or no!" and what could the poor man say? Murmuring about the law of gravitation did no good, for it only provoked another question, "Why is the law of gravitation?" To that, the only possible reply is that of the character in Terence's comedy who, perplexed by unanswerable questions, yelled, "I am Davus, not Oedipus!"

But our Davus was in the unfortunate position of having been mistaken for Oedipus, the riddle-solver, by the throngs that pressed around him. Their view was that if he wasn't Oedipus he ought to be. Presidents before him had posed as omniscient and, having never been put to the test, had managed to get away with it; but Hoover was face to face with the Sphinx and, failing of an answer, he was mauled.

Even if he had been Oedipus, the man of ready wit, it would have been next to impossible for him to give the correct answer, because he was committed to a point of view, which he could shift only by slow degrees. It was the point of view of Grover Cleveland, that government is entitled to support by the people without bearing any responsibility for support of the people. Bit by bit, driven by relentless fact, Hoover altered this, never to the point of admitting that direct support of the people may be a charge on government, but to the halfway point of admitting that it might be necessary to support the greater corporations who, in turn, would support the people by furnishing jobs. This was the theory of the Reconstruction Finance Corporation, which did issue public money to railroads and giant industries that were on the point of collapse. It was a partial remedy, but the malady was too well established to yield to halfway measures.

The truth was that until 1929 the United States had never faced up to the necessity of paying for its share of the destruction wreaked upon the world by the war of 1914-18. Even then it was one world, economically, if not politically. Even then there was no need to ask for whom the bell tolls. The ruin concentrated in Europe was in part our loss—in a larger part than we had been willing to pay. So, since we would not pay voluntarily, Destiny, that bailiff whom none can evade, levied upon our household goods and chattels, and relentlessly exacted heavy costs over and above the original debt.

Hoover certainly was not that cosmic bailiff, and most certainly he had not invited the bailiff in. He was merely the temporary head of the house at the embarrassing moment of the seizure; but he had to take the jeers and catcalls, just the same.

Wiseacres have since pointed out a dozen ways in which the crash of 1929 and the subsequent depression might have been avoided. Many of these schemes are logical and some of them perhaps might have worked; but all of them are subject to one insuperable objection—in order to duck a high-explosive shell successfully, you have to believe it is coming. If you are serenely confident that you are well out of the trajectory, nothing will induce you to duck. The average American had that confidence in 1928. There was no lack of Cassandras, even then wailing of the wrath to come; but it was the fate of Cassandra never to be believed, so her prophecies were perhaps the most complete waste of breath that history or legend records.

Certainly the warnings of 1928 were wasted, therefore the

precautions that apparently might have been taken were in fact unavailable, since realization of danger, the first requisite to prudence, was lacking. Twenty years later the question came up again under strikingly similar conditions. The combined resources of the world had been sacrificed again, in a new and even greater war; again what was left of liquid capital was largely concentrated in the United States; again we were faced with the necessity of redistributing that capital, not through the normal processes of trade, for they had been interrupted, but arbitrarily, in order that normal trade might be resumed. Naturally, this redistribution violates the canons of what we are accustomed to regard as good business practice. Naturally, it is full of danger, for if it is not managed resolutely, skillfully and discreetly it will be as useless and costly as was the effort of private business following the First World War.

For these reasons the operation was viewed with marked distaste by Americans—not merely by the average American, the man in the street, but also by his leaders, the shrewdest and best-informed commanders of business and politics. However, the abler leaders perceived and admitted the necessity and, against the clamor of the stupid and shortsighted, urged it upon the people. In the beginning, the people assented; the Marshall Plan was adopted and was carried through for at least the first two years. Whether or not the average man will be resolute enough to see the thing through remains a question; but he did agree to start.

Surely, then, one is justified in claiming that our generation has learned something in the horrifying school of two wars and a world-wide economic depression. That we learned enough remains to be demonstrated; but we did learn something, and a generation that has learned anything at all about the satisfactory conduct of public affairs is exceptional, and is entitled to plume itself, at least a little.

Furthermore, it is this slight advance in the education of the common man that made it possible to act. It is no depreciation of the courage and vision of such exceptional men as George C. Marshall and Arthur H. Vandenberg with their associates who worked out the details of the plan, to point out that they would have been helpless to do anything without the assent of the millions who make up the rank and file of the political parties. Certainly, intelligent leadership is indispensable if we are to have good government; but in a democracy an intelligent following is indispensable to the existence of intelligent leadership. Presumably our party leaders learned a great deal from the mistakes of Woodrow Wilson; but the knowledge would have done them little good had not party followers learned a bit from the mistake of those who voted for Harding in 1920.

Complacence is a word with evil connotations in American history. Complacence has been our besetting sin from the foundation of the Republic. Complacence at the critical moment marked by the end of the first half of the twentieth century could easily betray us into appalling disaster. But undue pessimism is also a breeder of disaster. Without doubt, we should study our mistakes more assiduously than is our custom, but not to the total neglect of our accomplishments, for that could reduce us to the apathy of despair.

Besides, in the case under consideration, complacency is rudely jarred by the facts. If we have acted on the whole somewhat more intelligently since the Second World War than we acted after the first one, the fact is not to be attributed exclusively to an increase in our wisdom and virtue. Much of the credit is due to good, healthy fright. We had seen Lenin pass by.

Even yet, we have no adequate realization—some, but not full realization—of the size of the contribution to the deification of Lenin that was made by the American panic of 1929 and the depression that followed. For be it remembered that Lenin had foretold the catastrophe at a moment when the United States was riding the very crest of the wave of prosperity. Therefore, when the storm burst exactly as he had predicted, the effect was not unlike that of the phenomena described in the eighteenth chapter of First Kings, when at the call of Elijah the thunderbolt fell squarely on the indicated altar and vaporized the works before the eyes of an awe-struck nation. If any Russian had been skeptical of Lenin's inspiration, his doubts must have been resolved by the horde of Europeans streaming back from the United States during the depression years, each a Job's messenger bearing tidings of woe and desolation. It was exactly as the dead leader had said that it would be; therefore his word was established ten times as firmly as it had been before.

The living presence of Lenin chilled us slightly, rendered us a bit uncertain; but after he had passed we inadvertently helped to make him immeasurably greater dead than he had ever been alive.

III

Roosevelt Passes

---

1. *Laughter Among the Trumpets*

WHEN the writer of the Book of Job undertook to describe how formidable is the warhorse, he resorted to a series of extravagant metaphors. "The glory of his nostrils is terrible," his neck is "clothed with thunder," and he "swalloweth the ground with fierceness and rage." But the thing that capped the climax, what the writer put last because he evidently regarded it as the acme of the redoubtable, is expressed in the words, "he saith among the trumpets, Ha, ha!"

It was a shrewd estimate. There are few things that strike the world with stupefaction more complete than gaiety in peril, or under stress of any kind. It is bitterly resented by some, it delights some, but most people it disconcerts. Everyone, however, is impressed by it, wonders about it, remembers it; and those who have come into collision with a laughing opponent usually remember it with mingled fear and rage.

The second Roosevelt, Franklin Delano, is the only President of the first order of importance who was not a solemn fellow. Even Lincoln, in spite of his Rabelaisian wit, carried an aura of the tragic about him. His face was mournful and his figure and bearing that of an undertaker. Washington had the solemnity of a monument, Jefferson was humorless, Jackson furious, Wilson austere. Of the first five Presidents who stand head-and-shoulders above the rest, not one was gay.

Roosevelt was. For that very reason every Gloomy Gus in the country flatly refused to believe that he could possibly be great. It was the more puzzling because he was a cripple, the first that had ever occupied the White House. It would seem that he had less cause to be merry than any of them, and especially less than vinegar-visaged Coolidge, who stated his own claim to the distinction of being the healthiest President.

More than that, his term of service in the Presidency began in the midst of calamity and ended in the midst of war. There was never a moment after he took office when the country was not racked by malaises of one sort or another, and few when it was not appalled by hobgoblins, some of which may have been fantasies but not all—some of them had teeth and horns that were very real indeed.

The fact that the President remained jocund through all this maddened the humorless. Roosevelt's economic and social policies aroused widespread detestation; but it is doubtful that any of these evoked hatred as deep, as relentless, as implacable as the fact that he frequently laughed at the very moment of impact of his opponent's most furious charges. As one looks back on it, the fact that Roosevelt held the office continuously into the thirteenth year without being murdered is rather wonderful. Cranks tried it, repeatedly, but the guards always picked them up before they could accomplish anything. His only narrow escape came while he was still the President-elect, when a madman in Florida fired on him but missed and killed Anton Cermak, Mayor of Chicago, who was standing by him.

The lighthearted man of ability is so extremely rare, in fact, as to make it noteworthy that the United States in its relatively short history has produced two who stand at the very top. The other was Benjamin Franklin, first American to make any perceptible impression on Europe, and in some sense the first genuine American; for old Ben threw off the status of a colonial Englishman long before Washington did.

But this rarity is also almost a guarantee that such a man will be underestimated while he lives, and for a long time afterward. The writing of history is an occupation that seems to have a dreadful fascination for the stodgy; most of our annalists, when they encounter a historical figure gifted with humor, treat him as they treat one afflicted with epilepsy; if they are friendly, they cover up the matter and pass it by hastily; if they are ferocious, they exploit it vigorously as an excuse for believing every campaign lie that whispering slanderers have spewed up about the man.

Franklin has suffered both ways for well over a hundred years; Roosevelt has suffered in like manner, and presumably will continue to suffer for a long time. Fortunately, though, the quality seems to contribute to longevity, literally and figuratively. Franklin lived to the impressive age of eighty-four; and although Roosevelt died at sixty-three, if one takes into consideration the experience of his last thirteen years, there is some logical basis for the contention that he did more living in this world than Franklin. Figuratively, Franklin is almost the only pre-Revolutionary notable who remains a living force in the modern world; how long Roosevelt will last is beyond conjecture, but he certainly will not be forgotten while any who saw him in action survives.

It should be noted carefully that Roosevelt was humorous, not witty. The distinction is important, for wit frequently flashes and sparkles in some very sad dogs. The mournful Lincoln was a wit, and so was many a less eminent personage who has ended as a suicide. The merely humorous man may rarely, if ever, say anything that will be treasured and repeated at dinnertables, or in smoking rooms, for generations. The wit laughs at others, and makes others laugh; the humorous man laughs at himself first of all, and if he makes others laugh it is by the infection of his good-humor, not by the sharpness of his perception of the absurd.

Roosevelt was a laugher, not a jester. Solemn fellows can never perceive the difference, but it is real and important. The jester is quoted endlessly, but he is rarely followed; the laugher may not be quoted at all—who can remember a single joke with any real point that Roosevelt manufactured?—but it is flatly impossible to deprive him of his following.

It is a curious circumstance that Roosevelt was effective for a reason that superficially might seem to be a guarantee of ineffectiveness—he was completely out of sympathy with the prevailing mood of the moment in which he came to power. That mood was one of unrelieved gloom. The very day he was inaugurated the banks of New York, Chicago, Philadelphia and Boston refused to open their doors. The banks of Maryland had been closed a week, and those of Michigan three weeks earlier; but the action of March 4 meant the collapse of virtually the whole banking system. Roosevelt's first official act was to make the course of the banks legal by declaring a "bank holiday" for five days until Congress should have time to assemble in the special session that he called for March 9. A gloomier situation could hardly be imagined.

Yet the tone of the inaugural address was one of such brisk confidence as neither Coolidge nor Hoover had been able to muster in times of lush prosperity. "All we have to fear is fear itself" was the keynote, and it was abundantly plain that the new President cherished no mystical fear of fear. If he erred, it would be on the side of overconfidence, not on that of pessimism.

We had lived through a regime, twelve years long, of serious-minded, prudent men, grave of face and sober in deportment; and that regime had brought us to ruin and despair. Now came a blithe, laughing man, and he was hailed with a delirium of joy, not because he laughed, but because his laughter indicated that he was different. The argument of the average man was that, since he could hardly be worse, to be different he would have to be better.

Presidents are sometimes molders of public opinion, but public opinion is always a molder of Presidents. If the country for any reason, justifiable or not, makes up its mind that a certain man is good, the odds are a hundred to one that he will be, if not really good, at least better than he would have been had the country deemed him hopeless. On March 4, 1933, the average American made up his mind that Franklin D. Roosevelt was not only good, but very good; and the opinion was a tremendous impetus to the President to make good.

It must have been an enormous reinforcement to his natural cheerfulness, and nothing could have had a happier effect upon the course of events. A tremendous job of reconstruction was imperative and the work had to be done with desperate speed. For a single, relatively small, item, every bank in the United States had to be examined just as fast as was humanly possible, and yet without serious mistakes. This was enough to appall, nay, to paralyze, the Treasury Department under ordinary circumstances. Had the work been undertaken in an atmosphere of hopeless pessimism, men would have broken under the strain and it would have dragged fatally. As it was, the new Secretary of the Treasury, William H. Woodin, did break; his health, precarious when he took the job, could not stand the strain. He lived barely a year; but he performed prodigies before he broke, and his organization never cracked, partly because of the efforts of certain Republican holdovers who helped Woodin. The banks were examined with startling speed and with remarkably few errors—none of grave consequence.

The same spirit animated the extra session of Congress known as the Hundred Days—the session lasted ninety-nine days, to be exact—which witnessed such a complete overhauling of the American system of government as had not been undertaken at one time since the Constitution superseded the Articles of Confederation. The merit of the changes effected is not germane at the moment; the point stressed here is that they were very numerous and merely to get them enacted into law in due form involved a prodigious amount of work on the part of Congress and on the part of the executive departments. Whether good, bad, or indifferent, this work could not have been performed at all had it not been attacked with a hearty good-will. An assembly of dismal souls, hamstrung by a sense of utter futility, would never have been able to plow through it. The Congress of the Hundred Days had its dismal members, to be sure, but they did not do the work; appalled by the magnitude of the calamity signalized by the bank closings, they did not even oppose the work except in the most perfunctory way. In general they were dazed and rendered almost completely inert; the work was done by a brisk, resolute, confident majority, who had no doubt that things were going to be pulled together.

There is no question that the attitude of the President strongly influenced the attitude of Congress. It is commonly asserted that Mr. Roosevelt dictated the bulk of the legislation of the Hundred Days, and in a sense it is true; but the fact establishes, not the dictatorial nature of the man, but the critical nature of the time. Anyone else could have dictated legislation had he shown equal assurance, poise, and general command of the situation. In the moment of catastrophe Congress was not disposed to stand upon its dignity, nor to haggle over fine points. Any cool, confident, unterrified man of reasonable intelligence can always take over when panic is general and confusion complete. In such a situation any rational course of action, taken promptly, is better than a waste of time seeking for the ideal; so the man who proposes prompt and rational action will not only be followed, but followed with a great sense of relief by the bewildered.

It was not the record of the Hundred Days that proved Roosevelt's mastery of the art of politics. That record proved only his imperturbability. The veriest tyro in politics would have had sense enough to seize the opportunity if he had himself been cool enough to see it clearly; but to remain cool in that fervent heat one must have been endowed with a temperament unusual indeed. One must have been, in short, as incorrigibly cheerful as F. D. Roosevelt.

Even before the end of the Hundred Days this gaiety was beginning to rasp all solemn and pretentious leaders in politics, but it delighted the ingenuous voter. To assert that the average American understood what Roosevelt was trying to do would be fatuous; but the common man did understand that the fellow was different from most political leaders—not fearful, not hesitant, yet careful to avoid any claim to omniscience, stating frankly that some of his experiments would probably fail, but in that case he would try something else. All this struck the ordinary voter as full of good sense as well as good-humor, so he was not merely willing, he ardently wished to give Roosevelt a free hand in practically anything he saw fit to do.

The yelling of the trumpets had split our ears, had shattered our nerves, had destroyed our morale to the point at which the weapons were slipping from our shaking hands. Then through the wavering ranks strode the new captain, and how did he look? Why, the man was laughing! "He saith among the trumpets, Ha, ha," and instantly the rank and file were galvanized. Centurions and tribunes might scowl, but the plain legionnaire felt an electric shock run through him, gripped his falling spear and lurched forward with a howl that drowned the trumpets of disaster. It may have been irrational, it may have been completely insensate, but it is true that when he heard his captain laughing, he was a fighting man again.

2. *Rumble of a Distant Drum*

O N MARCH 5, 1933, within twenty-four hours of the inauguration of Franklin D. Roosevelt as President of the United States, the German Reichstag passed the Enabling Act, conferring all but absolute power upon the Chancellor of the Reich, one Adolf Hitler.

A specialist or two in the State Department may have attached significance to this act. Some hundreds of newspapermen handled the news in a routine way, and possibly an editorial writer here and there may have commented on it. But it is a safe assertion that not one ordinary citizen in ten thousand paid the slightest heed to this law, or even knew that it had been enacted. Nevertheless, it was one of the most important dates our generation ever saw, for it marked the beginning of the great duel that was to continue for twelve years, to destroy both duelists, and to tear the world apart.

Adolf Hitler was one of the grisliest jokes the sardonic gods ever perpetrated upon mankind. He looked and acted like something dreamed up by Mack Sennett, that early movie producer famous for comedies that reached their climax when the actors hurled custard pies at each other. Somewhat below middle height, with the high, domed forehead of the stupid man—a dome covered with patent leather hair usually plastered down across half the forehead—and with an unkempt mustache of the Charlie Chaplin type, Hitler was a bantam rooster of a man who at first aroused nothing but amusement in the outside world.

In and of himself, indeed, he was nothing. During his infestation of the earth he poured out millions of words without leaving one line illumined by wisdom, or honor, or taste. Nothing that he said or did contributed a feather's weight to the art of statecraft, or to any other art or science. No idea that he ever expressed was above the intellectual level of low comedy. He was as complete a stranger to grace as he was to learning. Apparently he did not even contribute to the advancement of vice, as did Tiberius and Caligula, whose monstrous appetites were backed by an undeniable ingenuity. In and of himself, he was a nullity.

Unfortunately, he represented a great deal more than his own tortured and frustrated soul. He represented the torture and frustration of a large and powerful nation that had somehow lost its way, straying from the path of civilization into a horrible region of bogs and quicksands, brambles and stones. Therefore, far from being comic, he was sinister beyond the power of words to convey.

At the moment, however, his advent seemed to most of us a trifle by comparison with the collapse of the American banking system, the installation of a new President, and the summoning of Congress in extra session. Nor is there much reason to assume that this attitude was the monopoly of the plain, undistinguished citizen. In all probability it was shared by the new Chief of the State himself. There was no reason for Roosevelt to have supposed that all the sensational developments of the day in Washington were to be overshadowed by what took place in Berlin at the same time. He could not have imagined that in enacting this law the German Reichstag was drawing the warrant that would send Roosevelt into the fieriest trials of his career and eventually to his death.

But it was so. Filled with jubilation by the hope of seeing a way out, Washington danced. Filled with determination to break a way out, Berlin drummed. The dancing was the more spectacular, but the drumming was the more significant; for it continued incessantly, even after the dancers had grown tired, it increased in volume and intensity until at length it drowned out the music of the bands and merged into the roar of a falling world.

Roosevelt and Hitler were both potent men. It would be nonsensical even to question that. But by comparison with the impersonal forces that sweep through history, the strength of the most powerful individual is nothing. In a very real sense, therefore, Roosevelt and Hitler were both symbols, not themselves the contending powers, but the standards around which the powers gathered. This is an unusual event, therefore it is hardly to be credited until it is proved. In 1933 nobody supposed that it was happening. We estimated Hitler at his individual value—and laughed. The estimate was not inaccurate. He was comic. The trouble was that we should have been making an estimate, not of Hitler, but of the power behind him.

That was beyond us, for our political education in 1933 was still woefully parochial. The average American, schooled for five generations in self-government, doubted not at all that self-government was the aspiration of civilized men everywhere. His ignorance was not entirely excusable, because he had evidence to the contrary before his eyes. Every American business-man knew then as he knows now that one of his hardest jobs is to find people willing to assume responsibility; but not every one drew the obvious inference that millions of people want to be disciplined, desire to be controlled, long to be directed in word and act and thought. Even in this country, after its unprecedentedly long training in liberty, there are hordes who hate to be free.

Why, then, should we have assumed the existence of a burning thirst for freedom in a nation that had had no experience of self-government in the sense that we know it? The democratic republic that the Allies imposed upon Germany had little chance of success in any event; but with a large proportion of the German population hating the responsibility that democracy thrust upon it, that government had no chance whatever. In the early days of the Nazi regime it was obvious that Hitler was using trickery and betrayal to bring the German people into subservience, so we fell into the mistake of believing that trickery and betrayal accounted in full for his success. We dismissed the possibility that the German people were inclined to subservience, because, arrogantly attributing our own attitude to all the rest of the world, we did not believe that it is in the nature of civilized man to like subservience. Confident that Hitler's tricks and swindles would soon be exposed, we took it for granted that the exposure would generate a resentment that would destroy him; we overlooked the fact that the Germans will forgive much to the man who brings them the boon of a tyranny that relieves them of political responsibility.

But the Germans' most satisfactory achievement in the art of government had been a paternalistic state, that permitted its nationals little liberty, but that did furnish them with reasonable security. The alternative, in their experience, had been the exploiting state, that gave them neither liberty nor security. Democracy had been introduced to them in the guise of a carpet-bag government set up by a conqueror. In the eyes of the Germans it was a puppet regime, and could not be anything else. They detested it. The wildest extravagances of Hitler seemed to them less fantastic than the idea of living under a government that was the creature of a military invader.

The consideration that the Germans were, if possible, blinder than we were had no effect upon the situation as it existed. We were certain that eventually Hitler would revolt the conscience of Germany; but the conscience of Germany could not perceive that Hitler was more revolting than democracy (or, doubtless, any other form of government) imposed by a victor. Hitler at least was Austrian, that is to say, almost native, while this other thing was foreign to the core.

So before Roosevelt had been in the White House twenty-four hours his course was fixed and determined, not by anything he said or did, not by anything Congress said or did, least of all by anything the common American who had elected him said or did, but by the decision of a so-called legislative assembly three thousand miles away. That assembly abdicated its functions; and from the moment it quit, the long duel was inevitable. After March 5, 1933, the course of events was irreversible; the contestants were committed to the struggle and were to remain committed until one ended in a bunker under the flaming ruins of Berlin, and the other in a small house set among Georgia pines.

For the Congress of the United States did not abdicate. The assertion that it did so is merely one of those characteristic exaggerations to which partisan disputants are always resorting. It accepted suggestions from the President gladly; in general it submitted to his guidance cheerfully; at times, especially during the Hundred Days, it enacted legislation that it did not thoroughly understand simply on his assurance that it was necessary. But not for one moment did it surrender the right at any time to overrule his decisions and refuse his requests. In the twelve years that were to follow, it frequently did overrule and refuse, sometimes to its own regret later, but effectively. Congress, in all probability, would have overruled and refused oftener except for its healthy fear of the wrath of the voters, who wanted Roosevelt given a free hand. In other words, in the United States, although a powerful leader was exercising an authority comparable to that of any dictator, final control was still exercised from below. Neither Roosevelt nor Congress had the last word. That was retained by the people and both the President and Congress admitted that they could only be persuaded, never compelled.

In Germany, after March 5, control was frankly and openly exercised from above. This basic fact made collision of the two ideas inevitable. It happened that the sort of control exercised by Hitler was stupid and vicious in the extreme, but had he been a modern Solon, instead of an extreme psychoneurotic, still he must have come into collision with the American idea soon or late. As it was, the collision was swift and violent. The incidental hatefulness of Hitlerian control was extremely effective in bracing the American people for the shock, so the collision was also final, as far as the Nazi regime was concerned. Had he been a benevolent despot, we might never have had the heart to pursue him until he was buried under the ruins of his own capital, but we should have had to oppose him, or yield our own way of life.

The education of the average American in this particular phase of life was not, in fact, effected in March, 1933. The demonstration was given at that time, but it was more than five years later that the lesson really began to sink in—to be exact, it was in September, 1938, that we began to suspect that at the time of the inauguration of Roosevelt we had been watching the wrong show. It was in that month that the European democracies, desperate, made the infamous bargain of Munich. Even then, although the shock was strong, we did not perceive the full significance of what had happened. We thought that Czechoslovakia had been sold down the river; we did not see that Czechoslovakia was merely a token, and that what had really been sold was democracy, all democracy, including our own.

Our disgust with Britain and France, the agents in this transaction, was justified, but it might have been less freely expressed had we realized to how large an extent they were our agents. The bargain was forced because democracy's stake in the deal was not adequately protected. Our part of that stake was larger than any other, but we were precisely the people who had done least toward protecting it. Therefore, when the democratic agents defaulted, they acted for the whole democratic world, the United States included.

All this was unsuspected, however, on that gusty, cloud-dappled day when the second Roosevelt was sworn in as President of the United States. His inaugural address lifted us from the depths of gloom and gave us new hope and new resolution. What could be more important? In the eyes of the plain American, nothing. He was to be rudely undeceived, but the time had not yet come. A citizen of this Republic was he, owing no sort of allegiance to any other political organization, anywhere in the world.

Technically, this was correct, but actually he was already very much a citizen of the world, and any attack on world order was an attack on his homeland. The installation of Roosevelt was an effort to buttress the existing system; it was important, to be sure, but actually less important than the operations of the sappers and miners in Berlin who were cutting under the foundations of the structure. Our education in international affairs was as yet woefully incomplete; at the critical moment we were intent on the wrong show, and it was to prove a costly bit of negligence.

Yet to suggest that the basis of the error was either moral turpitude or irremediable stupidity would be to concede at once the impossibility of self-government among men. We failed out of ignorance. We had not yet been shown. The test of our capacity for self-government is not our ability to deal with the unknown, but our ability to act intelligently after we have been shown. That is what justifies an effort to look back over this disconcerting half-century and to arrange its events, if we can, into some sort of comprehensible pattern.

3. Arcadia Revisited

THE ordinary American whose years are numbered with those of the twentieth century has, like the woman of Scripture, "suffered many things of many physicians." If he feels that destiny has put him to the rack in a way that shouldn't happen to a dog, he can cite much evidence in support of his complaint; and he would be sordid indeed if he did not hope for this year's children a happier time. Nevertheless, he enjoys one advantage over the first voters of 1950, for there is in his dreary history an episode of such pure delight that the young fellows of today can hardly be expected to understand it, much less to experience anything like it. This episode was the first year of the New Deal.

Youth cannot hope to duplicate this experience because modern youth is not conditioned to receive the impression it made upon the generation that was mature in 1933. That conditioning was a conviction born of long experience that wherever the intellectual leadership of the nation might reside, it was not in the nation's capital. The best that could be hoped of Washington was that it might not lag so far behind as to drag the nation back, rather than lead it forward, in any mental operation more complicated than that of tallying the vote in Sandy Mush Precinct.

The first two years of Wilson's first administration had been an interlude, but a restricted one. Between Wilson's inauguration and the outbreak of the First World War the capital had been the scene of some vigorous intellectual activity, but it was almost entirely confined to the field of government. Wilson and his advisers had a great many ideas, some of them fresh and new, about cleaning, oiling and adjusting the machinery of democracy, and they did a remarkably thorough job in the brief time allowed them to work at it. Moreover, in the Land Bank System and in the program of labor legislation the administration did trench somewhat upon the fields of economics and sociology.

But the energies of that administration were soon diverted to the single problem of military defense, a problem so old that its conditions were determined many centuries ago and the intellectual questions it poses are strictly those of technology, not of philosophy. In general it is true that within the memory of living men no vigorous exploration of the ways of life open to Americans had been conducted from Washington. Colleges and universities, churches, municipalities, even State legislatures, produced and propounded such ideas as enriched American thinking; never Washington. The function of Washington was to suppress novelty as long as suppression was feasible; and then

to yield grudgingly, and only so far as was imperatively necessary to prevent an explosion.

The President himself was sometimes a man of force. Hoover
and Taft were unquestionably men of intellectual vigor, and the
first Roosevelt had not only an alert, but an inquiring mind. But
every occupant of the White House since Lincoln had in some
measure given bond to his party. Each owed his election to a
powerful party organization—even Theodore Roosevelt and
Coolidge, who came to the Presidency by the intervention of
death, had to depend upon the party machine for re-election—
and therefore had to fill the great offices of state with experienced and influential party leaders.

These leaders, as a class, are about as stuffy a group as can be
assembled. At least it is so as regards their public appearances,
and the average American has no other way of gauging them.
Correspondents of newspapers, and others who have business
with the government, know that in private the politician is frequently a salty and amusing personality; but in public he is no
more capable of bold, unexpected action along unexplored lines
than is one of the stuffed animals in the Museum of Natural
History.

The business of eminent party leaders, in fact, is to prevent
bold and unexpected action because its results are unpredictable;
and the essence of getting re-elected is the correct prediction of
public trends. The ultimate calamity for a politician is to find
himself leading public opinion; his study is to follow it while
giving the impression that he leads; and the most convenient
way to effect this is constantly to pronounce irreproachable and
insignificant sentiments in thunder tones.

The result of assiduous practice of this technique had been to
make Washington for the fifty years preceding Roosevelt—the
brief Wilsonian interlude excepted—rather less of a national
intellectual center than any first-class penitentiary. In fact, at

the very moment when Wilson was really doing something with government machinery, Warden Osborne made Sing Sing prison a more fecund producer of social ideas than Congress had ever been. Far from being the nursery of thought, Washington was its extermination camp, the Oswieçim into which the brain children of other places were herded, only to be gassed to death.

But in March, 1933, the customary rules were suspended. In the first place, Roosevelt had not been elected by a party, but by a conglomeration made up of everyone who had a grievance; and in 1932 practically everyone had a grievance. There is some color of truth in the assertion that Roosevelt hadn't been elected at all as a personality on his own account; what the country went out to accomplish on election day was to defeat Hoover and his party; the election of Roosevelt was merely a necessary incident to that. Again, Roosevelt had singularly few old-line Democrats of any perceptible size on his hands. McAdoo, having sated his vengeance by blocking the nomination of Al Smith in the Democratic National Convention, was safely embedded in the Senate. Smith had sulked through the campaign and therefore was due nothing. Bryan had been dead for years. Garner, the shrewd and aggressive Speaker of the House, had been stuck into the Vice Presidency, and was out of the way. The usual phalanx of inevitable office holders—what the polite call the party's Elder Statesmen and the impolite the Stuffed Shirt Brigade—was almost entirely missing. Cordell Hull, the able leader of the opposition in the Democrats' long exile, had to be taken care of, and Roper, an ancient Wilsonian, was given recognition. Swanson, a decrepit relic of neolithic times from Virginia, was taken out of the Senate and made Secretary of the Navy, partly as a conciliatory gesture to the ardent party men and partly, strange to say, to make room in the Senate for the apparently progressive Governor Byrd, who was to return the favor by knifing the administration as early and as often as he dared.

This left Roosevelt unusually free from party obligations. More important still, on March 4, 1933, not many sound party men really wanted high office. The situation was too appalling to make office attractive to hacks. It was plain to the dullest that the men who took over the conspicuous jobs would be compelled by dire necessity to think fast and take chances; an old-fashioned politician, of the type that had been holding the statelier jobs for the past fifty years, hates to think at all, and doubly hates having to think fast, while taking chances is as contrary to his nature and nurture as swimming is to cats. So if they conspired and contrived to capture the big posts, they did not put much heart in it, and when they were denied most of them were as much relieved as disappointed.

The circumstances being what they were, it was generally agreed that conventional politics might be considered adjourned for the moment. The new President was expected to bring in a Cabinet of a new type, and he did. Hull was made Secretary of State, but he, Roper, of Commerce, and Swanson at the Navy Department, presented the only faces familiar to Washington. The rest were people that nobody had ever heard of before— nobody, that is, except bankers, industrialists, lawyers, scholars, scientists and a million or two of unclassified people who read magazines and books, as well as newspapers, which is to say, nobody who had thitherto counted in Washington.

There were Woodin, Ickes and Wallace, all, until the election of 1932, lifelong Republicans, yet Woodin was given the Number Two job in the Cabinet, the Treasury Department, while Ickes got Interior, the job with the fattest pickings for party hacks with sticky fingers. There was Perkins, a social worker and, of all things, a woman! All New York State knew Frances Perkins, as manufacturers knew Woodin, farmers Wallace, and all who loved a gaudy intellectual circus Ickes; but none was taken seriously in practical politics; therefore the old-style jobholder and even the old-style Washington correspondent had never heard of any of them. One might as soon have expected the denizens of Washington to recognize the names of Socrates, Goethe and J. S. Bach.

But even more important than the reconstruction of the Cabinet—after all, it did include some conventional appointments, Roper and Swanson, for instance, and, of course, the customary award of the Postmaster-Generalship to the winning campaign manager, in this case James A. Farley—was the change in the character of the second-string men. Roosevelt himself had served in Wilson's day as Assistant Secretary of the Navy under a chief who was willing to let him act; so he knew by experience the tremendous potentialities of vigorous executive officers of less than Cabinet rank.

He brought such people into Washington by dozens and scores, most of them young men and even those who were middle-aged still lively fellows. In fact, the loudest individual in the crew was fifty-one years old in 1933, an ex-brigadier general named Hugh S. Johnson, but better described by his army soubriquet of Ironpants. Not many men in their twenties and thirties could maintain the terrific working pace set by Ironpants, and not one could emulate the stentorian roar with which he could startle from their sleep drowsy old boys in all the grander clubs from Boston to San Francisco. "The air," said Ironpants with obvious satisfaction as he assumed office, "will soon be filled with dead cats." It was. He saw to that. He was in position to do so since, as head of the National Recovery Administration he dealt with both industrialists and labor leaders and he handled them in the spirit of the smartest regular army drill sergeant. Naturally, they were soon throwing everything they could lay their hands on, including lawsuits. One of these, brought by a dealer in dressed poultry, was decided by the Supreme Court against the NRA; so in the end Ironpants was knocked out, not by a dead cat but by a dead chicken—a charmingly spectacular end to a charmingly spectacular career.

While he lasted, though, he furnished endless excitement and diversion to the nation. He was, perhaps, the most exciting individual in the New Deal, but if so it was by a narrow margin, for he had stiff competition. In his speech accepting the nomination in 1932 Roosevelt had promised a renovation of the public service;[1] but no one had any idea of the extent, and still less of the nature, of that renovation.

In the campaign Roosevelt, observing that the appalling depression had made the old-style partisan approach completely hopeless, had determined to make a different sort of appeal. He had the wit to perceive that when all the old reliances have collapsed, the usual conditions are reversed. When a conflagration is raging, dynamite may represent safety, not the utmost danger. Politicians regard novelty as dynamite, not without reason in ordinary times; but in the fearful year of 1933 Roosevelt boldly seized novelty and brandished it.

To assist him in formulating his appeal he assembled a group of advisers outside the usual party organization. The mechanics of the campaign he left to the veteran politicians, headed by Farley, knowing that they could handle that work more skillfully than anyone else; but his own speeches were hammered out in close consultation with a handful of experts, not politicians

[1] The closing paragraph of that speech, delivered to the Democratic National Convention at Chicago after the nominee had broken precedent by flying out to accept on the spot, read, "I pledge you, I pledge myself to a new deal for the American people. Let us all here assembled constitute ourselves prophets of a new order of competence and of courage. This is more than a political campaign; it is a call to arms. Give me your help, not to win votes alone, but to win in this crusade to restore America to its own people." Thereafter the Roosevelt domestic program was known as the New Deal so exclusively that many people forgot that he was technically a Democrat, as they forgot that Theodore Roosevelt in the Bull Moose campaign was technically a Progressive.

at all, but each eminent in some intellectual discipline. Prominent among them were Raymond Moley, at that time a professor of public law in Columbia University, Judge Samuel I. Rosenman, of the New York bench, R. G. Tugwell, an economist also at Columbia, and General Johnson, a genius at publicity. These men's best service, however, was not always in supplying answers to questions; frequently it was in knowing where to find the man who could give the answer. They were perpetually summoning others to Roosevelt headquarters; some came once only, others repeatedly, while others remained through the rest of the campaign.

Naturally, each man thus summoned was eminent in his particular field. The idea was always to call in the finest expert available and the group around Roosevelt had a pretty shrewd idea who was the best man in almost any field of human endeavor, machine politics perhaps excepted. A great many of them were connected with universities, a few with libraries or courts, a few from the higher level of journalism, while some without any institutional connection were known as the authors of authoritative books. The newspapermen assigned to cover the campaign, most of them veterans of many such assignments, watched them come and go with increasing amazement; never had they seen such a procession of pundits, sages, worshipful masters, and learned doctors of every description. One of them[2] at length set it down in print that Roosevelt appeared to be trying to establish a monopoly of all the learning in the country, a veritable "brains trust." The country, dropping the "s," joyously adopted the designation and the Brain Trust became an inseparable part of the mythology of the New Deal.

Immediately after the inauguration it developed that the Brain Trust was not a mere campaign device. Roosevelt brought

[2] Moley says it was James Kieran, of the New York *Times*. (See Raymond Moley, *After Seven Years*. New York: Harper & Brothers, 1939, p. 27.)

it practically intact to Washington and gave it official authority, usually in positions just below Cabinet rank. Moley, for example, was assigned to the State Department as an assistant secretary, Tugwell took a similar position in Agriculture, Johnson, as already stated, headed the NRA, and while Rosenman retained his judgeship in New York, he became an important consultant at the White House.

Many others were drawn into government service at the same time, and in almost every case the newcomer was assigned to a position in which he could wield an important influence upon the selection of personnel in the lower ranks. They then proceeded almost to denude the universities and great corporations of their ablest, most alert young men. Washington was inundated by a flood of vigorous and aggressive economists, sociologists, attorneys, engineers, historians, statisticians, geographers, agronomists, architects, linguists, publicists, in fact anything and everything except precinct captains and ward heelers.

The effect was electrifying. As a rule these swarms of minor officials were young and enthusiastic, sincerely desirous of performing genuine public service. Some of them thought, most of them acted, and all of them talked. Conversationally, Washington leaped at a bound from the dullest to the most brilliant place in the country. It was transformed into the great national center of ideas, and if a goodly proportion of them were idiotic, nevertheless they were stimulating and vastly entertaining.

Naturally, in this atmosphere of youth and unbounded enthusiasm the talk was not always judicious. On one famous occasion a group of these boys and girls picked up a serious old party from the Middle West and took him to dinner at a house in Georgetown; discovering that the gaffer was almost fabulously credulous, they proceeded to amuse themselves by stuffing him with the most horrendous tales their uninhibited imaginations could devise. They gravely assured him that the Revolution was already on. They asserted solemnly that it was all fixed and that the Roosevelt who so terrified him was really nothing—merely the American Kerensky, who would presently be set aside to make room for an American Lenin who would chastise with scorpions where Roosevelt had used rods. They scared the old man so nearly out of his wits that he promptly fled to his Congressman, poured out the bloodcurdling tale and precipitated a Congressional investigation which brought just retribution upon the humorists.

But such absurdities were comparatively rare. The spirit of the time in Washington was that of a vigorous, sincere and, on the whole, intelligent effort to bend the energies and resources of the government to the service of the common good.

To assert that democracy actually worked in Washington during the early days of the New Deal would be an imprudently broad claim. The collapse had been too complete and too ruinous for anything to work well at that time. But at least it was a moment when democracy tried to work. For almost the first time within the memory of living men cunning was set below intelligence and the winning of the next election was subverted to the promotion of the general welfare. For the moment the old capital pulsed with intellectual energy; for the moment it had that "more abundant life" that the New Dealers had promised; and it was a moment that will not be forgotten while any that experienced it survives.

4. *Economics for Simple Simon*

THE condition in which the country found itself on the day that Roosevelt was inaugurated has been the subject of studies that have filled literally thousands of thick books. Many learned and industrious economists, sociologists and historians have worn their brains out trying to understand it, and to convey their understanding to others. It is as intricate as any subject with which the human mind has grappled, and nothing could be more fatuous than an attempt to explain it in a few pages here.

Yet from the standpoint of the ordinary, undistinguished American it had the stark simplicity of death and taxes—with both of which, indeed, it was intimately involved. If that ordinary American was a workman, he had no job; if a farmer, he had no market; if a small merchant or manufacturer, he had no customers. More than that, his lack was patently nonsensical, because there was an enormous amount of work to be done, an enormous production (we dared even call it overproduction) of goods, and all the potential customers the market could need.

"The business of America is business," Coolidge had once remarked, to the delight of the scornful; but Coolidge was not the man to go on to inquire, what is the business of business? About that, the average man had no doubt whatever. The business of business is to furnish a living to the average man.[3] That

[3] The world does not owe men a living, but business, if it is to fulfill its ideal, owes men an opportunity to earn a living.—Owen D. Young, in Harvard Business Review, June 4, 1927.

is the only excuse for the existence of business. When business no longer affords a living, it fails utterly, completely, beyond all redemption.

In 1933 it had been failing progressively for four years. It was unquestionably the failure of business, too. The seasons had been good; crops had not failed. No earthquakes, or tidal waves, or volcanoes had damaged the land. No pestilence like the Black Death had swept away the workers. No invading army had burned down the factories and torn up the railroads and highways. No convulsion of nature of any kind had smitten the United States. Nothing had failed, except the economic system, that is, business. Yet hunger and despair had flailed the land, maddening the people to such an extent that in the previous year troops had been fighting milk farmers in Illinois and mobs had pulled judges off the bench in half a dozen States to prevent the foreclosure of mortgages.

The average man drew the inference that the economic system was extremely inefficient and in urgent need of renovation. What other inference could he have drawn, assuming that he was more than half-witted? He had relied upon business for a living, and he was threatened with death by starvation. Then to expect him to retain his old respect for business was to expect him to sink far below the intellectual level of Simple Simon.

A great many prominent business leaders apparently did expect just that. They persuaded themselves that the mounting unrest throughout the country was due primarily to the infiltration of foreign ideas, "foreign isms," as they delighted to say, mostly generated in Moscow. Why sane men should entertain the idea that chilblains and an empty belly are inventions of the Russians is beyond understanding, but so they did. Why they should think that a man in process of freezing and starving should need a foreign agitator to drive him wild, is equally beyond comprehension; but it was a popular doctrine in Chambers of Commerce.

Yet perhaps it is not an impenetrable mystery. The beans were spilled—there was no possibility of denying that fact. The only possible doubt was as to who spilled them. Nobody wished to assume the responsibility, especially businessmen, the most obvious suspects. To pass the blame to foreign agitators therefore was a natural, if rather silly, recourse. Needless to say, they convinced nobody but themselves. Unfortunately, they did convince themselves in so many instances that the contribution of business to the effort at reconstruction was reduced far below what it might have been.

The utter nonsense of the doctrine of infiltration by foreign "isms" is demonstrated by the eagerness with which the average man welcomed the Rooseveltian suggestion that all the American system needed was a thorough overhauling in the interest of the people, for basically it was sound. By comparison with the programs being adopted in other countries also suffering under the depression this was conservatism itself. It offered no challenge to the theories of private property and civil liberty; in fact, between 1933 and 1940—after which time the war upset all calculations—the index of personal income rose from 67.9 to 114.2, while the individual's right to drink what he chose to drink had been restored, the censorship of books had been restricted to local communities, and the right to worship had been sustained by a series of Supreme Court decisions, even the right to worship in ways favored by such minorities as Jehovah's Witnesses.

All this was very much in the American tradition and the ordinary citizen regarded it in that light. Therefore he paid no attention to the cries that it was socialistic, communistic and probably atheistic, and continued to vote for the New Deal, stolidly and solidly. Why not? To sustain the traditions established at the very foundation of the Republic seemed to the average man conservative, not radical; and government "for the people" was certainly one of those traditions. It did not originate with Lincoln. It went far beyond him, far beyond Jackson's fight against the Bank, back through the Declaration of Independence and the Mayflower Compact, all the way back to Captain John Smith and the gentlemen hoeing in the cornfields at Jamestown.

Business had failed to do its job. That was the central fact of the situation. People were starving in the midst of plenty, and free private enterprise seemed to be completely impotent to do anything about it. The obvious next step in such a situation is to abolish free private enterprise and try something else. It was the step taken in country after country. It was not taken here, however, because Roosevelt and his New Dealers offered an alternative; that alternative was, since business had failed to discharge its only social function, to try what government could do—our existing government, the old Republic with which we were familiar—to stimulate private enterprise before jumping all the way into Socialism or Communism.

To the plain, nonexpert American this sounded like good sense and he accepted it. More than that, he found that it worked, not perfectly, by any means, but well enough to give him some encouragement; therefore he clung to it with the same bland indifference to the outcries of the "rich and well-born" that had been exhibited by his forefathers, when they voted repeatedly for Jackson and, before that, for Jefferson and Jeffersonians.

From 1932 through eighteen terrific years the plain American has supported the central concept of the New Deal, namely, that government is not merely an umpire, but an instrument in the hands of the people to effect their safety and happiness. Intellectually, the revival of this ancient idea was the work of Wilson. His long study of the theory of government had disciplined his mind to the difficult task of applying an old principle correctly to new conditions. Every man in public life pretends to be applying old principles to modern conditions, and many sincerely believe that they are doing so; but to apply such a principle correctly is tricky business; it requires not merely an accurate historical perspective, but a solid philosophical basis never attained by any but exceptionally mature minds. When Wilson envisaged the Presidency as an agency as directly responsible for the general welfare as the Prime Ministry is in Great Britain, he drew the blueprints for the New Deal. This work was later obscured by his much more spectacular achievement in drawing the blueprints for an orderly world in the League of Nations; but historically the first feat of statecraft is not a whit less important than the second. He first accustomed the modern American to look upon the President as a party leader; and that modified the American profoundly.

But Wilson was permitted to work at the application of his ideas a scant two years only. His intellectual, although not immediate, successor, Roosevelt, had six full years to work at the task before his attention was diverted by the Second World War. It is doubtful, to say the least, that Roosevelt could ever have worked his way through study and sheer power of reason to the conclusions that Wilson reached; but he had ample power to understand them, and to assess their value, once Wilson had pointed them out.

For the rest, Roosevelt was better equipped, temperamentally, than Wilson for the practical application of an idea. The greatest master of the laws of optics is not necessarily the best landscape or figure painter. In statecraft, although it is an art, rather than a science, there is a distinction roughly corresponding to the distinction between pure and applied science, and as a rule the man who excels in one is distinctly weaker in the other. Roosevelt was as strong in application as Wilson was in discovery.

The supreme achievement of Franklin D. Roosevelt was not the United Nations, nor the victory in a double war, nor the Atlantic Charter, but the Fireside Chat; for it was the Fireside

Chat that gave him the power to accomplish all his other works.

There was where he proved his superiority, not only to Hoover and Coolidge, but in some degree to Wilson, as well. His enemies regarded this technique as a cheap trick, wherein they exposed their own ignorance of statecraft. They could not recognize high strategy when they saw it.

For in the Fireside Chat Roosevelt threw overboard all the idolatry of *expertise* that had hobbled and hog-tied his predecessors, and called in the only man who could really help, to wit, the commonplace, ordinary, nonexpert American. In the Fireside Chat the party leader sat at a microphone and told the people, sitting by their firesides with the radio turned on, exactly what he was doing, why he was doing it, and what he proposed to do next. These talks studiously avoided what is usually esteemed the eloquent (and is generally only the clinquant) in favor of the lucid. He really wanted the people to understand, and his close associates have testified that he worked like a dog to make these speeches utterly clear.[4] He did not hesitate to take up the most abstruse subjects—the abandonment of the gold standard and devaluation of the currency, for example—and talk about them to farm hands, garage mechanics, pick-and-shovel gangs, grocery clerks, housewives, school children, or anyone else who had a radio. He did not believe that it was enough for Treasury officials, financiers, economists and the leaders of the two Houses of Congress to understand the government's fiscal policy. He did not believe that it was beyond the power of the common man to understand, and he was confident that the common man, once he understood, would approve.

The miraculous part of it was that he made them understand at least his side of the question. Certainly he oversimplified great problems of statecraft. No human mind has ever stated a prob-

[4] Frances Perkins, in *The Roosevelt I Knew* (New York: Viking Press, 1946), is emphatic on this point, but Moley, Rosenman, Farley, Michelson and all the rest have said the same thing.

lem without oversimplifying it to some extent. Albert Einstein
oversimplifies when he declares that two and two make four, for
he ignores the question of why they make four; if he undertook
to explain that, he would get in so deep that he would still be
talking at the term of his natural life and could never consider
anything else. The important point is that with all his oversim-
plification, Roosevelt rarely distorted anything to the point at
which his argument was demonstrably false. When he finished,
the country did know the main reasons for the devaluation of
the currency, or of any other act of the administration that he
had discussed.

The people listened, understood, and approved; and that was
all there was to it.

But this the opponents of Roosevelt could never comprehend.
The very simplicity of the thing put it beyond their grasp. Like
the Senator Brabantio, father of Desdemona, they simply knew
that there must be witchcraft in it, and expended energy and
time beyond calculation

> To find out practices of cunning hell,
> Why this should be,

only to discover the electorate, like the lady of Venice, all the
more bemused after each installment of the tale. Sometimes it
was rugged stuff. The Fireside Chats were not all good news;
on the contrary, they commonly introduced some new austerity,
some additional reason why the taxpayer must pay, the worker
must work, the commoner must settle his shoulder to the wheel.
This, in the view of Roosevelt's opponents, should have ruined
him; yet upon inquiry their frail Desdemona averred,

> She wish'd she had not heard it; yet she wish'd
> That heaven had made her such a man,

and the infatuation was obviously deeper than ever.

The explanation is, of course, that the opposition had gravely underestimated both the intelligence and the sturdiness of the average American. They could not make him understand; so they assumed that his intelligence was weak, missing entirely the true explanation, that their own powers of exposition were utterly unequal to the task of explaining the simplest problems.

5. *Argus in the Dust Storm*

THE panic of 1929 was the settling down of twilight upon many gods. The businessman was perhaps the Wotan of that march to Valhalla, but he had no lack of companions. The invincibility of the Republican party was one. Even during the Wilsonian interregnum, "This is normally a Republican country" remained a political aphorism. It died hard. Four consecutive times Roosevelt subjected it to jolts of forty-five hundred volts, yet it survived, feebly, until 1948. What killed it finally was the revelation that the country would take Truman, rather than accept a Republican. Not even a legend could survive that shock.

Another was the illusion that pretended joviality is always successful with the people. Roosevelt was jovial by nature; he had no need to pretend, and he didn't. His lameness put it out of the question for him to participate in the sort of imbecilities to which many candidates have lent themselves in the hope of garnering a few votes, but it is doubtful that he would have done it even if he had had the legs of a tap dancer.

The decade of the twenties produced two news photographs

that were probably more hurtful to democracy than Albert B. Fall's bribe-taking. One was of Ebert, then President of the Weimar Republic, and Stresemann, his Foreign Minister, emerging from a swimming pool clad only in bathing trunks. Both were elderly, pot-bellied, and spindle-shanked; and the effect was so dreadful that good judges have attributed to it a considerable share of responsibility for the downfall of the German Republic. The other was a picture, taken in the West during a campaign year, of Coolidge in a cowboy suit.[5]

Roosevelt had the ability to talk in friendly fashion with every type of humanity without pretending to be anything but what he was. This was, in fact, an exhibition of far more genuine respect for the common man than the false joviality of the conventional approach. The common man knew that Roosevelt was a patrician, but that was all right as long as he acted like a real patrician, that is, a man who, knowing his own rights, is scrupulously careful to respect the rights of others. Roosevelt knew that the interest of the patrician coincides with that of everyone else at one point, the need of good government, so there was no necessity for him to pretend that he was at heart a cowboy, or a coal miner, or a Sioux Indian, to explain his preoccupation with that subject; and he thought that the cowboy, the miner, and the Sioux were intelligent enough to know it. Therefore in talking to the people he made no attempt to step out of character, and

[5] The social significance of the newspaper cameraman is a subject that deserves more attention than it has received from the learned doctors. H. L. Mencken once accused this fraternity of having contributed heavily, and with malice prepense, to the downfall of prohibition, by the device of choosing their subjects carefully whenever they had occasion to photograph ladies of the opposing factions. The lady wets were always delectable cuties, while to represent the lady drys the boys "dredged up some specimens so dreadful that it is hard to understand how a self-respecting God could have made them." The firmness with which Mrs. Harry S. Truman is said to have quashed every effort to photograph her husband on the beach at Miami during the campaign year of 1948 was probably an exhibition of rare good sense.

it seemed to work. At any rate, the people followed him with a fidelity unprecedented in our time.

But in these days of flattening reputations perhaps the most striking loss of prestige was that of the press. In the campaign of 1932 Roosevelt had some support, even among the larger newspapers. To be exact, it should be said that the Democratic party had some support, for in 1932 the candidate was known merely as a vigorous Governor of New York, assumed to be a politician of the general type of Alfred E. Smith, whose policies he was following with marked success.

However, as soon as the New Deal revealed itself in action, the metropolitan press swiftly fell away, and became increasingly critical until it was practically unanimously in opposition. From 1936 on Roosevelt's only press support as regards his domestic policies came from country and small-city newspapers of limited circulation and no national prestige.

But the opposition of the great papers had no practical effect whatever.

Here is a phenomenon that deserves far more careful, objective study than it has received. From time immemorial most of us had been accustomed to regard the great newspapers as powerful exponents of public opinion. Some even clung to Macaulay's opinion that they were molders of public opinion and for that reason in a very real sense a fourth estate of the realm. The more realistic journalists had long cherished skepticism as to that, but even the realists had an idea that the newspapers were expressions of public opinion. The very way in which they contradicted each other supported the idea, for public opinion in a democracy is always somewhat self-contradictory. Hardly anyone doubted that on those rare occasions when the press spoke with a single voice, it spoke with the voice of the people.

But 1936 demonstrated, and 1940, 1944 and 1948 offered corroborative evidence, that it is not so. In those election years the press practically unanimously denounced the Roosevelt leadership—for even in 1948 the basic objection to Truman was his boast that he was the political heir of Roosevelt—yet the people continued to prefer it. Obviously, therefore, whatever opinion the press was expressing, it was not the opinion of the majority. Four consecutive times the press attack collapsed disastrously. Four consecutive times it was demonstrated conclusively that the average American no longer accepts his political opinions from his journalistic monitors, if he ever did; and that the journals now do not even reflect, much less create, majority opinion.

When an attack breaks down utterly, three possible explanations come to mind at once. The first is that the attack was fainthearted. The second is that the enemy was invincible. The third is that although the enemy may have been vulnerable and the attack resolute, it may have been misdirected in such a way as to strike the enemy at the point where he really was invincible, instead of at the point where he was weakest.

In the case of Roosevelt and the American press the first explanation may be dismissed without a moment's consideration. There was nothing fainthearted about the attack; not only was it violent in the extreme, but so resolute that it rallied and returned to the charge three times after the first assault had been smashed so completely that Landon, the standard-bearer in 1936, got exactly the same number of electoral votes, eight, that Taft got in 1912 with both Theodore Roosevelt and Woodrow Wilson running against him. As an explanation of the failure feebleness is definitely out. Indeed, nobody advances that explanation seriously.

The second possibility, that the assault was aimed at an invincible foe, is more to the taste of the ardent Rooseveltians, and they are inclined to accept it blandly. But it can stand the test of examination little if any better than the first one. The New Deal certainly was not invulnerable at all points; on the contrary, it was full of glaring weaknesses, some so blatant that its most ardent defenders could do no more than offer explanations, many of them pretty lame.

To begin with, the program was tremendously expensive, relative to the then current standards of expense. True, by today's standards it looks rather trifling. In the seven years before war preparations burst upon the country the New Deal increased the national debt by about twenty billions, which represent only six months' expenditures of the government in 1949. But in those days twenty billions was an inconceivable sum. Doubtless mere expense is not necessarily a fatal weakness, but a weakness it certainly is, quite important enough to give the opposition a starting point.

In addition to that, the New Deal was wasteful, and this is a weakness without qualification. The New Dealers extenuated it, of course, by citing the haste with which the program had to be thrown together. This may have been a sufficient explanation as regards the first year, perhaps even for the second; but when the waste continued into the third and the fourth and beyond, the extenuation no longer held good. The waste was, in fact, somewhat reduced as time went on. For instance, the calamitous Civil Works Administration was fairly soon eliminated to make room for the somewhat better Works Progress Administration which eventually gave way to a comparatively sensible Public Works Administration. But right up to the moment when rearmament took over, the New Deal was still engaging in some business practices that no rational accountant could possibly justify. Here was a gaping breach in the fortifications.

More than that, and in the final result probably worse than that, the New Deal introduced into the public service a bureaucratic element hard for a self-respecting people to tolerate. Much too large a proportion of its agents were not merely young and enthusiastic, but also callow. There grew up in Washington a far too general tendency to pontificate. Along with the brilliant minds that the regime unquestionably brought to Washington in impressive numbers it brought also a certain proportion of beardless boys whose estimate of their own genius was as colossal as it was erroneous; and sometimes these slipped into positions which they were utterly incompetent to hold, but which permitted them to dictate to honest men in a lofty and infuriating style.

This was more than a breach in the fortifications. This was a standing invitation to the attackers to come swarming in.

The regime had another conspicuous weakness traceable to the character of its leader. Roosevelt was afflicted with a squeamishness about inflicting hurts upon an honest and loyal man that, however creditable to him as an individual, was very decidedly a fault in a leader. It was not an innate and pervasive softness of character that made him unable to inflict punishment. On the contrary, when he dealt with an out-and-out crook, he could lay on the bastinado with pious joy; and a man whom he regarded as disloyal he could pursue with a resolution that passed beyond strict justice into the realm of vindictiveness. But when a man's loyalty and integrity were beyond question, when a man was doing his level best and was guilty of no fault other than having not quite enough ability to handle his job, it was flatly impossible for Roosevelt to take the sort of action that his leadership required him to take. A flawless leader cuts off the incompetent promptly, cleanly and definitely, for good intentions cannot supply the lack of ability. This Roosevelt rarely had the heart to do. Instead of throwing out the honest incompetent and replacing him with an abler man, he would usually try to soften the blow by adding the abler man to the organization, frequently making it top-heavy, unwieldy and inefficient. This got him the name of a hopelessly bad administrator and added materially to the waste that marred his program.

Waste, bureaucratic arrogance, and clumsy organization were faults too glaring for the opposition press—which presently included practically all the big newspapers—to miss, and it attacked at all three points, doing considerable execution in the ranks of the new Deal. But it never delivered its main assault on these vulnerable spots. Its shock troops, its massed artillery, its armor, and its air force were concentrated on the one position they could not possibly take, and when the main attack was crushed, minor successes at scattered points along the line amounted to nothing.

This impregnable position, which the press attacked four several times with the fatal obstinacy of Hitler sending army after army to ruin before Stalingrad, was Roosevelt's motivation.

It was the unshakable conviction of the average man—not only the underprivileged, but merely the unprivileged—that Roosevelt was his friend. Why Roosevelt chose to be his friend the unprivileged and undistinguished American cared not to inquire; so the furious ascription of every kind of discreditable motive to the President passed by the voter as the idle wind.

Some said that the Squire of Hyde Park was really intent only on preserving the advantageous position of his own caste and class. Some said that he aspired to be a dictator himself, covetous of the glitter that Hitler and Mussolini had draped around themselves. Some said that he was inspired by malice, and was pulling down the pillars of the temple to avenge certain slights and insults, never clearly identified, to which he had been subjected in earlier years. Some said he cherished a crazy ambition to emulate the eponymous heroes of the ancient world, intending to give the United States an endless succession of Presidents named Roosevelt. Nearly all agreed that it was his fixed, firm purpose to destroy the American way of life and substitute something else for it.

As one looks back upon it now, the striking thing about this sort of attack is its incredible immaturity. To begin with, some of the charges were silly on their face and would never have been advanced by men whose reasoning powers had not been injured by hatred gone maudlin. In the second place, there was a complete lack of co-ordination in the attack, for some of the charges were contradictory; no man could harbor all those motives simultaneously. But the third, and fatal, flaw in the strategy was the fact that if every single charge, including the mutually contradictory ones, had been proved to the hilt, still that would have done nothing to break Roosevelt's strength with the people. That strength was their conviction that he was their friend and, as far as they could see, their only friend among the great lords of politics.

So in four successive campaigns, not counting that of 1932 when the opposition was not solid, the infatuated battalions of the American press "marched through a slaughterhouse to an open grave," and all that was proved in the end is that the newspaper press does not even reflect, much less mold, the opinion of the majority.

Even Thermopylae had one survivor, and it would be gross disregard of fact to deny that a journal here and there escaped this multiple massacre. The New York *Times*, for instance, skirted the holocaust by confining its own attack to the genuinely weak points of the New Deal; even more remarkable is the fact that the *Herald-Tribune*, of the same city, although it was a frankly Republican paper and had partisan ends to serve, restrained its criticism of Roosevelt within the bounds of credibility, at least. Here and there another journalistic attacker eschewed exhibitions of infantilism and emerged with some share of public respect. But the survivors were few.

What is the explanation of this curious instance of institutional suicide? To attribute it to a general degeneration of the craft is nonsensical. As regards professional competence, general education, and breadth of cultural background it is probable that the staff of the average American newspaper in 1933 stood higher than it ever had before. Certainly it was not conspicuously lower. Some other reason must be sought for an exhibition of intellectual futility, one may well say puerility, that might have made Greeley, Fourierism and all, and the elder Bennett, fisticuffs and all, stare and gasp.

Part of it, without doubt, was due to the modern organization of the press. More and more metropolitan newspapers have become Big Business, frequently holding a monopoly position. Inevitably they have taken on more and more of the institutional character of Big Business, a prominent feature of which is the tendency to make a fetish of the system. Every great corporation executive knows that one of the dangers that he must constantly avoid is that of letting his organization drift into a worship of the system that puts correct routine ahead of increasing production.

The great corporations that produce our large newspapers felt called upon to defend a system that they dubbed the American way of life. They saw this system boldly assailed by Roosevelt, so they instantly counterattacked, expecting to be sustained by a people they supposed to be devoted to that system. Their institutional organization was too inflexible to take into account a possible reversal of their fundamental tenet. The fact that the system, after 1929, had proved to be the American way of death for millions, who therefore desired nothing more than to have it attacked, promptly and successfully, was ignored by a large section of the press; for faced with a choice between fact and the system, it unhesitatingly adhered to the system.

Intellectually, of course, this was suicidal; but when did people in the grip of a rigid institutional system ever hesitate to commit intellectual suicide rather than risk damage to the system?

The crash of the national economy in 1929 had raised clouds

of dust which the winds of doctrine whirled to and fro for years. In the vortex the traditional vigilant guardian of the people's liberties, our Argus of the Hundred Eyes, went as blind as a bat. Startling, even shocking, it indubitably was; but Argus is not well equipped for traveling in dust storms.

6. *Dance of the Nine Tailors*

THE average American's acceptance of its basic principle made the New Deal impregnable but, unhappily, did not make it perfect. That basic principle was the dictum that in a democracy government is properly an instrument in the hands of the people to be used, in the language of the Declaration of Independence, in such manner "as to them shall seem most likely to effect their Safety and Happiness."

This was clear enough, but it left open the most perplexing and harassing question in American politics, to wit, who are the people? The Nine Tailors of Tooley Street began their petition to Parliament with the words, "We, the people of England," and everyone laughed; yet no one has ventured to assert that they were not people of England. The exact point at which "people" become "the people" is one that the most skillful mathematician has never fixed and determined; and that uncertainty is the Old Man of the Sea that rides upon the neck of the Ways and Means Committee of the House, the group that has to draft the national tax laws, which, in justice should bear upon the people.

In fact, all government would become a science, rather than an art, if rulers had an infallible means of determining exactly when "people" become "the people." Nine tailors are obviously not the people, but what about nine million members of the Congress of Industrial Organizations and the American Federation of Labor? Still too small a group? Then what about the twenty-four million who voted for Truman in 1948? Well, twenty-four and a half million voted for various other candidates. Even the forty-eight and a half million who voted at all were barely more than a third of the total population; and so we run into absurdity at the other end of the scale.

To deny that the party that wins a fair and free election represents the people would be to deprive the people of any possibility of being represented; which is no less preposterous than to assume that nine tailors do represent them. To seek out the golden mean that lies somewhere between two absurdities is the art of statecraft; and it is an art rather than a science because its most brilliantly successful experiments can rarely be repeated with equal success by others.

The New Deal certainly did not practice this art with unvarying success. On the contrary, there were times when it seemed to have lost sight of the goal altogether and to have been captured, horse, foot, and dragoons, by one or another set of well-organized, well-drilled, rhythmically moving protagonists of special interests. The national stage seemed to be occupied exclusively by an intricate and confusing ballet of dancing tailors, advancing, retreating, circling, swinging, having nothing in common but the government as a central pivot. We called them pressure groups, and pessimists over and over again abandoned all hope. There was a moment when John L. Lewis, *premier danseur* of the coal miners seemed about to carry the government off in triumph; and another when the farm groups did such a startling morisco around it that their bristling pitchforks seemed to forbid any other approach. At times the CIO swept up from the left to apparently complete dominance, only to give way as the AFL swept up from the right to a triumph that also was but momentary. There was a never-to-be-forgotten moment when the whole stage was shocked into immobility as the President himself leaped into a furious *pas seul*, denouncing "a plague o' both your houses!" But always and everywhere it seemed that some Tooley Street was about to become completely dominant, leaving Washington no more than an impressive, but empty, shell.

Yet it never quite came off. Always, at the last moment something happened to cause the most threatening group to recoil. Some other would instantly take its place, to be sure, so the pessimists never let up from their wailing. We were sold down the river—if not to Philip Murray of the CIO, then to William Green of the AFL, or if not to either, then to the Farm Bureau Federation, or to the railroad brotherhoods, or to the organized veterans, or to the government employees. The identity of the master seemed to matter little; the point was that we were sold.

This lamentation was easily understandable in the beginning, but now that it has continued without cessation for eighteen years, it takes on rather more than a tinge of absurdity. It is not without some basis of truth. In a democracy there is always danger that nine tailors may designate themselves as the people and be taken seriously. But it is an ever-present danger. The ballet did not begin with the New Deal; it had been going on from the foundation of the Republic and only the dancers were changed. Instead of labor unions, farm groups, and veterans' organizations, read the National Association of Manufacturers, the American Bankers' Association, and the protective tariff organizations, and all the rest stands.

From the standpoint of the average man it may be, indeed,

that no lesson taught by the past fifty years is more valuable than this demonstration that no matter what sort of government you have, the show goes on and it is essentially the same kind of show. You can switch from Wilson to Harding, or from Hoover to Roosevelt; you can switch from Republican to Democrat, from conservative to radical, from Federalist to Know-Nothing to Whig to Barnburner to Republican, but always there is someone trying to set himself up as "the people" when he is only a denizen of Tooley Street, someone trying to snatch the instrument that belongs to us all in order to effect his individual safety and happiness, no matter what happens to the rest of us. The Dance of the Nine Tailors is endless, and the fact that the participants may change frequently is incidental.

The change that attended the coming of the New Deal was simply that the pressure groups were drawn from a different segment of the population and included larger numbers of people; but they were none the less pressure groups and some of them were as ruthless and avid as the Aluminum Trust, or the Silver Bloc, or the Elgin Butter crowd, or even, to go back a generation, as Corporal Tanner and the Grand Army of the Republic. Corporal Tanner boasted that he would drive a two-horse wagon through the United States Treasury for the benefit of the veterans; his successors have abandoned that antiquated ideology —some of them aspire to drive bulldozers and ten-ton trucks through it, but nobody would fool with a wagon.

The power of the old-fashioned pressure groups derived from their money and that of the new ones comes from their votes. This is, perhaps, an improvement, but it isn't a cure. Power is power, and if it is used for the benefit of any restricted group, even as large a group as the twenty-four millions who voted Democratic in 1948, it is used unjustly. "Equal justice under law" is not to be attained under any tyranny, whether it be the tyranny of one Hitler, or of nine tailors, or of twenty-four million Democrats.

The common man who has lived as long as the century has learned, or has had a chance to learn, that astute gentlemen who know what they want can operate under any sort of regime. Perhaps they are not the same gentlemen, but they are equally astute, and equally certain that they know on which side their bread is buttered. Tom Girdler may have felt more comfortable under Harding, and James C. Petrillo under Roosevelt; but when we swap a Girdler for a Petrillo can the profit be seen without a microscope? Possibly there are more union musicians than there are stockholders in Republic Steel and one may talk of the greater good for the greater number; but it is a theoretical advantage weighing little against the very practical loss incurred when any restricted group profits by coercion.

Nevertheless, this is democracy, this interplay of contending interests, never at rest for a moment, constantly alert to seize an advantage, always aspiring, each for itself, to persuade the average man to mistake it for "the people." On second thought let that be revised—this is not democracy itself, but the condition under which democracy must exist. Liberal or conservative, Republican or Democratic, under a great man or under a nincompoop, the government is forever the selected prey of self-centered groups. Such a group may be commanded by an industrialist or financier whose ethics are indistinguishable from those of Captain Kidd, or by a labor leader whose ethics are indistinguishable from those of Captain Kidd, but in either case piracy is contemplated and piracy will be perpetrated if the common man allows himself to be beguiled.

The ordinary American who has watched the government swing from Wilson to Harding, and then from Hoover to Roosevelt, has witnessed changes as sweeping and as sudden as can be effected short of revolution by violence. But with all the upsetting that has gone on before his eyes, one change he has not seen, and that is any appreciable alteration in the prevalence of scoundrels. They may differ in degree of moral turpitude, although that is an open question. As lawyers distinguish between *malum prohibitum* and *malum in se*, there may be a distinction between scoundrels based on whether they do evil out of sheer perversity, or do evil that good may come. But let the learned doctors quibble over that; the ordinary man is afflicted by *malum* of any kind, and he notes with a heavy heart that it is all over the place, no matter who inhabits the White House.

To a young man it may seem that if this is the teaching of our clamorous times, it is a wisdom hardly worth acquiring since it leads only to cynicism and despair. But the man of fifty has seen enough to enable him to make another generalization, which is that the piracy constantly threatened never quite succeeds. Under Harding thieves almost took over the government, but not quite. Under Wilson, the Anti-Saloon League did take it over, but couldn't hold it permanently. Under Coolidge, for a time "the people" seemed to refer only to people with fat bank accounts; but the bank accounts dried up and blew away. Under Roosevelt, Washington was besieged by the massed idiocy of the country, but it was defended by intelligence stoutly enough for the country to emerge from the siege richer and more powerful in 1940 than it had been in 1933.

These things are on record. As to how they were brought about, the argument is endless, but they happened. The average man is a witness, because he was there and saw, heard, and felt them all. It must be admitted that this proves nothing for the future. There is a first time for everything, and there may be a first time for this Republic to be taken over completely by some pressure group and run thereafter for the exclusive benefit of a segment of the population. But it hasn't happened yet, although within the past fifty years there have been some powerful efforts, supported now by predatory wealth, and now by flannel-mouthed demagogy. If Andrew Mellon and his friends could never quite persuade the country that they were the people, and if, a little later, Huey Long and his friends were equally unsuccessful, it is a reasonable inference that in this whirling chaos of contending self-seekers there is a strong stabilizing influence of some kind.

Moreover, there is impressive evidence supporting the theory that this basic stability does not rest upon the genius of great men, who come and go, but upon the increasing political maturity of common men, who are always with us. "You can fool all of the people some of the time," observed Lincoln and we contemporaries of the twentieth century have seen them fooled more than once by preposterous fellows who shouldn't have been able to fool a child; but invariably, before the catastrophe became complete, realization has come to the common man that these were not the angels and ministers of grace they pretended to be, but a set of dancing tailors whom it would be ridiculous to identify with the people of the United States.

7. *Serendipity and the Commoner*

YET, although duplicity, cupidity and stupidity were certainly not banished from the land by the coming of the New Deal, stupidity itself would not claim that there was no change at all. For one thing, everybody brightened up after the inauguration, even those who had voted against Roosevelt, and for the moment there was a genuine Era of Good Feeling when nine-tenths of the population cherished splendid hopes.

This lasted throughout the Hundred Days as an all but universal sentiment and it altered by relatively slow degrees.

Then when it did change, it was not in the direction of the dull, leaden apathy of the previous year. Those who came to dislike the New Deal did not lose their new brightness; on the contrary, it intensified into a fine, red, welding heat that sprayed sparks and flashes at the slightest tap. One of the *New Yorker's* most successful jests was its portrayal of a *grande dame* saying to her Very Important but slightly apoplectic spouse, "Stuyvesant, you *know* the doctor warned you not to discuss Roosevelt!"

This emphatic change in emotional intensity must have reflected some change in conditions. The average man was quite positive about that change. In his opinion it related to Privilege, with a capital P. Today the most ardent friend of the New Deal can hardly argue with a straight face that Privilege was abolished under Roosevelt; but there was a material change in the identity of the privileged.[6] One of the most coveted privileges is that of living free of fear of destitution; and this particular privilege unquestionably was transferred by the operations of the New Deal.

Destitution is a relative term. To the very poor it implies starvation; but as soon as the New Deal got well under way the poor found that if worse came to worst, one could always go on relief. The menace of outright starvation was removed. But to a man accustomed to an income of $50,000 a year, a reduction to $5,000 is destitution; and as the federal income tax rose dizzily such men began to entertain very real fears of being reduced to what they regarded as destitution. As their fright increased, their howls became louder; and as they are at all

[6] Yet it may be apposite to quote the comment of James Boyd, the novelist, in 1938 after his first visit to Miami in five years. "Miami is pretty much the same," he reported. "Like the rest of the country, it is divided into the people Roosevelt ruined and the people he saved—those he ruined still living in Byzantine palaces in more than Oriental luxury, and those he saved still living in tar-paper shacks."

times by far the most vocal element of society, the din they raised became deafening. By 1936 many earnest souls were convinced that the country was, if not up in arms, at least on the rise; and the election of that year, in which Roosevelt not merely defeated, but almost obliterated the opposition[7] came to them as a surprise, even though most observers were convinced that Roosevelt would win.

Naturally, the crushing character of the New Deal victory did nothing to console them and for the next four years their lamentations increased both in shrillness and in volume until by the campaign year of 1940 they touched a crescendo that in many cases went clear over the border into sheer insanity. Now this unquestionably represented a change in the American scene, and a radical one. Ever since 1893, when Mary Elizabeth Lease[8] had gone screaming through Kansas, calling upon the farmers (and with immense success) to "raise less corn and more hell," it had been supposed that the chronic yellers in this country would always be the out-at-elbows, while the hush-hush brigade would include the wearers of the plug hats and striped trousers. Hence it was a spectacular change to find, after 1933, the millionaires doing the screaming and the impecunious converting all their sounds of woe into hey nonny, nonny! But it was a change that did not shock the average man; it merely interested him, which was to the woebegone, of course, proof that he was utterly degenerate.

About this time—and probably based upon the equanimity

[7] In 1912 Taft got only eight electoral votes, the same number as Landon in 1936; but in 1912 Theodore Roosevelt, the third party candidate, got eighty-eight, so Wilson, the winner, received only 82% of the total electoral votes. In 1936, with no strong third party in the field, Roosevelt received all but eight, that is, 98.5% of the total. To beat this record, one must go back to the election of James Monroe, in 1820, when only one electoral vote was cast against the winner.

[8] I follow the *Dictionary of American Biography* in making her "Elizabeth" although she was frequently called Mary Ellen—which her opponents joyously distorted into "Mary Yellin."

with which the average man witnessed the writhings of the well-to-do—there was built up the weirdest political delusion that has afflicted this country since the early nineteenth-century notion that the Pope and the Freemasons were conspiring to subvert the Republic. It was the theory that the majority had been bribed to vote as they did.

This idiocy was propounded with the utmost solemnity not only by members of Congress and other vote-seekers, who may be expected to accept any grotesquerie that seems to offer help in a hot campaign, but also by men and newspapers that had been accounted unquestionably sane and presumably judicious. They blithely ignored that fact that the whole philosophy of democracy presupposes a reasonable honesty among the people, so if the time comes when most of the voters are open to bribery, the Republic will be a wreck anyhow, and its wretched framework will not be worth salvaging. It was a blinding revelation of the extent to which the better nourished and presumably better educated Americans had made an idol of the system, forgetting that without the spirit that animates it the system is as lifeless as wood or stone. They talked in the same breath of the corruption of the electorate, and then of recalling that electorate to its duty, apparently convinced that with the proper framework a corrupt electorate can build a decent democracy! Maundering could hardly go to a wilder extreme.

But the New Deal brought into our national life another novelty extremely difficult to describe, because it was unplanned, unexpected, and unauthorized by the New Dealers, and is by its nature intangible and elusive. It is possible, indeed, that the great and important never perceived it at all, but the little fellow, the common man, the undistinguished citizen saw it vividly and it was one of the features of the regime that enchanted him.

To pin it down in words one must borrow an expression, and a staggering one, from Horace Walpole, an eighteenth-century precursor of the modern cookie-pusher, but a sharp-sighted fellow at times. He once ran across a fairy story entitled "The Three Princes of Serendip" (an early name of the island now called Ceylon), the heroes of which were characterized by a gift for discovering delightful things by accident while they were searching for something else. Walpole thought that the author had hit upon something interesting and true; he knew people who seemed to have that gift, and to name it he coined a word from the story's title, "serendipity."

It can be argued plausibly that one thing about the New Deal that fascinated the common man was its serendipity. Through it, he was always discovering interesting, or amusing, or delightful things while hunting for something quite different; and this tended to keep him keyed up and expectant. Sometimes what he discovered was a personality; sometimes it was an institution; sometimes a lifting of his mental horizon; but always it was something by which he was astonished and pleased.

Consider, for example, the outcome of the New Deal's excursion into one of the dreariest byways of sociology, the matter of crime prevention or, if you prefer fifty-cent words, social prophylaxis against delinquency. In 1933 things were so bad that it would obviously take a long time to get going again. Once all the factories are shut down or running on part time, you can't start them up overnight. It will take months, probably running into a year or two, to bring them all into full production again, even when conditions are favorable; when they are not favorable—as they certainly were not in 1933—the lag is even longer. In the meantime, the young fellows just out of high school who would ordinarily have gone into the factories are stranded.

One doesn't have to be a sociologist to know that when a healthy, able-bodied youngster is condemned for months to hang around streetcorners and poolrooms with his mind and his pockets equally empty, he is likely to go to pieces rapidly. It is not only that he may drift into hellishness of many fancy types; more than that—and some people say worse than that—he is in danger of losing all spirit, all drive, all capacity to buckle down to a job and give it the old heave-ho, so that even when jobs become available again he will be but a poor stick. The common man knows all that as well as any doctor of philosophy, and frequently better because he has seen the dreadful process operating on his own boys.

So when the New Deal quite early in its existence proposed to use public money to put young men to doing some kind of useful work, the average man saw it as a good idea, doubly good because it was confined to young men. Old loafers did not matter nearly so much because their work habits were either established already or never would be; at any rate, what happened to them would not greatly affect the future. So the Civilian Conservation Corps came into being with the general approval of the people, simply as a salvage operation.

The serendipity of it was that when thousands of husky young fellows were scattered over the public domain, both the domain and the youths profited to an extent that nobody had expected. For the first time we enjoyed a forestry service that really had manpower enough. The work that was done on forests, streams, and soils, not to mention other projects, added many millions to the present value of the public domain; and when the future values that will come from such things as reforestation and flood control are added there is no doubt whatever that the CCC created more wealth than it consumed. We didn't undertake it for financial profit. We were looking for something else, and the profit was simply a pleasant thing that we ran across accidentally. It was so much velvet; and picking up velvet is one delightful form of serendipity.

But in this case there were many other forms. As the average man saw it, the original idea of the CCC was negative; it was to prevent a whole generation of boys from degenerating into bums. No doubt there were uncommon men among the planners of the scheme who saw much more in it than that; but just to avoid the production of innumerable bums was enough for the common man, and with that he would have been content.

However, when you snatch a youth out of the environment to which he has been accustomed, and project him into one completely different, more happens to his mind than to his muscles. When a boy of eighteen or twenty who has walked all his life on concrete and asphalt, whose vision has been confined to narrow vistas down city streets, who has known vegetation only in curried, combed and manicured city parks—when such a youth has trudged and scrambled his way to a peak from which he can look out over a hundred miles of forests and crags, green valleys, tumbled mountains, untouched waterfalls, unscaled cliffs, more happens to him than merely a toughening of his thews and sinews. He becomes a bigger man, not merely by some twenty pounds of extra weight, but by the immense expanse of what he has seen.

As a rule, he is inarticulate about it, but it registers. Never again can he view the world as comprised in a few city blocks. Forever after he has some idea of the immensity of this country, some notion of the vastness of that to which he belongs by being an American. Hundreds of thousands of young men had this experience in the camps of the CCC. A little later many of them were called on to defend the Republic in dreadful places. No one doubts that the physical strength and endurance they acquired in the woods and fields helped them to undergo the rigorous army training and to meet the terrific strain of active service. But they must have been helped, too, by the knowledge that what they were defending was enormously greater than their small share of it. A freeman fights first for home and fireside, but it doesn't hurt for him to know that beyond his threshold, beyond his street, beyond his city, lies a continent, vast, magnificent, and that this, too, is his. One may believe, and certainly one wishes to believe, that many a man struggling through the tough and vicious hedgerows around St. Lo, or in some stinking, nameless Pacific island, or at sea with the Japanese suicide planes plunging down upon him, was helped a little by the knowledge that what he was defending was nothing petty and mean because with his own eyes he had seen something of its greatness. This would be a delightful thing picked up during the search for something else. This would be serendipity.

Be that as it may, there is no doubt that the commoner at home enjoyed during the six years before the government was turned into a war machine certain usufructs of the New Deal that were not strictly political, that were not expected and that usually were not planned. Aside from all other considerations, it was a magnificent show. Only a part of this was attributable to the New Dealers. Some of the reactions against them were as entertaining, and as packed with thrills, as anything they did. Every day the common man picked up his paper in the knowledge that the chances were at least three to one that he would find in it something from Washington that would give him a great kick.

Looking back upon it, one can remember at least three organized assaults upon the New Deal, each of which was wonderful in a different way and each of which was packed with information for the student of politics and government. Among them they illustrated three great branches of democratic drama.

The most startling of the three was the blood-and-thunder melodrama staged by Huey Long. In the beginning many of us mistook it for farce, as we had mistaken the first act of the Hitlerian melodrama for farce; and down to the last bloodstained scene, few had an adequate conception of its seriousness. Not until years later did James A. Farley reveal[9] the results of a secret poll taken just before Long's assassination that indicated, to Farley's horror, that the Share-the-Wealth movement was just about equally popular in all sections of the country and might take away enough votes in 1936 to assure Roosevelt's defeat. At that, the plain citizen came to realize that the Louisianan was organizing in this country the same elements that had carried Hitler to power in Germany, and when Long was shot in a corridor of his own State capitol, the relief was genuine and widespread. It was also more than a little uneasy; to feel relief over a political assassination was not pleasant to most Americans. But they did.

Of an entirely different order was the adventure of the Liberty League, associated with the name of Al Smith, although his name was the only perceptible contribution that Smith made to it. Where Huey Long's show had been grisly melodrama, this was low comedy. The Liberty League was an organization including a startling number of multimillionaires that set out to restore the ancient liberties of the Republic by saving the misguided masses from themselves. It loftily disclaimed partisanship, which the average man construed as an announcement that it proposed to buy up both parties. All it actually got for its money was, of course, a horselaugh. It exposed the incredible political naïveté of the very rich, to the vast amusement of the financially stunted; and in giving a nerve-strained country an opportunity to indulge in a deep-throated guffaw, it did better than it knew.

The third of these plays-within-the-play was the breath-taking one-man revolt of Wendell Willkie. At first this, too, was misapprehended. The New Dealers thought that it was merely a resurgence of the comic Liberty League, an idea implicit in Ickes' saturnine description of its leader: "A simple, bare-foot,

[9] In *Behind the Ballots*, New York: Harcourt Brace & Co., 1938.

Wall Street lawyer." But it was nothing of the sort. This was neither Dracula nor burlesque, but picaresque romance, to which Americans have always been strongly addicted. Before it was over Willkie had become, in the minds of millions, a modern Scaramouche, Cyrano, D'Artagnan, a wild, romantic, gallant figure with terrific odds against him, but with a knightly confidence that God and his good sword would be support enough.

Well, they weren't. The age of chivalry is dead, and although Willkie did conquer the Republican party singlehanded and seize its nomination, in the general election the massed battalions cut him down despite the very important support given him by the anti-third-term tradition. Nevertheless, his defeat, although decisive, was not ignominious. He had stirred up a passionate enthusiasm surpassed in modern times among Americans only by that stirred up by Roosevelt himself and he actually received more popular votes than ever were given to a Republican candidate before or since. Even his opponents had to regard that record with respect, and in the eyes of the common man he remained a person of consequence, not an item for the political junk heap.

His effort, in fact, illuminated the old American faith that an honest man, passionately convinced that he is right, is a host in himself and can accomplish wonders. This was delightful, although it was the last thing anybody was looking for. It was another instance of the serendipity of the New Deal.

8. *Herself*

ROBERT E. SHERWOOD has gained cash and reputation, both in considerable amplitude, as a playwright, a trade requiring no small skill in character analysis. It stands to reason, then, that when this able playwright describes a character as complex, his word may be accepted. Mr. Sherwood, after working in an exceptionally close relation with Roosevelt for several years, has asserted that he was complex to a degree that baffled the playwright's skill completely.[10] With this verdict the common man has no reason to quarrel. Certainly we did not understand the President half the time; oh, yes, when he sat down at the microphone and explained some particularly intricate bit of government policy, he made it as clear as crystal, but that gave no clue to the man himself. Our attitude toward him was, in general, the comfortable one of the ancient Negro story-teller toward the terrapin: "I don't have to 'splain what make him do like he do do." We had learned by experience that what Roosevelt did, although it might at first seem baffling, always turned out to be reasonable, and usually was right; so we continued to bet on him to the very end.

But the common man, not pretending to any particular skill at unraveling the tangled skein of human motives, yet cherished a notion that a great many things in the President that puzzled

---

[10] That is the opening blast (page 9) in Sherwood's book, *Roosevelt and Hopkins* (New York: Harper & Brothers, 1948), which nevertheless proceeds to devote several hundred pages to analyzing Roosevelt, certainly plausibly and probably accurately.

the expert analysts would have been much less puzzling if they had paid enough attention to the kind of wife he had married.

In the five years following her husband's death the country attained a much clearer conception of Eleanor Roosevelt's character and ability than it had had before, but she is no simple proposition to this day, and in the opening chapters of the New Deal story nobody, among the lords or among the commoners, had the faintest idea of what she was about. Many were still puzzled when they came to the last chapter of that story; and as late as 1949 no common man, but one of the Princes of the Church gave spectacular public evidence that he was still at sea.

No doubt this perplexity was attributable to what Walter Lippmann in one of his early encyclicals[11] described elaborately as "The Stereotypes," the mental process by which we attach a whole set of qualities to a name, and on hearing the name inevitably think of the qualities, whether they actually exist or not. We were credibly informed that such-and-such things were true of Mrs. Roosevelt, so we automatically assumed that all the qualities we had attached to those things also belonged to her, and when it turned out that they didn't we were left fumbling.

We were aware, for example, that she was an aristocrat to the fingertips, descended on both sides from a long line of prominent people who, if not sinfully rich, had had no cause for generations to worry about where the rent was coming from.

We were aware that she had been very active in social work for years, and had participated in party politics to some extent in New York State.

We soon discovered that she was, if not learned in the sense that a translator of cuneiform inscriptions or a scholiast of ancient codices is learned, still amazingly well-informed.

[11] Walter Lippmann, *Public Opinion*, New York: Harcourt, Brace & Co., 1922, Part III, pp. 79-130

We discovered that she was a person of apparently inexhaustible energy, physical and mental.

We discovered that she held definite, positive convictions on practically every subject of importance and had unfaltering courage in stating them.

Each of these things had long been a stereotype in the mind of the average man and to each of them he attached a set of qualities, that the word called up automatically whenever it was pronounced in his hearing. So Mrs. Roosevelt at first was given an extraordinary character which it took her quite a long time to live down.

The word "aristocrat," for example, evoked in the ordinary man's mind a picture of an arrogant individual, probably purse-proud and certainly contemptuous of the common herd.

A social worker, and especially one who had gone into politics, meant to many a brassbound, pushing female, snooping into everybody's private affairs, and lavish with unwanted advice; or if not that, then a Lady Bountiful, expecting lifelong servility in return for a Christmas turkey.

A learned, or even a very well-informed woman meant a blue-stocking, probably strident, and certainly a bore.

An energetic woman meant a busybody.

A woman of strong convictions, backed by the courage to express them, meant a battle-axe.

Thus the commoner was, in the early days, a victim of his own lazy mental habits. By permitting his concepts to harden into stereotypes he had drifted into a condition to be perpetually astonished by the truth; in some cases he had come to the point at which he could by no means recognize the truth when confronted with it. To this day there are Americans who are convinced that because Mrs. Roosevelt is, indeed, aristocratic, active in affairs, informed, energetic, positive and brave, therefore she must have all the objectionable qualities they have attached to those words. Cumulative evidence that it is not so goes for nothing; it must be so, because if it were not, they would have to revise a great many of their fixed opinions, which is out of the question.

Such Americans are a minority now, a small and diminishing minority, but back in 1933 and 1934 they were a majority, perhaps an overwhelming majority. We had never seen anything quite like the real Mrs. Roosevelt, so it was natural that at first we did not believe it when we did see it. Generally speaking, there was little doubt as to the outcome; the betting was not on whether she would ruin her husband, but on how soon she would do it. The optimists said perhaps not within two years; the pessimists said within six months.

For another rigid stereotype, and this one having much more factual basis than the rest, was the conviction that a President's wife who undertakes to be anything more than the White House hostess, is absolutely certain to damage her husband politically. People with some historical perspective remembered Mary Todd Lincoln, and shuddered; except that rock-ribbed Republicans, remembering her, gloated. For Mrs. Roosevelt seemed to be everywhere[12] and seemed to be into everything. Only after a long time did the more alert begin to perceive that her apparently limitless activities were in fact rigidly confined to things that she could handle. On matters of appointment to office, on administrative policies, and on relations with Congress, any influence she may have wielded was carefully concealed from public view. Not even the most frenetic assailants of the New Deal claimed that the way to get an ambassadorship, or a fat government contract, or a pardon for some crook in Atlanta Penitentiary, was to apply to Mrs. Roosevelt.

[12] Another of the *New Yorker's* great hits at the time was a picture of a coal miner, deep in the bowels of the earth, glancing over his shoulder and saying to a startled companion, "My God, here comes Mrs. Roosevelt!"

They did accuse her of trying to wangle appropriations to supply milk for starving babies, and jobs for starving artists, and dancers, and musicians—all people whom the typical politician studiously forgot when appropriation bills were being framed. But this accusation did not have much effect upon the common man, because he knew his own wife, had she had the opportunity, would have done the same thing, and would have boasted of it.

Here, perhaps, is the secret of the extraordinary career of Eleanor Roosevelt in the years from 1933 to 1945—not her native ability, but her acquired ability to conceal it from the common view. She was a woman of genius who had the capacity to seem to be no genius at all but exactly like the kindhearted, sensible, hard-working wife of any decent, but quite undistinguished citizen, anywhere in the land.

Housewives in crowded cities, in modest suburbs, in farm houses, in country towns, read her writings or read about her, and got the idea promptly. Women—not glamour girls, but serious-minded mothers of families—in Kansas, in Massachusetts, in North Carolina, in Wisconsin, in every one of the forty-eight States and the District of Columbia, laid down the newspaper or the magazine saying, "I see exactly what she means; I guess I would have done the same thing, if I had thought of it."

There never was much sparkle to Mrs. Roosevelt's writing, so the oversophisticated held it in low esteem. But the oversophisticated rarely move the world, or know much about what does move it. The working members of the craft, who write for results and not for art's sake, know that when your writing is of such quality that it makes the reader say, "Of course; why didn't I think of that?" you've got him! The keenest wit, the subtlest ironist, the cleverest juggler of paradox are futile and impotent as against the writer who puts in plain language what the reader has been thinking all along, but lacked words to express. He may enjoy, and applaud, and quote the clever; but he will follow the one who expressed his own thought.

Eleanor Roosevelt got them because she knew how, and usually what they were thinking and, above all, how they felt.

By slow degrees that came home to the great mass of the people; but it was so unusual that the first administration was practically over before the wiseacres awoke to the fact that perhaps she wasn't going to ruin her husband at all; and it was still later before they could credit the truth that she was one of his valuable assets.

What Mrs. Roosevelt actually did, or felt, or was, is not within the scope of this inquiry, which is concerned, not with her, but with the common man. About her effect on him, there is hardly any room for argument. Rightly or wrongly, he attributed to her a certain quality in the New Deal that had not been clearly perceptible in any other administration within his experience. This was a concern not merely with the underdog, but with the beaten and with those who were incapable of putting up a fight.

The President was a strong partisan of the underdog. Nothing stirred him more quickly, or more profoundly, than to see some fellow making a gallant resistance with his back to the wall; and he delighted in leaping into the fray to take the hard-pressed combatant's side. But the President was a man, with the characteristic masculine admiration of a fighter who doesn't know when he is licked. Other Presidents with generous instincts— Theodore Roosevelt, for example—had exhibited the same tendency. It was admirable, but it was not unprecedented; our generation had seen it before.

What was novel in this regime was a striking disposition to come to the rescue of people who were not fighters at all, who didn't know how to fight—babies, and small children, charwomen and cooks and housewives in remote places and practitioners of the gentler arts, music, painting, sculpture, the dance. The government was always giving a break to people no one had ever thought of helping before, Negro singers, aspiring playwrights, blind people, all the dispossessed and disinherited, incapable of battling their own way through a fiercely competitive world. This concern for the noncombatant struck the average man as a distinctly feminine trait, and he attributed it to Mrs. Roosevelt's influence.

So did the opposition, and they made great play with it. The opposition made the curious tactical error of assuming that the common man is opposed to giving a hand to the nonbelligerent. But he is not; he simply doesn't think of it, until his wife reminds him.

Therefore the furious assaults on the President's wife got exactly nowhere. Never before in American history has a respectable woman been subjected to such reckless and relentless attack; even the reputable press was bitter, while the scavenger press crawled to depths of brutal indecency that it had not touched since the attack on Rachel Jackson, a hundred years before, the foulest newspaper campaign in American history.

But it fell flat. The most curious phase of it is that it didn't even bounce. Here and there an indignant individual rose to a counterattack, but there was a marked absence of any widespread disposition to defend Mrs. Roosevelt. Somehow, the common man seemed to feel that she didn't need it; he soon observed that every flagitious act charged against her turned out, on examination, to have been an effort to help some poor devil down on his luck, and in the opinion of the common man such an act needs no defense, even when it is imprudent or mistaken. So he didn't worry much about the attacks; she was invulnerable, so they really didn't matter.

The common man reached that point much sooner than the brilliant thinkers, probably because he felt no need to figure

out why it was so. Logicians were driven wild by the fact that
Mrs. Roosevelt constantly did things that no President's wife
could do without disaster, yet disaster never followed; but the
common man, observing that what she did was generally service-
able to him, one way or another, wasted no time on the insol-
uble problem of "what make her do like she do do." He was
for her, anyhow; and if her influence tended to make the whole
regime somewhat gentler, he was content to have it so.

At the same time, he thought he could understand the perplexity of people like Mr. Sherwood. Roosevelt, *solo*, was hard
to understand, but he couldn't be taken that way; what the
analysts had to solve was Roosevelt multiplied by Mrs. R., and
the average man readily admitted that the sum was not a
simple R-squared, but ran into some dizzy mathematics of personality complicated enough to make Einstein tear his hair, and
maybe give even the Recording Angel a busy afternoon.

But the lady was a lesson, a bright and encouraging lesson,
in the political education of the American who is as old as the
century. Her career was a practical demonstration that exposed
an ancient, bitter fallacy. It proved before all the world that
aristocracy, inherited wealth, education, and great natural en-
dowments do not necessarily combine to form an Iron Curtain
that cuts their possessor off from intimate contact with common
humanity. Or if they do, the Iron Curtain is not impermeable
when it is attacked by certain strong reagents. Kindliness,
sympathy, compassion, and selflessness, will corrode and dissolve
it until it vanishes like the fabric of a dream.

9. *Shouts and Murmurs*

ALEXANDER WOOLLCOTT found in the text of an old play a stage direction that so fascinated him that he borrowed it for the title of one of his books. It read, *"Shouts and murmurs without,"* which struck Woollcott as one of those charming absurdities that are more realistic than steely logic; what, after all, conveys better the impression of a great uproar than a continuous murmur punctuated by occasional shouts? In the perspective of a dozen years the general impression of the New Deal in the mind of a man whose knowledge of it came exclusively from what he read in the newspapers, is a memory of shouts and murmurs, an incessant uproar, rising occasionally to tremendous peaks of excitement, and then sinking somewhat, but at no time subsiding into anything properly describable as tranquility. It was a time of strenuosity, political, intellectual, and moral; a day of glory to the optimistic, a day of wrath to the pessimistic, but not a dull day to anybody.

It failed, of course. The most ardent admirer of Roosevelt cannot argue away two facts: one is that the New Deal was a scheme to effect the safety and happiness of the people; the second is that the New Deal has passed and the people are neither safe nor happy. But because it failed, it does not follow that it wasn't worth trying. The Christian religion is a scheme to transform this earth into the Kingdom of God, and in that it has failed colossally; but an intelligent atheist, not to mention a believer, would hesitate to assert that it wasn't worth trying.

Every important innovation in political philosophy has failed to accomplish all that its proponents hoped. In fact, every innovation has failed to accomplish the principal thing at which its proponents aimed; for the principal thing was always perfection of the art of government, and it remains woefully imperfect. The fact that the New Deal failed is therefore not conclusive; it may be proof of nothing more than that it was an idea of great magnitude, since big ideas always fail. The question is, did it have any permanent effect upon the American way of life? As far as this study is concerned, the question narrows down still further, to this: what effect, if any, did it have upon the plain, ordinary voter? Never mind the statesmen, the philosophers, the diplomats, the business tycoons, and the scramblers for fourth-class post offices and deputy marshalships; consider, instead, the anonymous millions who never figure in politics except on election day, who fill the ranks of the army from master sergeant down, who file their income tax returns on Short Form 1045A, and who do the work of the world. If the New Deal has left its stamp on them, then it was an Event with a capital E, and the fact that it failed to attain its main objective is incidental.

It is hard to believe that anyone who lived through the period can doubt that the average American was profoundly affected. Whether one believes that he was improved as a political entity, or ruined for any further good purpose is beside the point; the point is that he was affected, that he emerged from the period thinking and acting in a manner perceptibly different from his former habits of thought and action.

The reason is not far to seek. In the period from 1933 to 1940 the plain citizen experienced politics, whereas up to that time he had merely observed it. It was the difference between watching a performance by one of the Theater Guild's cleverest young women, and being in the theater when Eleanora Duse was on the stage; one was a show, the pleasant entertainment of an evening; the other was what the Greeks called *katharsis*, an experience that made a lasting difference in one's mental and emotional attitudes.

Statecraft in a democracy—perhaps even more conspicuously in a modern absolutism, but that is beyond our purview—is a science only in the fields of legislative and administrative routine; beyond that, it is an art. A tax bill might, at least in theory, be framed on strictly scientific principles and yet be a success. A great governmental department ought to be, although none ever has been, organized on scientific principles. But it is doubtful that a man ever was elected to an office as high as township constable on strictly scientific considerations; and it is certain that no man ever persuaded vast numbers of people to support him in a new and untried project by the use of scientific methods alone.

A man becomes a successful leader of millions by the practice of an art that is obviously a branch of the art of dramaturgy. Franklin D. Roosevelt was, among other things, a very great actor. It is a biting commentary on our unrealistic attitudes that his enemies have stressed this much more than his friends. For some reason we are loath to admit that a man cannot be a statesman of the first order without histrionic ability, although the truth is obvious.

Doubtless the reason is that we do not commonly make the tricky, but important, discrimination between an actor and a mime. Imitation is a trade, or at most a craft; but acting, on its highest levels, has nothing to do with imitation; it is the art of revealing and strongly illuminating some phase of truth. We enjoy the performance of a clever mime; but with a great actor we actually live through his performance, not necessarily with enjoyment, sometimes, indeed, most painfully.

Roosevelt exceeded any other American of his time in making

politics the experience, not the entertainment, of the average man. He was assisted in this, of course, by the critical nature of the situation, but the crisis had existed before he came to power without producing the same effect. The people watched Hoover's struggle with the depression without ever identifying themselves with the protagonist; most of us never felt that we had a penny on Hoover. Roosevelt, on the contrary, got us somehow into the fixed belief that he was carrying our bottom dollar, that we had bet our shirts on him, and we pulled our very hearts out whooping him on.

His opponents did not overlook this, but somehow they got the strange idea that they could discredit him with it. They spent a vast amount of time and energy "exposing" the President's habit of dramatizing events and especially policies, ignoring the fact that the dramatization was based on a grim and solid truth. In effect, he *was* carrying our bets, and if he had failed completely we would have lost our shirts.

At the moment when he assumed office every great nation in the world was coming about on a new tack, not out of mere caprice, but because the wind had shifted and it was necessary. In a Ship of State that is an exceedingly ticklish operation always, and the thirties proved no exception. Germany, Italy and Spain capsized, France came shudderingly close to doing so, and even Great Britain had some extremely bad moments, but the United States made it relatively neatly, notwithstanding the yells and curses of the more excitable members of the crew, who were certain that we were going over.

The necessary readjustment was basically economic, but this country was the only great power in which it remained almost entirely economic. Free private enterprise[13] had proved unequal

[13] Private enterprise had never, of course, been entirely free. Certain enormously important enterprises—coinage and the postal system, for example—had been operated on a "socialistic" basis from time immemorial.

to the task of making good the losses sustained in the First World War, with the result that, beginning in Austria, one national economy after another had crashed. The operations necessary to a restoration of the world situation were simply too gigantic for private enterprise to handle; the choice was between governmental intervention and chaos.

But throughout Europe, any leader bold enough to advocate the economic readjustments necessary was also a man committed to advocacy of social and political readjustments as radical as the economic changes. In Germany, Italy and Spain these political and social changes were so bitterly opposed that violence exploded and civil liberty vanished in the turmoil. Even in Great Britain, steadiest of the European democracies, the advent of the ex-miner, Ramsay MacDonald, as Prime Minister at the head of a Labor government, signalized a vast social upheaval which only the amazing agility of the British upper classes in ducking from under falling walls prevented from becoming something uglier.

Only in the United States was the work undertaken by a product of Groton and Harvard, a man whose income was derived in large part from investments made by his father and grandfather, an Episcopalian—rather high-church, too—by faith, a member of exclusive clubs, a director of sound corporations, and bearer of a name that every snobbish hostess in the land ardently desired to see in her list of guests. In other words, here alone was the readjustment undertaken by a man with every reason to save as much of the old economic system as could

---

Tariffs, embargoes, excise taxes, pure food laws, building codes and so on left little, if any, private enterprise absolutely untrammeled; yet, except for money and the mails, the theory of governmental intervention in the national economy was rejected by this country, ostensibly, even though in practice the profoundly socialistic theory of tariff protection was accepted.

be saved, and with no personal animus whatever against the social and political system.

That is one important reason why the United States came through the crisis as smoothly as it did. Without doubt, Roosevelt was assisted by the relatively fluid social order here; it was unnecessary for him to disregard social distinctions and uproot privileges that had existed for a thousand years. But at that, it is remarkable, in retrospect, that we came through, not only without a single firing squad, but without suppressing a single book or newspaper, without outlawing a single political party, without suspending the writ of habeas corpus, without any special courts dispensing with juries, without touching the right of public assembly, the right of public worship, or the right of petition.

Indeed, at the moment when civil liberty was vanishing in many countries, it actually tended to expand in the United States. Not only was prohibition repealed, but instead of burning books we received a series of judicial decisions that flattened the self-appointed censors who strove to make their private view of morals and manners official; instead of closing churches, we had Chief Justice Hughes' famous decision that stands now as a bulwark of religious freedom; instead of having the leaders of opposition parties shot, we carefully preserved them, and when war burst upon us put them to work, running the army and navy, mobilizing industry and opinion, and carrying confidential messages from the President to the heads of allied states.

Not that Roosevelt got any thanks from the people he defended most successfully. Like Lafayette in revolutionary France, he was denounced as a traitor to his class by men who sometimes seemed, like the French nobility, to value their purses more than they did their heads. Before he became Governor of New York, Roosevelt had been a banker. In the early

days of the New Deal it was the laws establishing the Federal
Deposit Insurance Corporation and the Securities Exchange
Commission that converted the word "banker" from an epithet
into a common noun, if not quite into the title of nobility it had
been before 1929. If that be treason, make the most of it.

The charge most frequently brought, and most bitterly pressed,
against him was that the dominant tendency of his regime was to
set class against class. It seemed to occur to none of Roosevelt's
opponents that this charge carried its own refutation; if this
Republic had been indeed stratified into classes rigid enough to
make war on each other, then the Republic had failed, for its
original purpose had been to promote the *general* welfare, which
is a repudiation of class distinctions. The first words of the pre-
amble to the Constitution of the United States define the only
class recognized as legitimate by this government. Those words
are, "We, the people of the United States." If class distinctions
have since arisen among us, they are flatly antagonistic to the
spirit of our fundamental law, and a man who would encourage
their mutual destruction would be a hero, not a villain.

The election returns show that the average man gave little
weight to this charge. There are two possible explanations of
this indifference: one is that the average American thought the
charge was true, but approved, or at least did not object to class
warfare; the other is that he thought the charge was buncombe.

Subsequent history strongly supports the latter explanation as
the true one. When the pinch came, there was no difficulty
whatever in persuading the average man to defend this country
with a ferocity and a tenacity that would never have been exhibited for an institution of doubtful ownership. What Roosevelt brought home to us was the truth that we are all one class,
or, rather all one group. We stand together or we fall together,
and any other assumption is nonsense.

This he accomplished less by logical argument than by the

histrionic genius through which a great actor establishes the impression of truth the instant he opens his mouth, before he has had time to frame any intellectual appeal. It was said of Charles Macklin, the Irish actor, that he could draw tears from the eyes of his hearers by reciting the multiplication table; it is true that Roosevelt, sitting before a microphone and saying, "My friends," could establish friendship in the hearts of fifteen million radio listeners before he had said another word. There is no argument in those two words; there isn't even a statement, no appeal to the intellect of any sort. But when Roosevelt pronounced them there was magic in them, and it could have been nothing but the magic of high art.

So under his leadership we lived in a state of tension comparable to the tension of an audience witnessing a superb dramatic performance. Members of such an audience are not in fact witnesses; they are participants, not merely watching the drama, but living it. In the case of the New Deal the tension was even greater, for we knew that it was not something concocted by a playwright, but reality indeed, the embodiment of our fate. But living under dramatic tension is living at a high potential. That will not be denied by anyone who has emerged from a theater, limp and drained of emotion. It will not be denied by many, sufficiently mature to appreciate it, who lived through the New Deal.

The scornful sneered prodigiously when Roosevelt once expressed the desire to give the country "more abundant life." But the sneers were "the crackling of thorns under a pot," the Biblical description of the laughter of fools. For during those years we did live, intellectually and emotionally, faster than we had ever lived before. If he promised us more abundant life, he certainly delivered the goods.

10. *Classifying the Worm Fafnir*

IN AN earlier day, when men's thoughts were simpler—at the time when *Beowulf* and the *Volsunga Saga* were written—our ancestors described every footless, creeping thing as a "worm." The harmless caterpillar that Beowulf might have brushed off his hand, and the deadly serpents with which he did combat were both called worms; and the Volsungs described Fafnir, who lay along the edge of a cliff thirty fathoms high and easily drank from the river at its foot, as "the worm Fafnir." Not until the tellers of tales had acquired a considerable degree of sophistication did they adhere to the classification of snakes and dragons as very different from worms.

To some extent the average American of 1933 appears, in the light of 1950, almost as careless in his use of terms as were the makers of the sagas. At that time and for some years after he evinced a disposition to look upon the most appalling phenomenon of our times as the worm Hitler. It took a great deal of sophistication, painfully acquired, to accustom him to the idea that a fire-breathing monster with a neck a hundred and eighty feet long is not properly describable, and emphatically should not be thought of, as a mere worm.

To do him justice, it was not the common man alone who fell into this error in the early days. Very important persons were equally bemused. It is probable that even the President of the United States in the first twelve months after he assumed office viewed the activities of Hitler and the party he led with disgust, rather than with dread.

In any event, it is certain that the common man in this country heard the early proclamations of Nazi ideology with a mixture of incredulity and amusement. Both, unhappily, were based, not on cool reason, as we thought, but on lack of imagination. We had ample information as to what was happening in Germany, but not the power to calculate its inevitable effect, even though we had a strikingly similar case history under our eyes. We had seen a form of Naziism generated in a population with a long history of successful self-government, and generated by precisely the means that produced it in Germany, to wit, economic bondage imposed by a conqueror; we should have been prepared, then, for a much more direful and a much swifter effect in a population like that of Germany, with almost no experience of democratic self-rule.

It took fifty years to break down the spirit of American democracy in the Southern States to the point at which Ku Kluxism[14] became a real menace. The Army of Occupation was withdrawn from the South in 1876, but not until about 1925 did the obscurantists, represented by the Ku Klux, Huey Long's following and, in some measure, by religious fanatics, become startlingly strong; yet the South, throughout those forty-nine years, had been subjected to economic exploitation, largely but not entirely, by the protective tariff system that had drained it steadily. The South had paid reparations in sums that Germany never dreamed of; three billion dollars in slave property was only one small item in the list, and its economic exploitation had continued more than three times as long as Germany's fifteen years. Yet so powerful was the democratic tradition, that even when our version of Naziism did appear, it was relatively halting and ineffective.

But it did show one monstrous tendency in which it was not

[14] This refers, of course, to the modern Klan, not to the original Ku Klux of 1869, who were merely bands of vigilantes.

surpassed by the Naziism of Eurpoe—it was highly infectious: Ed Jackson and D. C. Stephenson controlled Indiana, not a Southern State; and Oregon and Illinois for a time were worse infected with Ku Kluxism than Virginia and North Carolina ever were. Here was a demonstration, had we not been too blind to see it, of what can happen even in the nation with the longest uninterrupted experience of democratic government.

The success of the ranting of the Imperial Wizard should have prepared us for the success of the ranting of *Der Führer*. The fact that an appeal may be nonsensical is, unfortunately, no proof that it is not an appeal to strong, deeply-rooted, human impulses. After all, a blow to the jaw, if hard enough, does end an argument, and a man harassed, bewildered, and exhausted by an argument too complicated for him to follow is strongly tempted to end it by whatever means he may. There is nothing peculiarly German about this impulse; it is human; people of any nationality feel it, and if pressed hard enough will follow it.

As the program of National Socialism in Germany unfolded, it became, in American eyes, more and more monstrous, less and less related to any rational procedure, therefore—and this is where we miscalculated—more certainly doomed to early repudiation by any rational people. The burning of the books, the rejection of individual freedom, the attack upon learning, the development of a bloated and hideous racism, the apostasy to paganism, and eventually the resort to pogroms not only against Jews, but against unpopular minorities of all kinds— these seemed to the average American successive steps on the road to destruction of the whole regime by the Germans themselves.

What we forgot, or chose to ignore, was the fact that these things are not fundamentally unpopular, in Germany or anywhere else. Judge Lynch has had a long and spectacular career in our own country. In the first five years of the present century lynchings in the United States averaged over a hundred a year; and nearly two generations later we have not quite eliminated them—that in a country whose government for a century and a half has represented some rough approximation of the will of the people. The man-hunt is exciting, entertaining, a magnificent release of pent-up emotion, the very apotheosis of outdoor sport. It is natural. What is unnatural, is suppression of the tendency to indulge it, and substitution of the tedious, dull routine of legal process. Barbarism is natural; civilization is the unnatural, the artificial creation.

Fundamentally, civilization is annoying, and it is doubly annoying in a relatively free country, because there it becomes the responsibility of every freeman. In an absolutism the despot determines the degree of civilization of the whole country and the ordinary man has nothing to do but conform; if the despot decides to revert to barbarism, the ordinary man will follow readily enough and, whether we like to admit it or not, that is as true of Americans as it is of Germans. With our own eyes we have seen the State of Louisiana converted into something closely resembling an absolutism, and we have seen that the despot had no trouble in securing popular support for acts very much like Hitler's earlier moves in Germany. But the people of Louisiana, like the people of Germany, had had precious little to do with running their own government for many years before Huey Long appeared. They were too poor, too ignorant, too firmly gripped by a ruling oligarchy, skillful at employing the people's prejudices to tighten the people's fetters.

Yet it is possible that the average man in pre-Long Louisiana may have been happier in some ways than the average man in more progressive States, where popular rule has had some semblance of reality. The innocent Cajun at least escaped one oppression, the heavy oppression of having to make up his mind about public affairs. He may have been exploited by the sugar interests, the oil interests, and half a dozen other interests, but while exploitation was the prevailing way of life he did not have to decide between various ways of escaping it, all of them dubious. In more progressive States the average man cannot escape that task, and it wears him down. Being free is difficult, as well as dangerous, and the love of freedom has to be strong in a people if they are to undertake the labor of maintaining it.

This became clear to Roosevelt long before it did to most of us. The truth is that Hitler was the natural man, and Roosevelt the artificial creation, the product of forces that had been operating slowly and often blindly at least as far back as Runnymede, as Sempach, where Winkelried gathered the spears into his own breast, as the Albigenses in France and the Beggars of the Sea in Holland. He had the blood of all these nations in his veins, and in his mind the traditions of Erasmus and Luther, of Voltaire, and Locke, and Milton, of all the uncommon men who had gladly undertaken the labor and the peril of being free. He knew that the average American shared those traditions with him to some extent; but he also realized, much more clearly than the average man, how thin and fragile is this overlay, this crust, of civilization.

So he was frankly terrified by Hitler. The Brown Shirts were not what bothered him. A hoodlum is a hoodlum, whether he wears a brown shirt, in Berlin, or a Ku Klux nightshirt, in Mississippi, or a zoot suit in the neighborhood of Times Square. A blackjack, smartly applied behind the ear, will dispose of the strongest of them, and the fact that he is called an SS Man, instead of a hood, will not cause him to hit the ground any less promptly.

What alarmed the President and made him accept the challenge of Naziism swiftly, was the danger of invasion not by Nazi thugs, but by Nazi ideas; for the thugs were detested by everyone, but the ideas, unhappily, had their protagonists even here. Most of us did not see that at the time. Why should we? Naturally, the President did not declare in so many words that the infiltration of Hitler's ideas was what was causing him most concern, for his enemies would have translated that into an insult to the American people; but one reading his speeches now can see plainly enough the cause of his uneasiness.

Always he stressed the danger to the intangibles. "What I would emphasize is the maintenance of successful democracy at home."[15] "The arts cannot thrive except where men are free to be themselves and to be in charge of the discipline of their own energies and ardors."[16] "The military strength of a country can be no greater than its internal economic and moral solidarity."[17] Such quotations could be multiplied a dozen times from the President's public utterances in the years preceding the explosion. He did not harbor any great fear that Hitler could whip us in the field of battle, provided the Nazi ideology did not disintegrate us before the battle began. Like the legendary heroes, he feared the claws of the dragon, and even its fiery breath, less than the venom it spat that corroded and destroyed whatever it touched.

In theory, at least, he was right. As a leader, it was his business to see somewhat further into any situation than the average man could see. As regards the Nazis, most of us feared definite, objective losses if they triumphed. If we were Jews, we feared for our lives. If we were Catholics, we feared for our church. If we were tradesmen, we feared for our business. If we were intellectuals, we feared for our liberty. If we were artisans, we feared for our living, our liberty, and to some extent for our lives. The Nazi system was horrible enough, considered exclusively as a force imposed from without.

[15] Address at the University of North Carolina, December 5, 1938.
[16] Dedication of the Museum of Modern Art, New York, May 10, 1939.
[17] Graduation address at West Point, June 12, 1939.

Yet it is incontestably true that none of these perils is to be compared to the peril of coming to like the sort of thing for which the Nazis stood. A dead American is a spectacle less mournful than a Nazified American. An America wrecked and ruined as completely as Poland was at the end of the war would be less dreadful to contemplate than an America accepting totalitarianism and liking it.

Nor was that peril by any means a fantastic impossibility. There is in every man something that responds to Naziism, some remnant of the abysmal brute, some trace of kinship with ai, the three-toed sloth that cannot be spurred to any worthy activity, yet at the same time some suggestion of Alouatta, the howling monkey, whose delight in excitement and uproars has no basis in intelligence. There is a Nazi in each of us, and if he doesn't break out, that is simply evidence of the strength of the controls that have been built up by civilization. The strongest of these is self-control gradually built up by experience in self-government.

It proved strong enough in the United States, but only just strong enough. Here and there the control snapped, and we had Bundists, and Silver Shirts, and similar groups in small numbers. In the mass, though, the average American did not revert to the anthropoid level. At the same time, the danger that he might do so was by far the greatest danger that threatened the nation and the President was right in so esteeming it. We were a long time in discovering that the worm Hitler was really Fafnir, the fearful dragon; but we never regarded him as delectable, even as a worm.

That much, at least, the common man had learned by the schooling of a century and a half in democracy.

11. *Fifty-Nine-Minute Men*

TEN YEARS is too short a period in which to gain anything like true perspective on a catastrophe of such magnitude as the one that struck the world in 1939. Forty years hence historians will still be examining the event and probably constructing new theories to account for this or that phase of it—always assuming that it is not, ere then, blotted from memory by a fresh catastrophe so tremendous as to make the war against the Axis take on the look of a mere preliminary bout.

Yet after no more than ten years certain aspects of the affair begin to stand out conspicuously. One is an impression of how dangerously close we came to missing the boat. So reluctant were we to face the facts that on August 12, 1941, less than four months before Pearl Harbor, the House of Representatives failed by one vote to pass a measure disbanding the major part of the army.

This is enough to make any man shiver in 1950; and since such reluctance to move in time appeared twice in one generation it has driven pessimists to despair of the survival of democracy. If we were incapable of learning anything from the frightful lesson of 1917, is it certain that the even more frightful lesson of 1941 has been taken to heart? And if we are incapable of learning from two such lessons, is it not a mathematical certainty that in the course of time some disaster will overwhelm us because of our inertia?

This danger cannot be dismissed as imaginary. A people that

nothing can induce to take precautions until the situation is desperate is not well adapted to survive in this world, and perhaps does not deserve to survive. Nevertheless, it is not true to say that we learned nothing whatever from 1917 and did no better at all in 1941. In 1939 we began to arm promptly, and when the blow fell at the end of 1941 the army had a million men who had been given at least twelve months' intensive training, while the navy had on the stocks in various stages of completion enough warships to replace the fleet sunk in the surprise attack. We lost the Philippines through the defeat at Pearl Harbor, not because we had neglected to build a fleet strong enough to contest the mastery of the Pacific. It was a defeat in battle, not a failure of democracy to look ahead; and defeat in battle can happen, and does happen, to the most alert and warlike nations.

Even more significant as regards the political education of the average American was the character of the opposition to preparedness in the second instance. The vote to disband the army in 1941 did carry a strong taint of partisanship, but the move was defeated because a sufficient number of Republicans, putting the safety of the country ahead of their desire to embarrass a Democratic administration, voted against it; but outside the halls of Congress, the opposition was for the most part nonpartisan. The two leaders were Senators Wheeler and Borah, and Wheeler was a Democrat; one of the most conspicuous agitators was Charles A. Lindbergh who in a speech in Des Moines, Iowa, in September, 1941, attributed war sentiment in this country to the British, the Jews, and the Roosevelt administration, in that order, not putting the party issue first, or even second.

Unquestionably, the disposition to employ the war issue for partisan purposes was distinctly less apparent in 1941 than it had been in 1917. Borah, ablest of the opponents of action, did not take his stand in order to advance the fortunes of the Republican party, nor were many of his followers moved by the fanatical party loyalty of Lodge and Theodore Roosevelt. So, at any rate, it seemed to the ordinary voter, to whom the isolationists—with the exception of Lindbergh and a few of the more frenzied members of the group—made appeals carefully divorced from party advantage. The politicians unquestionably were persuaded that any effort to make the war threat a party issue would react disastrously because the average American would resent it.

This represented an advance in political maturity—small, it may be, but a distinct advance. If the common man got nothing else out of 1917 and what followed, he did at least learn that there is a limit to party loyalty, and that when the safety of the country is concerned, too great loyalty to party may be treason to the nation. Thus to say that we learned absolutely nothing from the First World War is to deny the plain facts on the record.

Nevertheless, isolationism did exist, right up to the moment when the first bomb fell on Pearl Harbor. As regards the leaders of the movement, who were, or should have been, better informed than the ordinary voter, it can be accounted for by several factors. There were a few embittered men who had come into collision with Roosevelt at one time or another and whose judgment was utterly debauched by personal hate; there were a few who secretly—and not always too secretly—hoped for a Nazi triumph; but both classes were small, nor did they command much public respect. Borah, for example, certainly did not fall into either group.

Perhaps the strongest factor in making an isolationist of an able and well-informed man was simple vanity. There are always in Washington men, especially among those who have been long in public life, who have nothing but disdain for the

President of the United States, whoever he may be. No matter what he may do, there are always twenty men on Capitol Hill who are absolutely certain that they could have done it much better. In the summer of 1939, at a White House conference on a pending military measure, the Secretary of State presented an appalling picture of conditions in Europe, most of it reported by skillful and experienced agents of the government, and not a fifth of it made public. But at the end Senator Borah curtly informed the Secretary that there would be no war that year. He knew it, he said, because his own information was better than that of the State Department—an instance of presumption hardly surpassed since Marsyas announced himself a better flute-player than Apollo.

But this explanation cannot account for isolationism among ordinary Americans, who had no disposition to set either their ability or their information above that of the President and his Cabinet. Yet it did exist, by no means as extensively as in 1917, but still in perceptible measure. It vanished in the smoke of the Japanese attack, but it had held some people back up to the very moment of that attack. With negligible exceptions, the average American was willing to fight for his country, but not every one was ready to fly to arms at a minute's notice. Minute Men, in fact were rare, and some were not even Thirty-Minute Men. Some refused to move until the clock was striking the hour—Fifty-Nine-Minute Men at best.

Ruling out vanity and partisan bitterness, which certainly did not control many plain Americans, leaves only ignorance as an explanation. But even this theory is tenable only under careful restrictions. The average American certainly was not ignorant of current events; on the contrary, he was better informed than the average citizen of any other country for whatever its faults the American press has not neglected its duty as a gatherer and disseminator of news. It was ignorance, rather, of some fairly recondite matters, particularly logistics and psychology.

So stated, it seems fairly reasonable. Why should a farmer, or a hay-and-grain merchant in Iowa, for example, be expected to know much about logistics and psychology? Who else knows much about them except military men and professors? The answer is, of course, that the average man has no need to know much about them; but if the citizen of a democracy knows nothing at all of these subjects, the outcome is likely to be that he will find himself blown out of his own house some fine night. For logistics is the science of moving a striking force to the selected point of attack; and psychology is the science that tells, among other things, who is likely to strike.

It is the general impression that isolationism was more prevalent, in 1941, among the common people of the Middle West than in any other section. The reason is plain. These matters had not been forced upon the people of that region, and no man studies what has not been brought forcibly to his attention. A great savant who could hold up his end in an argument over mathematics with Einstein has been known to drive a new car until he burned out the bearings because he didn't know that you have to renew the oil occasionally. Sherlock Holmes, according to the veracious Dr. Watson, did not know that the earth goes around the sun; and having been informed, strove to forget it because he had no use for the information.

But plenty of common people, standing on Atlantic beaches, had seen the glare of torpedoed tankers burning at sea. Then and there they learned enough about logistics. That lurid glow taught them that a striking force could be, and had been, brought within sight of American soil. Plenty heard the tales of refugees and of our own representatives abroad about what the Nazis were doing in Europe. Then and there they learned enough about psychology. It was plain that this gang would not, indeed, could not, tolerate the existence of a free nation anywhere in the world.

The disloyal, the self-seeking, the vengeful, and the vain we shall always have with us. They will always be a nuisance, always a handicap, always cause for regret and shame. But they are not in themselves a serious threat. The quality of the Republic is the quality of the great mass of honest citizens; and 1941 demonstrated that these were not Fifty-Nine-Minute men. Some held back until the desperate last moment, but not many, not as many as in 1917, and not the fact that there were some, but the fact that their number had diminished is the important thing in comparing the two crises.

More than that, the isolationists among ordinary people command respect for their idealism, at least. The man who refused to support the rearmament program because he considered his wisdom greater than that of anyone else was a fool. The man who refused because he secretly hoped for a Nazi triumph was a traitor. The man who refused because he hated Roosevelt, or hoped to embarrass the Democratic party, was a swine. But the typical isolationist among the plain people was not moved by any of these sordid motives. He was moved by a civilized man's hatred of war as a barbarous and generally futile method of settling international disputes; and by a creditable, if mistaken, belief that governments are as civilized as he is. In the excitement and emotional strain of war the isolationists were damned by their fellow citizens much too roundly; they were, in fact, an element in the population far removed from barbarism, perhaps further removed than the majority.

Unfortunately, though, moral excellence is no guarantee of survival in the world of the twentieth century, or of any other century, unless it be one far in the future. The traveler in Scripture who went down from Jerusalem to Jericho was, as far as we know, a man of unblemished moral excellence; nevertheless he "fell among thieves, which stripped him of his raiment, and wounded him, and departed, leaving him half dead." His moral excellence was by no means impaired if, on his next journey, he was attended by a couple of muscle-men equipped with stout clubs; and his judgment, far from being impaired, was improved. He had learned something from the first experience. His political education was advanced. So was that of the average American between 1917 and 1941. When, in 1939, it appeared that the way ahead was infested with bandits, he did not go unattended. He had bad luck in that his guards were shot up in the first explosion of firearms, but at least he had acquired the wit to have them. His wisdom was little enough, in all conscience; but it had increased somewhat as the years advanced.

12. *The Unhappy Warrior*

SUPERFICIALLY, at least, the most striking difference between the war of 1941-45 and all prior combats in which the United States had been involved was the relative silence, both of the men engaged and of the people behind the lines. It was the first big American war that never produced a song. "Praise the Lord and Pass the Ammunition" quickly wore out, and had no successor among the people at home. Among the soldiers, "Dirty Gertie From Bizerte" and "Roll Me Over" hardly came up to "Mr. Zip-Zip-Zip" of 1918, not to mention "Mademoiselle From Armentieres."

It is the more curious, because we never fought better. After Pearl Harbor our arms did not encounter a single major defeat, anything comparable to, say, Long Island or Camden in the Revolution, or to Bull Run, Chickamauga, Chancellorsville, or the Wilderness in the Civil War. At sea, especially, many of the encounters of the Second World War were desperate and very costly. The Battle of the Coral Sea and the first fight off Savo were defeats, although not major ones; and the great, culminating Battle of the Philippines was a frightfully close thing, but it came off. On land, the Battle of the Kasserine Pass was a tactical error, and the Battle of the Bulge was a strategic miscalculation, but both were swiftly recovered. The Bataan-Corregidor campaign was lost, of course, but it was lost at Pearl Harbor, not in the islands; and as a delaying action it served its purpose admirably.

Quite a number of generals and admirals proved incompetent, and had to be replaced, but only once after Pearl Harbor was a top commander removed. That was Stilwell, commanding in Burma, a side show, relatively speaking; and he was relieved, not because he failed to whip the enemy, but because he couldn't whip a so-called ally, Chiang Kai-shek, into line. Subsequent experience proved that nobody else could do it, either, so the change of command does not tarnish the military record of Vinegar Joe, which surpasses that of Forrest and approaches that of Stonewall Jackson in the Civil War.

For the rest, after the initial defeat the war on two fronts moved inexorably toward its appointed end. Doubtless military experts will quarrel for decades over whether it might not have moved faster if some other dispositions had been made here, and a different style of attack had been chosen there; but the plain, undeniable truth is that on December 8, 1941, we started toward Tokyo and Berlin, and while the vanguard suffered occasional checks the main force was never turned back on either front.

In short, never before in a great war had we had such good cause to sing. But we did not sing.

The satisfaction that the United States took in the triumph of its arms between 1941 and 1945 was profound but, to one who can remember the delirium of 1918, remarkably sober. Joy, gratification, pride were all present, but not much exultation. The dominant emotion of the time was profound relief.

The flat truth is that we did not want to fight, never had wanted to fight. The men who smashed the German, Italian and Japanese empires did so with a profound distaste for the job. The men who had smashed the German, Austrian and Turkish empires a quarter of a century earlier had done so with grim joy.

Better than in any treatise of sociologist or psychologist, one can see this difference in the work of the most popular army cartoonists of the two wars, Walgren and Mauldin. Walgren, in the earlier war, was a happy-go-lucky fellow, greatly interested in the soldier's gripes, to be sure, but inclined always to give them a humorous turn. Mauldin, a better artist and a keener wit, was much less the humorist. Walgren laughed at the whole war. Mauldin never did. Walgren's soldier was frequently full of indignation, but he was essentially a jocund fellow who could not be kept depressed very long, not even by those two banes of his existence, top sergeants and second lieutenants. Mauldin's soldier could laugh at the absurdities of army life, but at bottom he was a melancholy type, whom not even the most brilliant victory could lift out of his depression for very long.

But both were highly successful cartoonists and no cartoonist can be highly successful without being a fairly accurate mirror of his times. Mauldin's Willie and Joe were average Americans, and being put into uniforms changed them only superficially from the average Americans left at home. Walgren's Doughboy developed a profound disgust with the whole dirty business, but he got at least an occasional thrill out of it, too. Mauldin's Dogface got nothing but the disgust. In this, the soldier differed little from the civilian.

But it is characteristic of the immature mind to regard the happy warrior as the only successful warrior. No veteran campaigner cherishes that delusion. In the first collision dash and enthusiasm may count appreciably; but after that, the steadiest troops invariably are the tired, dirty, cynical and usually pessimistic survivors of many battles, who never want to fight.

Romantic historians have frequently described profound distaste for war as infallible proof of the degeneration of a nation; but it may be evidence of its political maturity, especially in a democracy. In 1939 neither the British nor the French wanted to fight; but in the years that followed the British fought better and the French worse than either had fought in the preceding century. The fact that the warrior is unhappy therefore means nothing until one has learned why he is unhappy.

The factor of leadership enters into this equation, and all the opponents of the Great Man theory of history cannot argue away the truth. In 1939 the French had nobody remotely comparable to Clemenceau, not to mention Churchill, and that contributed to their collapse. But from 1914 to 1917 they stood up sturdily, before Clemenceau came to power, so it is clear that leadership is not the only, perhaps not the controlling factor.

In a democracy in which the average man has attained anything like political maturity, what makes the warrior unhappy is his profound conviction that modern war is a lawsuit over a dime. Even the winner must incur costs vastly exceeding the most that he may hope to gain. However, if he is persuaded that there exist other and better ways of attaining social justice, he can fight, if he must, in the hope that his victory will demonstrate the folly of war.

But if he is not convinced that there is any better way, then to fight or not to fight must in the end come to the same thing. In France, during the ten years preceding the war, events had run a course parallel, up to a point, with the course of events in this country. France had sunk into a depression as appalling as our own. France had undertaken something resembling the New Deal in the Popular Front led by Léon Blum. But there the parallel ended; Blum's effort had been sabotaged and destroyed by a coalition not unlike the Liberty League that attacked the New Deal in this country; so the average man in France had had no demonstration that government could be used as an implement to effect his safety and happiness. The Frenchman in the ranks had had no recent experience leading him to believe that things would be appreciably better, whether the war were won or lost.

The average American had had exactly the opposite experience. The New Deal had not assuaged all his woes, it is true; but it had relieved some of them, and it seemed to the average man that, if it had been let alone, it might have relieved more and more. So when war interrupted it, he was bitterly resentful and heartily in favor of making that war as expensive as possible to those who had precipitated it. He didn't want to fight. He resented having to fight. But far from being disheartened, he was grimly determined to follow Polonius' advice—

> Beware
> Of entrance to a quarrel; but, being in,
> Bear 't that the opposed may beware of thee.

That he did so is written, not in words, but in graveyards of armies and fleets, and in ruins of cities all across the world. Eisenhower, Nimitz, MacArthur and the rest led dismal warriors, but they hit hard. Roosevelt led a nation having no joy in combat, but one that was out for unconditional surrender and would have had it had the war lasted twice as long.

But this resolution was not rooted in thirst for glory, or hope of pillage. The American people were politically educated beyond that adolescent nonsense. Their determination was based upon a fixed belief that there is a better way than war to achieve what all men desire, and that Americans knew that way. If others rejected that belief and clung to the sword, then the sword must be shattered in their hands, not for the glory of the act, but to convince them of their error.

Once more, like Woodrow Wilson, we plunged into war in the spirit of a policeman plunging into a barroom brawl. A squad of policemen who rushed into a riot singing would be suspected of insanity; but their silence is no indication that they cannot or will not break it up with all possible speed.

Nevertheless, we deceive ourselves if we assume that this political maturity is the common possession of all mankind. The adolescent attitude toward war is still widespread; and the adolescent characteristically regards the unhappy warrior with contempt. There is, regrettably, some evidence that the American attitude toward the war of 1941-45 has been misunderstood abroad and construed as moral deterioration, rather than as moral firmness. If this misconception prevails, the chance that we shall be attacked again is good. The worst of it is that there seems to be relatively little for the American to do about it. Warlike preparation is essential, but not conclusive, for our potential enemies will be relying on the theory that all our armament is as hollow a shell as the French army proved to be in 1940.

The true preparation, in fact, is not in fleets and armies and airfields, but in the fighting spirit to which all these things are adjuncts; and the fighting spirit is to be maintained only by

keeping the average man convinced, as he was convinced in
1941, that what he has to defend is worth the fight. To make
this government an ever more efficient instrument to effect the
safety and happiness of the people is the only way to make
sure that the atom bomb will be hurled upon the spot where it
is needed; and the one that hits the crucial spot is the only atom
bomb that is worth a nickel.

A Great Man we shall certainly need if war comes again, but
he is not indispensable. What is indispensable is an average man
with such confidence in democracy that he will fight, sadly,
perhaps, but well.

13. *The Commander-in-Chief*

THE second aspect of the war of 1941-45 that is already
clear enough to make a fair appraisal possible is the extraordinary vigor with which Roosevelt exercised the political,
without entangling it hopelessly in the military, command.
The Constitution vests both in the President of the United
States; but no man has ever been found who was equally adept
at both. Washington, perhaps, might have qualified, but he
never had the political command, and even his military authority was subject to constant interference, which is one reason why
the War of Independence dragged on for seven years.

Franklin D. Roosevelt's genius in statecraft was never ex-
emplified more brilliantly than in his success in exercising political, while delegating military, command. His first great political
stroke came a year before the actual outbreak of hostilities, but

when it was evident even to the man in the street that war was highly probable. It was the appointment of two Republicans to head the naval and military establishments.

This was a triple play. In the first place, the two selected were administrators of proved ability. Henry L. Stimson, Secretary of War, and Frank Knox, Secretary of the Navy, had both been in public life for years, Stimson in the Cabinets of Taft and Hoover, and Knox as the Republican candidate for Vice President in 1936 and as an eminently successful newspaper publisher. There was no possible doubt of the intelligence of either. In the second place, it was open, public recognition of the principle that in moments of national crisis, partisan politics must be adjourned, and this met with the strong approval of the plain people. In the third place, it convinced the public that, however else they might be influenced, promotions in the army and navy certainly would not be made in the interest of the Democratic party and could not be made in the interest of the Republican party. Under a Democratic President, but with Republican secretaries, the armed forces were well protected against the cheaper sort of politics; and this gave the average man no small satisfaction.

The second great political stroke came in August, 1941, when the President, on an American warship, met the British Prime Minister, on a British warship, at sea, and gained the formal assent of the British Empire to a statement of peace aims that accorded exactly with the sentiment of the average American. As a matter of fact, the British had never had any objection to the terms of what became known as the Atlantic Charter, but their enemies in this country had constantly denied that they were in substantial agreement with us; so to have them on record, publicly, greatly strengthened the hope of the ordinary American that something worth having would come out of the war.

But the most important achievement of the President in this

field came after the outbreak of hostilities. The war began with a military action that was disastrous in a double sense. By a surprise attack on our greatest naval base, Pearl Harbor, in Hawaii, the main Pacific fleet was disabled and we lost command of the sea. The loss in ships and men was bad enough, but still worse was the suspicion that the disaster was attributable to gross negligence on the part of the high command. To go into a fearful war under officers of doubtful competence was a strain upon the morale of the nation that had to be lightened if it were humanly possible. Unfortunately, not much could be done, but what was feasible was done with speed. The general and the admiral at Pearl Harbor were instantly removed from command, and the Chief of Naval Operations at Washington resigned. This could not repair the damage, but at least it did something toward allaying fears that the war would be lost by incompetence covered up by influence at Washington. The average man may have had an uneasy feeling that disciplinary action was pretty light, and that somebody should have been shot after an affair like that; but at any rate, action had been taken, and American tradition on such matters is mild. The important thing was the proof that authority did exist, and could move with speed and decision.

Evidence on that point was never lacking thereafter. Indeed, after the war got into full swing and our forces were engaged all around the world, it became rather too plentiful for the ease of mind of the American public. Slowly, but definitely, the man in the street learned that the President was taking desperate chances. He showed up in the oddest places, which he could have reached only by flights and voyages so perilous that they might have stopped an athlete, not to mention a crippled man.

One of the great bits of folklore of the time told of one of our aviators, who shouted to his companions in a billet at Casablanca, "Don't drink any more of that whisky! Don't touch it! I took only one drink and looked out of the window and saw Roosevelt in a jeep!"

Casablanca, Cairo, Tehran, Yalta—he was all over the place, conferring, pleading, arguing, threatening, working desperately to hold the great coalition together. The average American, to his comfort, had but a dim idea of how hard it was to maintain a combination including such disparate elements as Churchill, Stalin, and Chiang Kai-shek; but he was aware that the political side of the war needed constant attention, and the activity of the President assured him that it was getting attention. It bolstered his confidence.

He did not altogether approve. Naturally, he did not share fully the desperate exasperation of the military men directly responsible for the President's physical safety; but even the man who knew nothing except what he read in the papers knew that Roosevelt was carrying his life lightly, and he didn't like it.

On the other hand, he didn't altogether dislike it, either. After all, a military victory would be worthless if it were attended by a political defeat, and to fight the political war was the President's job. The common man's son—or his nephew, or some young fellow in whom he was interested—was out there in the African desert, or under "the red-hot rake of war" in Italy, or in France, or in the Pacific. The boy was taking frightful risks, so the fact that the Boss was taking some too was not altogether displeasing to the man who read about it. At least the Boss wasn't shirking his job. A common peril that threatened President and Pfc alike gave a wonderful sense of solidarity to the American. He wished Roosevelt wouldn't do it, but at the bottom of his heart he loved him for it.

Furthermore, as he looks back on it now, it is much easier for the undistinguished man to appreciate the sharpness of the necessity that drove the lame man to undertake those appalling journeys. Throughout his career he had been most effective when he

talked to people face to face. In this he was the opposite of
Wilson, who was most effective when he set down his ideas on
paper. Roosevelt would have been recreant to his duty had he
failed to employ in the great contest the best weapon in his
armory, which was personal persuasion. How fragile was the
alliance recent history has demonstrated all too well; the fact
that it survived the strain of a four-years' war is proof positive
that someone did marvelously fine work in holding it together,
and there is no doubt that a large part of this work was done
by Roosevelt. Nor is there any convincing evidence that he could
have done it at home, being the sort of man he was.

In justice, the others should have come to the crippled man,
as Churchill did, repeatedly; but since they would not, he
deemed it his duty to go to them. The fact that the journeys
were perilous and twice as arduous for him as for a man in
normal health, counted for nothing. He was a manful man.

The cautious medical faculty may hem and haw and refuse to
commit itself, but there is no doubt whatever in the mind of
the ordinary American that these journeys shortened Roosevelt's life. He came of long-lived stock and infantile paralysis,
once the acute attack is beaten off, is not necessarily a precursor
of an early death; many of its victims have survived to a green
old age. When he entered the White House he was notably
sturdy, and even after eight years there, at the beginning of the
war, his fine physical condition was attested not only by his
looks, but by the examination of competent physicians. Had
there been no war, or had he been content to sit out the war in
the comparative ease of Washington, he would not have died
at sixty-three. So, at least, the common man believes, so he lists
this man among those who died of wounds received in action.

This being the case it is reasonable to add to the list of Roosevelt's wartime trips one more journey, one that he did not consciously plan, and perhaps did not know that he had made, but

one that carried him farther than Cairo, or Tehran, or Yalta. It was a journey into the affections of his people deeper than any but one or two Presidents had made before him. He penetrated into the shrine where they keep the memory of their young men dead that they might be free; and no human being may go beyond that.

14. *Solitary Way*

THE genius of John Milton, say the critics, achieved one of its finest effects in the last two lines of *Paradise Lost*, which relate how Adam and Eve, at the end of the stupendous drama—

> hand in hand, with wandering steps and slow,
> Through Eden took their solitary way.

The simplicity of this exit, the effect of a sudden hush after the storm, touches a level of magnificence that could have been achieved in no other way; and to end on a note of magnificence is assuredly one of the most difficult feats in the art of dramaturgy.

But Destiny can be a greater poet than Milton, and the Hand that wrote the drama of Franklin D. Roosevelt made a master stroke on April 12, 1945. The twelve-years' duel was over. In his flaming, falling city the dragon still thrashed furiously, but he had received his death-stroke. By one last, mighty effort at the Russian town of Yalta the great coalition had been held together, and the champion of the West could set his blade back in the sheath. Far from "the thunder of the captains and the shouting" where the armies of the civilized world were closing in for the kill, far from the pomp of great capitals, in a modest cottage set among Georgia pines, he rested for a moment with only a handful of friends around him.

Roosevelt put his hand to his forehead. "I have a terrible headache," he said, and died.

Who will ever forget the stunning effect of that sudden silence? Truman said that in that moment the weight of the moon and the stars fell upon him, and we all knew what he meant, for we were all crushed. The feeling of emptiness, the blank vacancy of the future, that the average man and woman in America experienced that night was one of those things that bend mind and character into new shapes from which they can never be restored to the old. "With wandering steps and slow" we took a way that was solitary beyond anything we had ever imagined.

But the political education of the common man strode in seven-league boots that night. Atlas was down, and the weight of the world that he had carried pressed upon our sagging shoulders. We wept for him, we shuddered for ourselves, but we learned. Great men go, but the average man is immortal. If the load is to be carried from generation to generation, he must carry it most of the time, for he alone is ever-present. If occasionally a giant appears to ease his burden and guide his steps, the relief is but momentary. Wilson is dead, and Roosevelt is in the grave, but the labor of building a government that will effect the safety and happiness of the people remains, and the average man, only the average man, can carry it on.

Is it any wonder that the sweet draught of victory turned to brine upon our lips that night? The tears that filled the cup were not all for the lost leader; in some measure, in great measure, we wept for our own weakness and futility facing the heavy toil that lay ahead.

It was a sharp and bitter coming-of-age, but the process of maturing is never ecstatic, and perhaps in no other way could so much have been accomplished in so short a time. For there is some reason to believe that the average man did brace himself after Roosevelt's death and attempt to take over the task. For the professionals politics has been more difficult in the last five years than it was at the beginning of the century. The election of 1948 demonstrated that the old methods no longer serve to herd the people in any direction that professional politicians wish to drive them. There appeared in that campaign a new disposition to independent thought, a new stubbornness with which the professionals were unable to cope; so the result was a paralyzing surprise.

Whether or not this tendency is permanent remains to be seen; but if it is, it means that political campaigns must henceforth be fought on an appreciably higher intellectual level than was necessary fifty years ago. There is no lack of indications that it may be transient. The wave of anti-Communist legislation, for example, is convincing evidence that many of our people are still so immature that they harbor a hysterical belief in the efficacy of force against ideas. But it remains to be proved that this hysteria has overcome a majority. It can be accounted for as the affliction of an active and highly vocal minority, and in that case it will soon be remembered in the same shamefaced fashion that we remember the similar hysteria in 1920 and 1921.

Such matters, however, lie far beyond the scope of this study, which is confined to the experience of the common man in a century that can by no possibility be regarded as common, in the sense of ordinary. For its first fifty years have been dramatic beyond all precedent; perhaps they have been great, but it is incontestably true that they have not been dull.

Nor has there been an episode, even in this amazing time, more gigantic than the contest between Roosevelt and Hitler. It was an immeasurably ancient contest, to be sure, one that has raged since history began, the old struggle between reason and emotion for dominion over the minds of men. Yet rarely, if ever, has the setting been as spectacular or the stage as vast. The fact that the emotion embodied by Hitler was hate made it inevitable that the contest should involve flames and blood; and the fact that he led one of the most warlike nations the world has ever seen assured that it would be tremendous.

But the artistic perfection of the thing, attributable to no human factor, doubled its effectiveness. Probably most of us were at first deceived into thinking that the play had been spoiled because Hitler outlived Roosevelt for some weeks. It seemed ill-adjusted, out of symmetry, disappointing. But the Dramatist knew better. One can imagine Him looking over what He had written and considering how to end it most effectively: "The thrust has reached the dragon's heart. The wound is mortal. After that, for the hero to continue delivering blows would be bad art. No, let the eager spearmen come crowding in to finish the creature; as for the champion, I will now have him lower his point, turn away, and rather indifferently, almost disdainfully, quit the field."

No audience can witness such a drama and come away quite the same kind of people that they were before. There is no question that the ordinary American who lived through it has been changed. There is room to argue that he has been enlarged, for he understood some of it, and if Bertrand Russell is right in asserting that we are equal to what we can understand, then we must have been enlarged.

At any rate, the experience aged us, and much more than by the mere procession of days. To love and to hate, to triumph and to fail, to rejoice and to grieve, all intensely, is an aging process of great efficacy. "Better fifty years of Europe than a cycle of Cathay," said Tennyson in 1842; if his lordship had lived in America in 1942 would he have said "better"? On one's answer to that question depends his classification as an optimist or a pessimist.

So Roosevelt passed, leaving us very much alone, but with a glowing sense that we had seen a Notable. For the common people, although they did not always understand him, trusted him from the beginning and loved him in the end; nor can they be convinced that he was less than a mighty champion and their friend. They would say of him as the Sagaman wrote of Sigurd the Volsung, who slew the dragon:

Of many words he was, and so fair of speech withal, that whensoever he made it his business to speak, he never left speaking before that to all men it seemed full sure, that no otherwise must the matter be than as he said.

His sport and pleasure it was to give aid to his own folk, and to prove himself in mighty matters, to take wealth from his unfriends and give the same to his friends.

Never did he lose heart, and of naught was he adrad.

IV
Stalin Passes

1. *The Dark Tower*

BROWNING'S hero, struggling forward across the featureless plain as twilight closed in, saw evil in everything on
which he cast his eye—the "hoary cripple" who gave him direc-
tions, probably misleading, the blind, starved horse alone on the
great plain, the circle of ground trampled into bloody mud by
fighters whose identity he could not guess, the rusty, broken
wheel, plainly part of some instrument of torture, finally a
blinding vision of the other knights who had set out on the same
quest and whom he had known when they were young, and gay,
and debonair, but now all gone, one a coward, one a traitor, all
gone to death and shame—evil and foreboding everywhere, with
darkness coming down,

and yet
Dauntless the slug-horn to my lips I set,
And blew *"Childe Roland to the Dark Tower came."*

In that ghostly poem there is something that the ordinary American can feel deeply as the century turns into its second half. The featureless plain is familiar enough to us who for five years have been pushing forward, not knowing that we are on the right track, not knowing that we are on any track, but aware that no other direction promises anything better. The lowering presence of evil is familiar to us who are warned every day that war may burst upon us momentarily, war in forms unimaginably hideous and for causes that we long ago gave up trying to understand. The land through which we have been traveling, our postwar world, is starved and smitten, trampled and seared by recent fighting, littered with rusting engines of torment, inhabited by living skeletons. The day has been dreary and darkness thickens.

Nor is the plain man whose years run with those of the century altogether free from such disturbing flashes from the past as multiplied the woe of Browning's knight. It is not so much the men as the ideas of his youth that recur to him now without bringing him any sense of cheer. So many of our fine notions have gone wrong!

There was the League of Nations, first of all. It doesn't matter now who did that dream to death, for the common man stood by and saw it done; and the memory haunts him as Paul, when he was old, was haunted by the memory of that youth who stood by and held the cloaks of those who were stoning Stephen. The quest of a form of government that should effect the safety and happiness of the people by administering equal justice under law was the quest to which the League of Nations was committed. It was a brave and splendid idea and millions rejoiced in it untroubled by any doubts of its strength and firmness; but the poisoners were about and their philters were potent; like an unwary knight for whom some Circe has mixed a draught, the League of Nations ended in futility and derision. It is a memory that brings no comfort to men plodding across the plain on that same endless quest.

Nor are the specters that cross our path these of ideas alone. The ghosts of dead nations rise along our line of march. They also set out upon the quest, blithe and confident in the early years of this century. Ethiopia, Spain, Czechoslovakia, Poland, Finland, China—some of them fought well, but the odds were too great and no help was at hand. Some were recreant, some were murdered. All were our friends and comrades once, admired and trusted, and all are gone. We meant well by all of them, but when the critical moment came for each we were confused and uncertain. We were of no help. Perhaps we could not have helped them all, but the one certainty is that we did not help any soon enough and generously enough to avert its fate. In the twilight of a gray day there is no pleasure in remembering them.

Such things as these sap a man's strength and undermine his courage far more effectively than any menace from without. Armed men and lions in his path had no power to chill Childe Roland's heart; he faltered only when he thought of how long was the quest and how many setting out upon it had failed. If the American of fifty comes to the year 1950 plodding, rather than marching, somber, rather than gay, more grim than hopeful, there is ample reason. He has seen the great men come and go; he has seen the brilliant, the brave, the noble, spend their strength and break their hearts; and still the thing remains undone. His hopes have been shattered, his idealism chilled; and he is weary, with the inexpressible weariness of the old campaigner.

And yet—

On June 7, 1947, we sounded a blast that echoed around the world. George Catlett Marshall was the trumpeter, but that is a detail, for he was sounding in behalf of the average man; all that the identity of the individual did was give a name to the call. It carried the defiance of the commoner, whose heart and hand must make it good; and the great herald was, after all, merely a herald. Every American who has assented and who has supported the Marshall Plan is entitled to say, "the slug-horn to my lips I set," for at Harvard University that day the Secretary of State was speaking for us all.

It is certainly true that our motives were not unmixed. The Marshall Plan would never have gone through Congress so quickly, and it might not have gone through at all, had not some members been spurred by fear of Communism. Its sup-posed efficacy as a stopper of Communism gave the Plan the last group of votes necessary to a majority, and to that extent it is correct to say that terror, not boldness, was the deciding factor.

But it is equally correct to point out that there was a heavy vote in Congress, and a strong sentiment among the people in favor of the Marshall Plan before terror was introduced as an additional argument. Fear gave it the final shove, but it was al-ready close to success. Fear is nothing new. Fear has been dic-tating action since history began. Fear will always be a factor in the decisions that any nation makes. The presence of the oldest of human motives in this decision signifies nothing as regards the political education of the American people. The appearance of a new motive does. Realization that the restoration of Europe is a part of our task was such a motive; and it was powerful, if not controlling.

It is appropriate to the moment that the poem ends with the trumpet call. What happened after that, Browning does not say. What is to happen after our bugle blast we do not know as yet.

But the fact that we had the spirit to sound it is one of the great incidents in the tale of our times.

For it was not a defiance of any specific man or of any specific society. It was a challenge offered to certain ancient ideas, stronger than any man, a defiance of traditions older than history. What will come swarming out of the Dark Tower we know no better than the knight errant did, but it will be trouble in multitudinous forms. Perhaps one of those forms will be war, but perhaps not. We got through the first two years and well into the third without war, but it may well be upon us before these lines are in print; or it may not come at all. But we have already precipitated plenty of trouble by our defiance and there is more to come.

Why not? No one has attacked an ancient evil yet without starting trouble, and the evil we attacked is one of the oldest in the world. It is the belief, rooted in the human mind before history began to be written, that *Vae victis!* is the supreme law of nations and that diplomacy is simply war in another form. This belief had been challenged before, but never as flatly, never as uncompromisingly as in the Marshall Plan. Here for the first time a conqueror assumed that in destroying any part of the world, even that part held by an enemy in arms, he was destroying values in which he had a share, and that the woe that ensued should in justice be shared by him also.

The Marshall Plan on its face is a financial measure, by which the American people—not the President and the Secretary of State, but you and I and the man next door—undertake to contribute sums of the order of five billion dollars a year for at least four years to a pool from which stricken nations may draw to restore their shattered economic life. But its financial aspect is its superficial aspect. That is proved by the fact that some nations, including some of the worst devastated, refused the offer.

In view of the fact that the money does not have to be returned, except in certain restricted cases, and in view of the fact that the offer was made to all alike, it must have been a powerful motive indeed that induced any nation to refuse an offer so much to its advantage. It is evident that the Marshall Plan, in the estimation of these nations, includes much that does not appear on the face of the financial transactions.

It does, indeed. It includes a tacit agreement on the part of beneficiary nations that they will make every effort to restore, not only their domestic productive power, but also that free and friendly commercial exchange necessary to support the economy of the world. This economy is not sustained but damaged by a policy of aggression on the part of any nation or group of nations; hence the Marshall Plan by its very nature requires abandonment of the idea of aggression.

In theory a strong nation—Russia, for example—might have accepted the Marshall Plan with no intention whatever of living up to this responsibility; but in practice it wouldn't work. The leaders of the Communist State were well aware that if they accepted the benefits of the Marshall Plan, intending all along to follow a policy of aggression, they would be left in a position so indefensible morally that they could not make even their own people regard it as justifiable. The Soviet system is powerful; but even so, it is not powerful enough to accept a man's money and then stab him in the back without incurring the condemnation of its own supporters.

But Russia, debarred from accepting the plan, must inevitably regard its success elsewhere with great apprehension, and was compelled, by her own stern logic, to employ every resource to prevent its success. Those resources have been employed, with considerable effect. The blockade of Berlin, for instance, compelled us to resort to the airlift, costing us hundreds of millions and many lives; and that was but one item in a long list. Oh, yes, when we put the slug-horn to our lips we started something that will be difficult to carry through.

The worst of it, though, is not Russian obduracy and ingenuity, but our own fatigue. The moral endurance of the American people has astonished the world, but it is not unlimited. The antagonist who rose before us after 1945 is well aware of the fact and has employed it with great shrewdness. His game has been to facilitate a psychological collapse by every means in his power, and to play for time until it comes about. It is a style of warfare to which Americans have never been subjected before, and the manner in which the average American will sustain it has yet to be determined.

Stalin is the first great European antagonist who has had the wit to see where the strength of this Republic lies and to aim his stroke at that point. The cold war is a device to break the spirit of the average man. To the President and the Secretary of State, to the admirals and generals, to the Senate and the House, he has paid little respect, other than to make his official relations with them coldly correct. His attack is upon the emotions, the intelligence, and, above all, on the endurance of the plain people; for he knows that if he can break them down, he can sweep the Very Important Persons aside like so many jackstraws.

Of the four giants whom the American of fifty has encountered in this tumultuous century, Stalin deserves the most careful consideration; for he is the one with whom the average man must come to grips, since no one else can handle him. Yet he is precisely the one about whom our information is least enlightening. Not without reason did Churchill call Russia "an enigma in a mystery." It is the Dark Tower, all right, and we have challenged it, frankly guessing; if we have guessed wrong, it is going to be just too bad. But when the American people accepted the risk, they advanced enormously their claim to the right of self-government, for no one has a right to rule unless he will accept the risks of rulership.

2. *The Colossus*

IOSIF VISSARIONOVICH DZHUGASHVILI is a man, but Stalin is an Idea.

This separation of the personality from that for which it stands is a stumbling block to the average American, for it is a convention from which our long experience of political freedom has released us. Although in moments of mass hysteria we tend to forget it, in principle we have repudiated the doctrine of Dangerous Thoughts. In theory, and in practice except when we are frightened out of our wits, an American is accountable to the law only for his acts. The Supreme Court has held that shouting, "Fire!" in a crowded theater is an act that may be held criminal, even though it consists only in uttering a word; but the point of that decision is that the circumstances must be very exceptional indeed to make mere speech a crime.

This is a reversal of a rule that was universal until our Sedition Act expired by limitation in 1801 and that is still valid over most of the world. Highly intelligent men have known for generations that it is a bad rule, but it is too convenient to constituted authority to be abandoned except under some such pressure as our Revolution. But when authority cannot be induced to revoke a bad rule, the intelligent always contrive means of evading it. In Europe one such evasion was the pen name. In eighteenth-century France, for example, intelligent men could pretend that they did not know that Monsieur Arouet was the author of stinging comments on public affairs as long as they were signed "Voltaire."

Eventually the custom became so firmly established that it lost its original significance and passed from a measure of protection into a standard of propriety. Gentlemen began to regard it as in bad taste, if not actually indecent, for a man of quality to publish anything over his own name. The authors of *The Federalist* stood in no danger of prosecution, but it would have been a little infra dig for people as prominent as Madison, Hamilton and Jay to sign letters to the editor with their own names, which is why "Publius" appears at the end of each. It took nearly a century to dissipate this idea even in America, where the pressure of law had been removed.

It never has been dissipated in Europe, where even professional newspaper writers are given to adopting such pseudonyms as "Pertinax" and "Sagittarius"; and in Russia it has always been, and still is, a matter of life or death for a critic of the government to preserve his anonymity. Vladimir Illich Ulyanov called himself "Lenin" for a very good reason indeed—to save his neck. Where ideas are held to be criminal, personal notoriety can only be ruinous to an intellectual; and in such an environment Iosif Vissarionovich Dzhugashvili spent his youth and early manhood.

Stalin means "steel," and the average American is not disposed to question the appropriateness of the word as the name of the head of the Communist State. For Stalin has been the sword of the Idea, as Lenin was its pen. A harder man has not appeared on the horizon in this century, so prolific of hard men. Stalin's metal is alloyed with intelligence, which has had the effect of the admixture of a little chromium in ordinary steel.

He came up the hard way,[1] but there is no record of a terrific

[1] My authority for biographical data is *Stalin*, by Leon Trotzky (New York: Harper & Brothers, 1941). In view of the mortal enmity between the

shock comparable to that administered to Lenin by the execution of his brother. Stalin apparently was a hard case to begin with. In the remote province of Georgia, cut off by the tremendous barrier of the Caucasus from the rest of Russia and facing Turkey to the south, life was very different from what it was in Simbirsk (now Ulyanovsk), relatively close to Moscow, where Lenin's youth was spent. Georgia was poor, rural, Asiatic. It was a harsh country in which soft characters did not survive. But Stalin survived and flourished. He was in trouble with the law before he was of age, but in Russian Georgia in his day that had no great significance; a little banditry now and then was practiced by people who were regarded as quite respectable.

Stalin was a revolutionary from his youth, but that he was inspired by any idealistic passion is open to doubt. He was much too business-like. He was willing enough to defy the imperial government, but he had no suicidal tendencies whatever. He was willing to take a calculated risk, but it was carefully calculated. He slipped once or twice, and did short prison terms, but he was never in serious danger of the gallows.

Yet the risk was there and more than one of his associates ended with his neck in a noose, nearly always as a result of trusting the wrong man. Under such circumstances a man acquires a keen appreciation of the necessity of having reliable people around him. One has to be certain when the penalty of the first mistake is death. Stalin was certain. He is still certain, and that is why he is still alive.

Unlike most revolutionaries, he displayed early in life a genius for organization—not the genius of Leon Trotzky, the fiery enthusiast, who could build an army out of a dispirited

---

two men, I have no doubt that Trotzky told every lie he thought he could get away with; but every other book about Stalin is equally stuffed with lies, and in following Trotzky one has the advantage of knowing that Stalin is certainly no worse than this bitterly hostile witness makes him.

mob, but that of a master of routine, a giant among office managers. In the early days it was the genius of Lenin that made Trotzky commander of the Red Army and Stalin secretary of the Communist party. It is highly doubtful that Stalin could have defeated, seriatim, the converging White armies in 1920 and 1921; but it is certain that Trotzky could not have organized the party into the smooth-running mechanism that Stalin created. Later he tried to do just that, and failed lamentably.

At the time of Lenin's death, in 1924, the relative positions of Trotzky and Stalin were roughly comparable to the positions of Ney and Fouché under the Napoleonic empire. All France knew the brilliant marshal, but the relatively obscure master of the secret files was by far the more potent man. In 1924 all the world had seen Trotzky and his army corps, and almost nobody knew Stalin; but the man who had the card indexes was in a better position than the man who had the soldiers. It may be that Stalin had not a single general attached to him personally; but for years he had been filling the lower party positions with his people, so when it came to a contest for power, the smooth political worker was able to overcome the dashing military leader.

At that, it was a close thing. Stalin's power was so far from absolute that he dared not have Trotzky shot; even exile could be imposed on him only by degrees, and the final elimination of Trotzky had to be accomplished by an assassin, instead of by an executioner. But accomplished it was. The bulldog tenacity of Stalin never lets go, and no crack in the monolithic state that he rules can be tolerated. In the simple environment of Russian Georgia Stalin mastered the incontestable truth that dead men do not bite. In a primitive society that may well be the dominant consideration, but in the management of a modern state it is overridden by another, to wit, dead men do not think, either. For twenty years Stalin's reliance upon homicide as the one effective retort was his strength, as it was Al Capone's strength during his heyday in Chicago; but in the end, this argument is always a weakness. In destroying his critics, Stalin has been destroying the brains of Russia, and the process, if carried far enough, can end only in giving him an entourage of fools, who will ruin the state.

All this is the picture of a very definite personality, apparently a flat contradiction of the assertion that Stalin is not a man, but an Idea. But it is not a contradiction. As far as Russians are concerned, Stalin is unquestionably a man, and a very formidable one; but as far as the average American is concerned, which is to say, as far as this book is concerned, his personality is of relatively small importance, and the Idea he represents is what counts.

Intellectually, he has given us more trouble than all the others combined, in part because he represents a reversal of the process to which we were accustomed. Roosevelt enlarged Wilson's concepts; Stalin has contracted Lenin's. Wilson, like Washington, undertook to raise a standard to which the wise and honest can repair; Roosevelt erected a standard to which pretty much anybody can repair. Lenin conceived one universal faith, but in the New Economic Policy he admitted the necessity of living amicably and for a long time with heresy; Stalin has struck away that concession. Lenin and Trotzky were frankly out to Communize the world, but Stalin has a narrower aim—it is not merely Communism that must prevail, but Russian Communism, which may be Marxist, but is far indeed from being Marxism.

Basically, Stalin's thinking is identical with the kind of thinking that the average American indulged until he encountered Stalin. Thirty years ago there was little doubt among us that democracy, and American democracy at that, eventually must prevail, and the sooner the better for all the earth. At first we were incredulous when that idea was challenged as arrogantly as it was propounded. We couldn't believe that anybody meant it; but hard experience has taught us that they do mean it, and little by little we have matured sufficiently to accept the fact that all men do not think alike, not even all honest men. In this we are a step beyond, not Stalin perhaps, but beyond the idea that Stalin represents. Thus far, the concept of an honest difference of opinion is beyond the grasp of the Communists, and while that is true they will continue to imperil themselves and everyone else.

It is conceivable that the death of Lenin at fifty-four was as heavy a blow to us as the assassination of Lincoln was to the South. It is beyond belief that Lincoln would have consented to the more vindictive measures of Reconstruction, and it is a certainty that he would have restrained the incendiary brutalities of the army of occupation. It is apparent that from 1921 to 1924 Lenin was preparing Russia to accept a *modus vivendi* with the rest of the world; it is imaginable that had he lived ten years longer he might have come to an understanding with the democracies that would have checked the spread of Fascism in its early stages.

But it is much more likely that he died at the right time. Communism was already taking on the fanaticism of a militant religion, and it is doubtful that any man, even Lenin, could have prevented its development. Had he not died in 1924, he might have gone the way of Trotzky; for the idea of the Holy War to extirpate the infidel is deeply embedded in the Russians as it is in every politically immature people. It could have destroyed even Lenin.

It didn't destroy Stalin because he employed it, instead of opposing it. That Stalin himself cherishes any illusions as to the holiness of Russia is incredible. To begin with, he is not a Russian, but a member of a small nation overrun and for centuries ruthlessly exploited by the Russians. In the second place, every detail of his political career exhibits him as a typical political boss, contemptuous of all ideas except the idea of power. In this country a Hague, a Pendergast, a Crump, found no difficulty whatever in being an ardent New Dealer as long as it was clear that the New Deal commanded the votes; but few realistic observers doubt that the bosses would just as readily have accepted Republicanism, or Populism, or Rosicrucianism, if any of them had been the obvious avenue to power. Stalin is a Communist for the same reason that many an American big-city boss was temporarily a New Dealer. In the heart of Africa a century ago the same kind of man would have embraced cannibalism as fervently as Stalin did Communism.

Stalin, the man, therefore has really taught the average American nothing that he did not know before. Only in size does he differ from a type with which we are thoroughly familiar. But the idea that he represents, a contracted and intensified Leninism, which is, in turn, a contracted and perverted Marxism, has taught us a great deal, so much, in fact, as to make the Russian dictator one of the four powerful influences that have molded our lives.

3. "No Less Renowned Than War"

STALIN has forced us along the road to maturity by a spectacular exhibition of excellence. It is the immature mind that sees the world all black-and-white. It takes an adult intelligence to perceive and appraise correctly the virtues of the vicious, without ignoring their vices. Stalin, by compelling the average American first to dislike him, then to like him, and then to dislike him again, has loosened the American's emotional joints, has forced him to make use of his reasoning powers and to act in international politics like a rational being.

This applies, to be sure, only to the typical American. We have many minds that have been frozen in one attitude or the other, but these are not typical. There are among us minds so stiffened by a sort of intellectual arthritis as to be held permanently in whatever attitude happened to be theirs when the affliction came upon them. Some were ossified in hatred of Russia back in the days of Coolidge and could not unbend even when the Russians were pinning down two hundred German divisions, giving us time to arm and attack. Some were ossified in the days of the Grand Alliance and could not unbend even when it became obvious that Russia had replaced Nazi Germany as the chief threat to human freedom. These represent the Fascist and Communist elements in our population, and they are alike cases of arrested development—a burden and an annoyance at all times, and sometimes a menace, but at no time to be regarded as embodying the opinion of the country.

The typical American has wavered between the extremes and in the process of wavering has acquired a suppleness and resili-ence of mind that are attributes of maturity. For the world isn't all black-and-white. The vicious are sometimes endowed with great and admirable virtues. Stalin, less in himself than in what he represents, has been both our hope and our peril, and our best course from the beginning has been, not toward his aboli-tion, but toward increasing the hope and reducing the peril that he offers.

For the organizing genius that was the ruin of Trotzky was also the ruin of Hitler. We profited nothing by Trotzky's fate, but Hitler's end was helpful. The Stalinist cynicism that drove Trotzky into his wild and fatal revolt restrained Stalin from plunging into a wild and fatal attack on the West immediately after the fall of Hitler. So that cynicism was not a total loss from our standpoint. The very ruthlessness that exterminated all who even thought of betraying Stalin wiped out a great many who would willingly have betrayed us. We might easily have had worse to deal with than this gigantic edition of Boss Tweed.

The Russo-German War startled all the world, and nobody more than the military experts. Perhaps the people least sur-prised were the members of the German General Staff, who went into the affair with foreboding; but even they did not ex-pect to have their worst fears realized.

Those realists had always known that the weakness of Russia in her earlier wars had not been in any lack of courage, of strength, or of skill in her troops, but in an almost complete lack of organizing ability on the higher levels. This lack enabled Germany to defeat Russia in 1917, but in the process she was so weakened that she, in turn, was defeated by the Western

Allies. In 1939 Hitler undertook to reverse the strategy of the previous war; he would defeat the West first, and then deal with Russia. Unfortunately for him, he did not understand that as long as Britain survived, the West was undefeated, and so launched his attack on Russia before the first part of his program was completed. This his generals understood, and it accounted for their pessimism. They would have committed suicide en masse had they suspected that not only was the West undefeated, but Russia for the first time had a first-rate organizing genius in a position of authority.

But it was true. Russian strategy during the first year of the war was Fabian, which is an admissible, although frightfully expensive, strategy; but Russian tactics seem to have been as calamitous as they had been in 1914, and the early battles were as ruinous as of yore. The difference was that behind the retreating line training and supply were organized with a competence never before approached in Russian history. The result was that as fast as one division was lost, another came up from the rear to take its place, and when the army stood on the Volga it was larger and better equipped than when it stood on the Bug. Had Hitler dreamed of any such outcome even he must have known that Germany had no chance.

Needless to say, this was anything but clear to the average American while it was happening. Most of us had accepted the experts' opinion that the Russian army was no good, and the events of the first few months of the war seemed to prove it. But at length it became clear even to the ordinary newspaper reader that although the Russians were staggering back, they were not going to pieces as they did in 1915 and 1916. Yet the German drive was much fiercer than it had been in the First World War. With no French army clawing at his back, Hitler was able to hurl practically all of his land power against the Russians. Still they didn't go to pieces. Then came the long pause, with Lenin-

grad, Moscow and Stalingrad remaining in Russian hands; and
at last the beginning of the surge to the west. By that time, we
were kicking in the back door to Germany, and her defeat was
plainly a matter of time.

So much we could see, even while the war was raging; but
the thing was close to its end before most of us began to appreciate the miracle of organization that had been effected. Even
then we did not grasp its full significance, because it was an old
story to Americans. Knutsen, Nelson, Somervell and their col-
laborators were doing more wonderful things in this country;
but they were not working in Russia. When we landed guns,
trucks, ammunition and supplies on the Murmansk coast, or in
Persia, and those things showed up promptly on the battle front,
a tremendous change had come over the spirit of Russia; for in
the old days four-fifths of all we sent would have been lost, or
stolen, or at least delayed until it was too late for the stuff to do
much good.

So it became plain even to the man in the street that Stalin
knew his business; and high efficiency is a quality that the average American admires, even in a dictator. We modified our
opinion of the Russian leader. We had to admit that at least he
had cleaned out the grafters who had been the ruin of Russia in
the earlier war; and we did not hear from Moscow a constant
succession of tales of thievery, madness, and perversion in high
places, such as poured out of Berlin. Stalin was obviously sane,
one hundred per cent masculine, and extremely intolerant of
stealing by the boys in the back room. We began to wonder if
it might not be possible to get along with him in spite of his
dizzy economic and political ideas.

Roosevelt came back from Yalta fully believing that it could
be done. True, he had hardly reached this country before he
began to wonder, and on the day before his death he sent a
strong protest against what looked to him like a repudiation of

pledges given at Yalta. However, Truman came back from Pots-
dam thinking that it was not impossible. It is significant that
both men dealt with Stalin personally; they had little or no contact with the other thirteen men who constitute the Politburo.
They found the dictator at least partially amenable to reason,
and they assumed that when they had Stalin they had Russia.
Only some months later did it begin to appear that this is as
bad a mistake as is that of a foreign diplomat in Washington
who has talked with the President and thinks that is enough
without ever considering the Senate.

But so it was. By 1948 the plain man could see that Russia
was no more bound by what Stalin had said at Yalta and Pots-
dam than the United States was bound by what Wilson had said
at Paris. Here was another step forward in our political education—the realization that the Idea on which a nation is founded
is stronger than any man, and that the promises of the most
powerful leader are valid only to the extent that they are consonant with the spirit of the nation behind him. Stalin is dictator
only because the Russians tolerate him. If he becomes intolerable to the masses of the Russian people, he will vanish like a
puff of smoke; and he, or any leader, may make himself intolerable simply by getting so far in advance of the masses as to
lose contact with them. So Stalin has faded from a personality
into the mere embodiment of an idea, and the effort to understand that idea is the most difficult intellectual feat the plain
citizen has had to undertake in many years.

More than fifty years ago Kipling reduced the whole thing to
the simplicity of the doctrine of Original Sin—"Make ye no
truce with Adam-Zad—the Bear that walks like a Man." Unfortunately, the time has come when we have no choice. It is either
a truce with the Bear, or an endless war in which all the bel-
ligerents will be defeated and the whole of the civilized world
reduced to the desert that Germany was at the end of the Thirty

Years' War. But a truce without understanding is no truce; so it is understand or perish.

To this stern necessity have fifty years of laborious and bitter political education brought the American people. Yet is there anything new in it, except the magnified scale of the operation? Has not this same necessity confronted us from the beginning? Is it anything more than the primary condition of self-government? True, until 1914 our problems were largely confined to this continent, and almost entirely to this hemisphere, whereas now they spread from pole to pole, and from the International Date Line around to the Date Line again; but it is still a problem first of finding out what the other fellow really has in mind, and then of determining to what extent he can be accommodated without ruining our own plans and prospects.

In dealing with the Russians it is already clear that a large factor is one with which we are drearily familiar, since we have been struggling with it on this continent ever since 1607, and with none too much success. This is simply the old problem of political immaturity, that fruitful mother of every kind of bigotry.

If Stalin were the mightiest warlock in the annals of wizardry, he could do little about this, for, in Cleveland's phrase, it is a condition and not a theory. The Russians from time immemorial have held to the faith that the Israelites cherished when they invaded Canaan—the doctrine that there is one God, one State, one Chosen People and that any deviation from this idea is treason, any differentiation from this standard a rebellion that must be crushed. The overthrow of the Czar did not disturb the idea. It merely substituted Lenin, and then Stalin, for God, the Politburo for the empire, and Communists for Muscovites. There remained one God, one State, one Chosen People.

It is a heresy that afflicts us all to some extent, for no nation is entirely mature in its political thinking. It afflicted Germany so sorely as to destroy that nation. It afflicts isolationist Americans to such an extent as to make them a handicap upon the Republic at all times, and in times of crisis a threat to its existence. It afflicts extreme Zionists, Ku Kluxers and other Fascists, and, of course, American Communists are eaten up by it. In 1830 Charles Dickens found it afflicting practically all Americans, but in 1950 the typical citizen of this Republic has partially emerged from the dominance of that idea—only partially, be it noted. If one were to claim that Americans have wholly escaped, he would be instantly confounded by the published programs of the Daughters of the American Revolution, the American Legion, and other powerful organizations that frankly proclaim their intent to stamp out any deviation from what they call "Americanism," which on examination turns out to be not very different from Fascism. These organizations, however, although they are strong, represent a minority; the people as a whole have held pretty consistently to the theory that there are other legitimate forms of government, and if other nations prefer them, they have a right to do so.

No such idea seems to have penetrated the Russian consciousness as yet. The Russians have not passed the stage of political development at which it seems to them that there can be only two kinds of government—their kind and the wrong kind. This makes it hard for us to deal with them, but there isn't anything monstrous about it; a hundred years ago we felt the same way, and it took long and very rough experience in self-government to knock the childish notion out of our heads. Probably nothing else will cure the Russians; but another generation of trying to manage their own affairs will certainly cure them.

Fortunately for the world, at the time when we were cocksure of our own righteousness and wisdom—about the time of Dickens' visit—we were still a minor power, hardly more important in world affairs than Albania is today; therefore we did not constitute any great danger to international order. But the Russians have arrived at that stage at a moment when they are certainly the second, and consider themselves the first, Great Power. Their nonsense is backed by immense strength, both economic and military. It is a very definite threat to all nations that are politically more mature.

So for five years the ordinary American has been subjected to the most rigorous test a man of his type has ever undergone. The uncommon Americans are catching it, too—the statesmen, the diplomatists, the leaders of public opinion, all who have to do with shaping the national policy—but they are better prepared; all of them have some knowledge of history and political philosophy and not a few are deeply learned in those subjects. Yet the final decision is in the hands of the plain voter, whose knowledge of such matters is pretty much confined to his own experience; if that experience leads him to adopt a certain attitude, all the learning and skill of his leaders will not prevent that attitude from prevailing.

He has adopted the attitude of uncompromising opposition to Communism, but for five years he has refused to carry it to the extreme of blind hostility. Thus far, the position of most of the plain people has been clear—if the Russians want it, by all means let them have it, provided they don't try to cram it down our throats, or the throats of our friends. We are no Master Race. We were not, as Rumbold and Jefferson put it, born booted and spurred to ride on the backs of the rest of mankind by the grace of God. We are not the only honest people in the world, and wisdom will not die with us. That being the case, we deem it prudent to hear what other men have to say, for sometimes they may speak truth which we have overlooked.

Therefore we need no Iron Curtain. It is only children—and adults with childish minds—who must be protected against knowledge of what actually goes on in the world. A grown man, mature and responsible, must know; and the more dreadful the truth, the greater is his need to know it all. The American people, in possession of all attainable facts about Russia, have not burst into a senseless clamor for war; and that is irrefutable evidence that they have attained some degree of political maturity.

But it is none too much. After all, we are a long, long way from being a nation of philosophers, and we have been subjected to strains that might try the patience of Job. Stalin has passed from the status of a man, formidable, indeed, but comprehensible, into that of an Idea so vague and formless that we have great difficulty in grasping it at all; and what we do understand seems so inane that it is hard to believe that rational people could entertain it. Yet in the face of this we have—so far—kept our heads; and this is a feat in which an American can take more just pride than he takes in the Normandy landing, or in the Battle of the Philippine Sea.

4. *Trained Fleas*

DAVID HARUM enunciated the striking theory that perhaps a reasonable number of fleas are good for a dog, in that they may keep him from thinking about being a dog.

If David is too abrupt for your taste, consider that he was only restating the medical theory of the employment of vesicants as antiphlogistics, the principle of the counterirritant, which undoubtedly has some validity. Mr. Harum's theory is cited here to sustain the thesis that the American Communist party has had a very definite educational and moral value to the ordinary American since the year 1917.

This thesis will be challenged instantly, earnestly, and widely. To millions of Americans who can understand how Russian Communism came to be, although they have no sympathy with it, the very existence of an American Communist party is without explanation or excuse. Daily observation has convinced them that the consistent effort of the American Communist party has been to disseminate anything but truth, so they perceive no educational value in it. They have observed that the customary method of the party is that of the double cross, so they can see no moral value in it. They argue, very plausibly, that an organization which is, as far as they can see, reasonless, truthless, and faithless is bound to be valueless.

But in so arguing they miss the point. The beneficial effect is not necessarily a property of the article itself, but lies in the reaction that its stimulus produces. Cantharides is a deadly poison, but a plaster made of that poison has been used to good effect against conditions that would yield to nothing less violent. If the American public were to swallow Communism, its goose would be cooked, as certainly as that of a man who would swallow cyanide; but hitherto it has been applied externally, and there is much reason to believe that its application has helped. At least it has reduced certain swollen and congested complacencies, and in so doing it may have eliminated some dangerous foci of infection.

Two instances come to mind at once. The Communist attack on race prejudice may be utterly insincere, but it has been utterly violent, and its violence has focused attention on that carbuncle on the body politic. The Communist infiltration into labor unions has been the sharpest of spurs to labor leaders who might otherwise incline to be at ease in Zion with their twenty-five-thousand-dollar salaries. We think more about oppressed minorities than we would without the Communists. Labor leaders work harder and think faster than they would without the Communists. These are benefits that the existence of this party has conferred upon us.

There are corresponding disadvantages, to be sure. One of the most conspicuous is the fact that the existence of this small group has made the United States a very heaven for a regiment of parasites. Hordes of shrewd fellows constitutionally averse from labor have been and are now living in Byzantine luxury on the millions poured out by terrified rich men for protection against the Communists. These range from plug-uglies hired as bodyguards all the way to Doctors of Philosophy hired to edit handsome and expensive periodicals aimed against Communism. The number of ex-advertising men, ex-newspapermen, ex-school-teachers, and even ex-parsons in this country who toil not, neither do they spin because shivering millionaires support them handsomely as guardians against Communism, is probably much larger than the membership of the American Communist party.

These parasites are, of course, natural and relentless enemies of honest men everywhere and at all times. In the United States their most insidious attack upon the people who do the work of the country has been by using the terror of Communism to undermine both civil liberty and economic justice. Almost every scheme whose real aim is to handcuff labor and gag effective criticism now wears the mask of anti-Communism. All too frequently the deception has been complete, and the schemes have been enacted into law. But enough of them have been exposed to give the average man some suspicion of what is going on. The deception has to be constantly more elaborate, which is evidence that the ordinary man's perceptions are becoming sharper.

But this is education. The howling and counterhowling may be a vexation to the spirit and a grief to the judicious, but it keeps the average man awake. It is deplorable that it flames into open rioting now and then, and it is terrifying to think that it may flower hideously in judicial lynching comparable to the Salem witchcraft trials and the Sacco-Vanzetti case; but against these perils should be entered the advantage that it is an antidote to apathy. It is a small advantage, perhaps, far too small to balance the account, yet an advantage it is; and we owe it to the existence of the Communists.

Perhaps a much greater advantage is the fact that it becomes clearer every day that ideas cannot be put down by law, and that the only real defense against Communism is not blackjacks and bayonets, but good sense in the average man. If that is lost, then either Communism or Fascism must inevitably triumph; and if either took over, the country would no longer be fit to live in. The responsibility slides off the apex of the pyramid and comes to rest at the bottom. The President, the Cabinet, Congress, the Governors, the mayors and chiefs of police—none of them, nor all of them combined, can stop Communism, or Fascism either. The only man who can stop it is the plain citizen. He can kill it as dead as King Tut, but no one else can, and this he realizes more clearly every day.

Yet this is the meaning of democracy. A man who is to govern himself must be prepared to take care of himself. Mr. Truman is no feudal baron whose castle walls are our refuge in times of stress. Mr. Truman is merely our agent, charged with the duty of making our will effective. When it comes to fighting off raiders, especially raiders who come armed with ideas instead of swords, every man must stand up and do his own fighting, or it will not be done. It is a hateful necessity, but learning that it is a necessity is the beginning of political wisdom. Within the past five years the Communists have probably taught us more of this wisdom than any other group of comparable size.

Indeed, the raucous challenge of the Communists has driven

the average American to do more hard, steady thinking about first principles than he had done in a generation. This is due to something beyond the fact that they are no mean dialecticians; they also have a moral earnestness that puts into their argument weight that it could acquire from no other source. Few of the rank and file share the cynicism that seems to be the basis of Stalin's philosophy; most of them believe their own bunk with a single-minded intensity that carries them to martyrdom for an idea.

This is a quality that cannot be dismissed with a shrug, because it gives the Communists a strong appeal to idealistic youth. The young American knows by observation that it is a rare Democrat or Republican who is inclined to risk wounds, imprisonment, and even death for the party's sake, while it is a rare Communist who will not do so. This makes it clear that the sincerity of the Communists reaches a pitch not approached by that of members of the conservative parties; and young people inevitably respect a man who believes in something. Many an American father who has found a son or a daughter flirting with Communistic ideas has had to scratch his head and go back to notions to which he had given no serious attention since he was a schoolboy, to explain his own stand. In many cases he finds it difficult to collect his ideas and is sorely embarrassed, which is good for him. It contributes to his adult education.

Incidentally, it tends to make him angry with his teachers in grade and high school who, he now perceives, stuffed him with a highly adulterated brand of history. The unfortunate pedagogues have come in for much denunciation since the close of the Second World War, largely because we find ourselves ill-equipped to argue with the Communists, and feel that the teachers should have prepared us better.

Up to a point this denunciation is no doubt just, for there is plenty of bad teaching in American history classes; but, after all, the best teacher in the world cannot make immature minds capable of grasping subtle ideas. The difference between faith and superstition is subtle in the extreme, so much so that many powerful minds have been unable to distinguish between them in all cases. Sincerity emphatically is not the test. Moloch had martyrs in greater numbers than Jehovah, and Mencken points out that no more than five centuries ago Huitzilopochtli, utterly forgotten now, was so great a god that in one year fifty thousand youths and maidens were slain in sacrifice to him. Thus the fact that American Communists are willing to go to the stake for Stalin is no proof that Stalin is a greater god than Baal—no proof, indeed, that he is greater than a bundle of sticks and feathers tied with a red string, the fetish for which members of the obeah cult in the West Indies have willingly suffered the rigors of the law.

For all that, faith is powerful, and faith based on reason backed by observation and experience is the most powerful force in the world. If the ordinary American has been forced by the Communists to review and reconsider his faith in democracy, they have done him a good turn. Hardly any man who has lived through this turbulent century will deny that the Communists have compelled him to do some vigorous thinking; and to that extent their influence has been beneficial.

Thirty-five years ago Brooks and Henry Adams despaired of democracy and, in the existing circumstances, not without reason. Thirty-five years ago American democracy was close to meeting Milton's description of what he could not praise—"a fugitive and cloistered virtue, unexercised and unbreathed, that never sallies out and seeks her adversary, but slinks out of the race." Thirty-five years ago nobody had seriously challenged democracy within living memory, and if it had grown somewhat fat and lazy, what wonder? The Adams brothers' error was in mistaking the evidences of lack of exercise for an irreversible fatty degeneration.

Today the danger lies in the other direction. This hard and

lean democracy that has emerged, scarred, but laureled and powerful, from two world wars is in no danger whatever of stifling
in its own grease. Its peril is rather that it may loose the ferocity
it summoned up to meet and destroy its enemies upon people
who might be converted into friends. The danger is not apathy,
but too much action, too little considered.

For Stalin, the man, has passed and what we are confronting
now is an idea, against which the sword is useless. An idea is
more dangerous than any dictator, and must be opposed more
resolutely; but not with force. The average American has understood this, at least in part, at least far enough to refrain from
trying to shoot down a philosophy with artillery; and since that
is true, even Brooks and Henry Adams would have to admit
that some progress in political education has been made. While
any progress at all is being made, great progress is not impossible.

Finally, the passing of Stalin from person into philosophy has
had something, probably much, to do with one negative aspect
of the postwar period through which we are now struggling.
This is the firm refusal of the plain man to tolerate a repetition
of the "back to normalcy" degradation. An emotional reaction
after a great war is as natural as postoperative shock after major
surgery, and as much to be dreaded. We have had some evidences of that sort of reaction since 1945, but the worst was the
wave of hysteria which has made government service a distasteful
profession for an intelligent man, and even that was hardly as
bad as A. Mitchell Palmer's witch-hunt after the First World
War. As for the financial scandals, they have been, as compared
to those following earlier wars, much as an office boy's pilfering
of stamps and petty cash is to embezzlement by the treasurer of
the company. We have had nothing approaching Teapot Dome,
or the Crédit Mobilier, after the Civil War, or the speculation
in government scrip after the Revolution. Even George Wash-

ington is supposed to have made half a million by buying up veterans' claims at a few cents in the dollar; it was regarded as quite legitimate then, but George himself couldn't do it today without raising a stench, which is a clear indication that the level of public morals has risen somewhat in a century and three-quarters.

If it seems to you that the Communists had nothing to do with our refusal this time to rush from the crusade to the hog-trough, consider what was the final argument that assured adoption of the Marshall Plan; what was the final argument against reduction of taxes before we had discharged our obligations to the rest of the world; what is the argument against demolition of countless government services to save money. The answer in every case is the existence of the Communist power.

Every form of error battens on human misery; so if we let Europe drift too far into misery, Communism must triumph there. We are the sole remaining nation with military strength enough to cope with Russia, so we could not disarm to pocket the cash. Communism's claim to consideration is its service to its people; therefore we could not turn our own people over to the exploiters. With that threat hanging over us, such indecency as that in which we wallowed after the First World War would have been suicidal; so we remained quite remarkably decent.

David Harum's dictum can easily be adapted to fit the political education of the American citizen. A reasonable number of Communists may be good for a democracy; for irritating as they are, they do prevent its thoughts from drifting to the canine level.

5. *Salutary Alarm*

IT MAY be argued with some plausibility, however, that the most profound effect the passing of Stalin has had upon the destiny of the average American was that of propelling him beyond his own hemisphere.

This has occurred so recently that the ultimate effects are far beyond the reach of conjecture; but there is no reasonable doubt that the Atlantic Pact—forced upon us by the existence of the Soviet power—was a vast extension of American citizenship. For citizenship is not exclusively a matter of privileges; to at least an equal extent it is a matter of responsibilities. A citizenship that assumes new responsibilities is expanded, whether or not any additional privileges are involved. Faced by the Russian threat the American has had to assume a share of responsibility for defense of the whole group of nations facing the Atlantic. His destiny is henceforth linked with that of the Low Countries, the Scandinavian countries, France and Great Britain. It is not so much that the United States has become a European power as that all distinction among Atlantic powers has been obliterated, as far as their defense is concerned. Stalin has extracted the significance from the terms "European" and "American" and merged them all in the single category, "Atlantic."

This is a tremendous achievement, and the fact that Stalin did not plan it and takes no joy in it does not lessen its magnitude. It will make the American of the next generation an entirely different man, politically, from the sort of men his forefathers were. The American hitherto has been a citizen of a nation, and no more; today he is already a citizen of a hegemon with a very fair prospect of finding himself tomorrow a citizen of an empire. To say that this does not alter his political status is to say that there was no difference fifty years ago in the political status of an Englishman and a Swiss. There was a very great difference between a national of the greatest empire in the world and a national of the smallest confederation. Where the advantage lay is irrelevant; at this moment it seems to have lain with the Swiss, but the point is that the difference existed.

It was no greater than the difference in status between the American of 1900 and the American of 1950. The fact that the change was none of our choosing, and emphatically not of our planning, has nothing to do with the case. Empery has frequently been acquired inadvertently and sometimes reluctantly, but it is none the less real for that. Mommsen implies that Rome itself was strongly isolationist on the eve of the conquest of Sicily, and was forced to support the Mamertines (the first step toward creation of the transmarine empire) by the Carthaginian threat to overrun all Sicily.

His report of the debate sounds, indeed, strangely like the debate in this country over ratification of the Atlantic Pact. The Romans perceived, and did not like, the prospect of military involvement.

But there was the more important objection that by crossing the sea the Romans would depart from the purely Italian and purely continental policy which they had hitherto pursued; they would abandon the system by which their ancestors had founded the greatness of Rome, to enter upon another system the results of which no one could foretell. It was one of those moments when calculation fails, and when faith in men's own and in their country's destiny alone gives them courage to grasp the hand which beckons to them out of the darkness of the future, and to follow it they

know not whither. Long and seriously the senate deliberated on
the proposal of the consuls to lead the legions to the help of the
Mamertines; it came to no decisive resolution.[2]

The deadlock was broken by the vote of the burgesses, who
were readier to take a chance than were the Senators. Twenty-
two centuries later (the Mamertines were received in 265 B.C.)
the situation was much the same; few observers believe that the
United States Senate would have come to a "decisive resolution"
on the Atlantic Pact, which required a two-thirds vote, had it
not been for the pressure of public opinion, our equivalent of
the Roman burgesses. The burgesses, says Mommsen, were
animated by their military successes in Italy; but the Americans
were animated by the danger that without the pact Communism
would sweep Europe. It was the idea represented by Stalin that
did it.

The eventual outcome of the decision regarding Sicily was the
consolidation of the Western World for the first time into what
Toynbee calls a "universal state." It must be admitted that there
is no clearly apparent obstacle that will certainly block a similar
outcome of our decision on the Atlantic Pact. It is a repellent
idea. The suggestion that the Republic founded by such men
as Washington, Jefferson, Hamilton and Franklin is destined
to develop into a monstrous driver of slave states comparable
to Imperial Rome is enough to sicken every lover of liberty.
Nevertheless, it is a suggestion that must be considered. Logic
compels us to consider it, and were we wholly devoid of logic,
the yells and dances of such characters as Messrs. Molotov,
Vishinsky and Gromyko, echoed by our home-grown Communists, would make sure that it could not escape our attention.

The hegemony already exists. American arms and American
money are today the backbone of the Atlantic alliance, and

[2] Theodor Mommsen, *History of Rome*, vol. ii, p. 43 (Dickson's translation,
edition of 1873).

when one member of any alliance is in possession of both the sword and the purse, that member must necessarily lead. The next strongest member of the alliance is Great Britain but does any sane man believe that Great Britain would or could deliberately defy the will of the United States on any matter of supreme importance? So far, on all matters of supreme importance we have been in agreement, but the fact remains that no country in the world, Russia alone excepted, is in position to challenge the United States. Therefore hegemony is thrust upon us, regardless of our preferences in the matter.

It is a matter of fact also that in the past hegemony has been, almost without historical exception, the anteroom to empire. It is nonsense to say that it cannot happen in this case. It can happen. More than that it is extremely likely to happen unless vigorous and unprecedentedly skillful efforts are made to prevent it. There is, indeed, no lack of pessimists who hold that it is inevitable and that efforts to prevent it will be wasted energy. Nor can this view be dismissed lightly. It is supported by an appalling unanimity of precedents, as well as by theoretical reasoning. It must be taken very seriously indeed.

We resent with bitter indignation the Stalinists' accusation that we are moving toward imperialism by choice, whereas every move we have made in that direction has been forced upon us by the Russians. But it is a matter of small moment how we get there, if we eventually arrive. The important thing is neither to drift, nor to be driven, into imperialism at all. Yet to arrive at hegemony without going all the way into empery would be a feat of statecraft not yet accomplished by any great world power. It was a problem that was too much for Athens, too much for Rome, and in the modern world too much for England and Prussia.

Toynbee takes the discouraging view that it has not been accomplished in any of the twenty-six civilizations he has been able to describe[3] save where some exterior force interposed to divert events from their normal course, which he regards as the extinction or subjugation of one after another of the constituent states until only two remain, whereupon one deals the other a "knock-out blow." Western civilization has apparently followed that normal course to the point at which it consists of two super-states around one or the other of which all the rest are grouped. Russia has definitely subjugated most of her associates. We have not proceeded that far. Shocked by the example of Russia, we have in fact made definite efforts to arrest, rather than expedite, any such process; but they have not been conspicuously successful. The military alliance has had to be strengthened by economic bonds which tend to grow tighter and stronger. The British army, for instance, cannot be effectively supported by the American army unless the British pound is supported by the American dollar. The alliance of democracies is plainly moving toward a federation of democracies, and a strong federation is very close to a monolithic empire.

But when one super-state has dealt its only rival the "knock-out blow" the event has never yet represented the triumph of the civilization to which both belong. The triumph of the super-state in becoming what Toynbee calls a "universal state" has invariably signalized the beginning of the end of that civilization. There is no apparent reason to doubt that the collision of the United States and Russia would represent, not the triumph, but the beginning of the decline of Western civilization, not alone because of the physical destruction that such a war would involve, but also, and more importantly, because of the moral and intellectual petrifaction that would inevitably follow the establishment of a world-wide empire, whether American or Russian. "Absolute power corrupts absolutely" applies to nations even more rigorously than it does to men.

[3] See *A Study of History*, by Arnold J. Toynbee, *passim*.

Nevertheless, even in this country contemplation of the possibility of such a collision does not cause all men to wring their hands. There are those who rub their hands. Enraptured by the prospect of some transitory gain, they are blind to the ruin that would attend defeat, and would certainly follow victory.

If men of this type constitute the majority, not necessarily in numbers, but in influence—that is to say, the effective majority —in this country, then there would seem to be no convincing reason to doubt that to Toynbee's twenty-five civilizations already dead or paralyzed, we shall eventually add ours as the twenty-sixth. In that case, speculation on the subject of the American as a political entity is impossible, for there is no speculation where there is no uncertainty.

In whatever involves a human element, however, there is always uncertainty; *homo sapiens* is unpredictable; he may do anything, and in extreme cases he may even act rationally. For a case in point, consider a policy adopted by the American Republic in the latter part of 1949 at the urgent advice of President Truman—the issuance of considerable subsidies to arm the allies of the Atlantic Pact.

With all due respect, one hesitates to suggest that the Honorable Harry S. Truman is a wiser man and a greater statesman than Aristides and Themistocles combined. Nevertheless, the policy of rearming Europe, if adhered to resolutely, would avoid the mistake made by the two famous Greeks which Grote considered primarily responsible for the degeneration of the Delian Confederacy into the Athenian Empire.[4] This error was in turning over the defense of the confederacy almost entirely to the Athenian navy, instead of arranging for the confederates to defend themselves with Athenian support. In the course of time the confederates forgot the art of war and thereafter had to

[4] Consult George Grote, *History of Greece*, vol. v, chapter 45, especially the footnotes in which Grote explains his interpretation of Thucydides.

depend on Athens, paying her tribute for their defense; which, of course, was empire.

American policy has started in the other direction. At present, we are paying our confederates for our defense; but there is little danger that the payments will degenerate into tribute, because none of the confederates is now, or is likely to become strong enough to exact the payment if we do not choose to offer it. This makes nonsense of the Communist assertion that the Atlantic Pact, as it now stands, is a step toward empire.

But it does not make nonsense of the assertion that it might easily become just that. With what might appear to be a slight alteration of our present policy, we could turn into the path followed by all prior imperial powers—a path that invariably has led to ruin. If we avoid that fatal turn, it is not likely to be because of the intervention of some exterior force. At present the only dangerous force that could be brought to bear upon the United States is that of Russia; and so far that force has been exerted to drive us into the path of empire, not away from it.

The only considerable thrust in the opposite direction comes from the distaste of the American people for imperial adventure. But to be effective, this force must be applied with a relatively high degree of political skill; which is to say, it can be effectively applied only by a people whose political thinking has reached a relatively high level of maturity. At this, Henry Adams would have thrown up his hands. A good many living Americans, especially among the intelligentsia, do throw up their hands. If our only hope, they say, lies in a consistent and continuous exhibition of good sense on the part of the mass of the voters, we are sunk.

It may be that this dismal crew are prophets. It is incontestably true that the American electorate from time to time and from place to place has shown a tendency to vote for Silly Billy rather than for Socrates. That can be demonstrated conclusively by an unprejudiced inspection of the membership of the Senate and House of Representatives in any year you choose.

It is possible, too, that in some future crisis a single mistake on the part of the majority may wreak damage that can never be repaired. But it is not true that the electorate has to be infallible at all times, or we should have been ruined long ago. If the people are right oftener than they are wrong when they go to the ballot box, we shall survive, unless fate has in store for us the combination of a great crisis and an egregious error which would be irretrievable. Against that possibility there is no defense, so it is profitless to consider it.

But the course of American history thus far suggests strongly that our worst mistakes proceed from overconfidence. Surely, there are not in the list of Presidents two worse choices than Grant and Harding, each of whom was elected in a moment of triumph when the country was briskly confident of its ability to deal with any antagonist. It certainly is not briskly confident now, nor is it likely to be as long as the Communist power is formidable. That threat upon the horizon is a powerful inducement to the average American to think carefully before he marks his ballot; and when he thinks, his choice, if not always the best, is at least reasonably good.

On the whole, it may be fortunate that Iosif Vissarionovich Dzhugashvili has passed from a mortal man into an Idea invulnerable to wounds and pathogenic organisms. It at leasts strips us of the delusion that we may rely on arteriosclerosis or a dynamite bomb to solve our problem for us, and that all we have to do is play for time. The man will die, but the Idea will go on until it is liquidated by a better idea generated by hard thinking on the part of the plain, ordinary American.

V

One Abides

I. *The Vision of Abraham Lincoln*

IN LINCOLN'S dream someone said, "He is a very common-looking man," and Lincoln replied, "Friend, the Lord prefers common-looking people. That is the reason he makes so many of them."

At the moment he pursued the matter no further; but at another time he advanced a reasonable explanation of why the Lord prefers common people. Standing among the graves of men dead in defense of the republic he said, "It is for us the living . . . to be dedicated here to the unfinished work which they who fought here have thus far so nobly advanced . . . that government of the people, by the people, for the people shall not perish from the earth."

For us, the living, is the unfinished work, the work that will never be finished because it is an advance toward perfection, that may be ever approached but never attained. Unfinished work is necessarily for the living, for the ever-present, the never-dying; and the only immortal among us is the Average Man. There have been many periods in our history when the Great Man was conspicuous only by his absence; it is, in fact, the normal situation. But the Average Man is always on hand, not individually, but in the mass. Individually, he may be as transient as the polyp, but in the mass he is as persistent as the coral.

In the vision of Abraham Lincoln the Lord prefers the common mass because it tends to thrust upward, toward the light. It is not necessarily true because Lincoln believed it, nor because Jefferson and Jackson believed it before him, and Wilson and Roosevelt believed it after him; or because many minor figures in our national history have shared the belief. It is not necessarily true at all. But the possibility that it may be true is the only hope for this nation and this civilization.

For come what may, the Average Man will not be thrust back into the complete impotence that shackled him before the beginning of the democratic age; or he will not be thrust back without the extinction of what we call Western civilization. Government by the people is a partially accomplished fact and on it the whole structure of our culture is based; if the people cannot govern reasonably well, that culture will inevitably collapse.

To support of the theory that they can govern, we pledged our lives, our fortunes, and our sacred honor one hundred and seventy-four years ago. It is far too late to draw back. The Average Man must make good, or the nation dies.

We who have lived throughout the twentieth century have seen it demonstrated with a finality not experienced by any previous generation. We have seen not one, nor two, but four giants undertake the task of making government an implement in the hands of the common man to effect his safety and happiness. We have seen them opposed by at least three great despots, and by a dozen smaller ones. We have seen the world twice thrown into the convulsion of such wars as had never been known, unless the mists of mythology and prehistory conceal struggles more ferocious. We have seen the Great Men destroy the despots, although the world was wrecked in the process.

But we have seen them, one after another, fall before antagonists mightier than Hitler, Mussolini and Tojo. They could conquer human foes and shatter their man-made empires; but Time and Mortality they could not overcome. They passed, and the work was left unfinished.

But work unfinished is not necessarily work that has failed. It all depends upon us, the living. In the vision that inspired the great liberals of the democratic tradition it is a safe dependence. In the vision of the giants of the despotic tradition, it is no dependence at all.

Which is right remains a moot question. Bland confidence that democracy has already proved its competence, as well as its desirability, is childish. Democracy has won, at most, a chance to prove its ability to furnish the kind of government that all men desire. It has not furnished it, even in the United States, except in a few aspects of life. The American does enjoy the right to worship as he pleases, assuming that he does not disturb the peace, or violate public decency. It is unlawful to arrest and hold him without trial, or to extort a confession by torture. Such things are still done occasionally, but furtively, not boldly and openly. It is unlawful to hold him to involuntary servitude except as punishment for crime of which he has been convicted in open court. That, too, is still done, but by trickery and fraud, and when it can be proved the people who do it are subject to punishment. It is unlawful to deprive him of his property even for public purposes without just compensation. It is unlawful to interfere with assemblies to petition for the redress of grievances, that is to say, with political and labor conventions.

In short, the American has derived from his democratic government a considerable number of individual rights that are respected, on the whole, about as well as other rights are respected elsewhere in the world. But this is a long way from the sort of government that Lincoln imagined, and that was in the minds of Jefferson and Jackson, Wilson and Roosevelt. They envisaged a government that should be a potent instrument in the hands of the people to effect their safety and happiness—the "welfare state," if you choose to give it a name that some people now employ as an epithet. Democracy has not yet furnished this sort of government. Doubtless it never will furnish it in perfection. But every step closer to that perfection is what the great liberals called progress; and this sort of progress they believed that the people are capable of achieving, once what Wilson called their "generous energies" are released.

Roosevelt summarized the objective of democratic government under four heads, two political and two social—freedom of speech and freedom of worship, political, freedom from want and freedom from fear, social. We have gone far toward achieving the political aims, for they are relatively simple and can be attained by force. A sufficient number of policemen with a sufficient number of clubs can prevent interference with speech or worship. But all the policemen in the world cannot deliver us from want and fear. "Therein the patient," as Macbeth's physician remarked, "must minister to himself."

From the beginning of history it has been the opinion of many able men that he cannot do it. It is still the opinion of many able men, which is the reason why the world still has oligarchy, monarchy, absolutism and totalitarianism. It is why we have reactionaries in this country—reactionaries, not conservatives. Conservatives are men who question the pace, not the direction, of our movement. Reactionaries are those who believe that we move in the wrong direction.

It is not yet proved that the reactionaries are wrong. The experiment called the United States of America is the best evidence as yet offered to indicate that they are wrong, but that experiment is far from conclusive. At least five times in our national history we have demonstrated that under the leadership of a great man we can do well, extremely well. Oftener than that we have demonstrated that we can do fairly well under the leadership of a man of moderate talents—an Adams, a Madison, a Monroe, a Polk, a Cleveland, a Roosevelt the First, possibly a Truman. But, unfortunately, we have also demonstrated that we can fail miserably even under the leadership of a man of respectable attainments—a Van Buren, a Taft, a Hoover. George Washington is really out of the picture because the average man did not figure importantly in politics until he had retired. Washington's moral dominance was so complete that he could have made himself king with a nod of the head, and, indeed, had to take some pains to prevent a crown's being thrust upon him against his will.

The critical test of government of the people by the people for the people is still to come. That a democracy can survive, we have proved. That it can become formidable in battle, we have proved. That it can allow its citizens a very wide range of political liberty without serious danger to its structure, we have proved. In short, the experiment is well-nigh, perhaps quite, conclusive as regards the first aim of government, which is to effect the safety of the people. But the second aim, their happiness, is a goal that retreats as the quester advances. Like the Grail, it may be glimpsed, but never seized; yet the sight of it is the idealist's earthly reward.

The great liberals have understood this perfectly, and have

not been in the least dismayed. An intelligent liberal, devoid of any trace of greatness, may understand it in part and at times without being dismayed. A nation moving steadfastly toward a high goal is a mighty nation, even though its goal may be unattainable. The difficulty, touching impossibility, of complete success, is immaterial. The question is as to the resolution and endurance of the people.

In the vision of Abraham Lincoln and his peers the answer was affirmative. In the vision of Alexander Hamilton—"Your people, sir, is a great beast!"—it was negative. But Hamilton was an able man, and he has had able followers even unto this day. For the liberal to assume that he has been completely refuted would be folly; for the Hamiltonians have a mass of evidence that has not yet been contravened.

The time element with which some of them make great play is not impressive. The hundred and seventy-four years since the Declaration of Independence are but a moderate space in the life of a nation. Who remembers that a branch of the Comneni ruled a completely independent empire at Trebizond? Yet they lasted for more than two hundred and fifty years and until relatively recently—they collapsed in 1462. If, then, an empire may endure for a quarter of a millennium yet leave no more impression upon history than "a wisp of fog betwixt us and the sun," it is fatuous to berate the United States, only two-thirds as old, for not having solved the problem of the ages, and to ask dolefully how much longer it must take.

The time element does not enter for the simple reason that, as a people, we have all time. If the solution of the problem is to make government perfect, then we do not expect to solve it, ever. But if the solution is not to attain but constantly to approach perfection, then it has already been solved many times, and as many times missed again, a process that may go on for-ever.

It is senseless to imagine that by taking thought we can make every citizen of the Republic wise and upright. It is not of record that, solely by taking thought, one man has been rendered wise and upright, to say nothing of a nation. Character is something above and beyond the product of thought. You may call the extra factor emotional balance, or you may call it God, but in any event it is not exclusively mind. But it is not senseless to imagine that by taking thought we may attain an increasing intellectual maturity. That is the way it is done. A high level of intellectual maturity would solve most of our governmental problems, for the political evils that beset us are compounded of at least nine parts of stupidity to one of wickedness.

Already we know that an intellectually mature leader can spur democracy to accomplish wonders. The Hamiltonians concede that. Their theory of the survival of a nation, in fact, is predicated on the possibility of securing a succession of intellectually mature leaders to control the hopelessly immature. They defend it by the formidable argument that in six thousand years of recorded history, no nation has as yet lifted the mass, or even a large proportion, of its people to a level of maturity at which their government could survive for more than a few generations.

The great Americans who have shared the liberal vision have been compelled to admit that the feat has not yet been accomplished; but to a man they have insisted that not all possible means of accomplishing it have as yet been tried. Even in the United States our experiment with the means of self-government has been tried under many obvious handicaps. Even in the United States there are, and have always been, artificial barriers that tend to hobble character and ability. Ignorance, poverty, disease, prejudice have always existed here. Each of them is a handicap upon any mind, and when intense enough any of them can defeat the best mind, as far as a significant contribution to the proper conduct of public affairs is concerned. To a man, our great liberals have striven to eliminate as many artificial barriers as can be eliminated; for to a man they have believed in the existence in the mass of the people of sufficient character and ability to create, if existing talent could be released, a finer civilization than the world has seen, and to maintain and improve it.

The vision has some basis in fact, or it would hardly have persisted so long in minds of such caliber. It is not difficult to pick out signs of increasing maturity in the thinking of the average American since he began to become effective in public affairs about 1800. These signs can be made to look impressive by the simple process of omitting all indications of an opposite trend; but if one is honest enough to take them into account, categorical assertions become foolish and the effort sinks into the harassing and indeterminate business of balancing probabilities. Yet one thing is clear—since 1900 the average American has been subjected to a series of stresses any one of which was as severe as the worst experienced by any earlier generation. A test so rigorous ought to justify one of two conclusions—either that the capacity for self-government on a highly civilized level is not in him, or that the capacity not only exists, but in a degree that permits stronger hope for the future than could possibly have been entertained before the test was applied. The man who is as old as the century is about ready to quit the scene; he will not count for a great deal for more than a few years, so it is idle to inquire what he is likely to do. He will not do much of anything more. But the shape he is in at this moment does furnish some indication of how much the average American can take. Any evidence that he is not a complete wreck, as a political entity, adds substance to Abraham Lincoln's vision.

2. *He Has Lived*

"WHAT, then, is the American, this new man?" asked French Crèvecourt in 1782, and wrote a whole volume without framing any very definite answer. In Crèvecourt's time this new man was, in fact, faith, as Saint Paul described it: "the substance of things hoped for, the evidence of things not seen." A hundred and sixty-eight years later there is not much more to be said. The American is certainly not yet what every liberal believes he may be, and hopes he will be. All hands agree that he is the evidence of things not seen; but what sort of things is the subject of endless debate.

Yet Crèvecourt really answered his question in asking it. If the American is a new man, it necessarily follows that he cannot fit into any frame of old ideas. If he could, he would be new only in the sense that the last Ford off the assembly line is newer than the one just ahead of it. When Crèvecourt said "new" he meant "different"; and whatever is different is pretty sure to puzzle many minds and to disappoint some.

Evidence that this new man is both puzzling and disappointing to many minds may be found in the latest issue of any serious review. Since 1929 especially, since 1932 doubly, and since 1945 quadruply, the average American has been held up to scorn and contumely by Jeremiahs who have sprouted like mushrooms in a rain-soaked meadow, both to the right and to the left. They agree that he is the evidence of things not seen as yet, but sure to be seen pretty soon, and they agree that they are horrible things; but with that, agreement ceases.

The Wailing Women of the extreme right paint a dreadful picture of apostasy from the true faith as it was delivered unto Adam Smith. The Children of the Covenant (that is to say, *The Wealth of Nations*) ensorcelled by the Fiend Roosevelt, have wandered so far from the truth that the apparition of Socialism arouses no terror but only a mild curiosity in them. Obviously, they are far on the way toward accepting Communism, with all the usual appurtenances—tumbrils crowding the streets, the gutters awash with blood, and the women nationalized.

The Wailing Women of the extreme left—excluding the Communists, who have no ideas of their own, but must wait to be told by Moscow what they are thinking—paint an equally dreadful picture of sodden refusal to hear the gospel as it was propounded by Karl Marx. The Children of the Covenant (that is to say, *Das Kapital*), seduced by Caiaphas Roosevelt, are giving their offspring stones for bread and serpents for fish; the final result is bound to be an apocalyptic terror, attended by plagues, conflagrations, seven-headed beasts and horsemen of hell.

Such addlepates we have always had with us, and doubtless always shall have. Such people held special services when George Washington retired and rendered thanks to God that now the country was delivered of a tyrant. Such people agreed with Editor Dwight who could see this side of hell no spectacle more dreadful than the Jefferson administration. Such people saw in Lincoln a baboon, in Wilson a Casanova, in Roosevelt a thinly disguised Robespierre. If the average man had ever held them in anything save derision, he would have ruined himself and the country long ago.

But while the hysterical old women, of both sexes and all factions, may be dismissed with contempt, it is impossible to deal so with certain well-poised, thoughtful men, not given to seeing "ghoulies and ghosties and long-leggetit beasties," but well aware that false prophets do exist and many there be that are deceived thereby. These men know that the world does move, and that the thinking of 1900 is not adequate to deal with the problems of 1950. To class them with the Wailing Women because they are profoundly apprehensive is out of the question. They have reason to be apprehensive; none but a fool proceeds upon an uncharted way with no trepidation whatever.

Perhaps the genuine liberal has more cause to be apprehensive than anyone else, for he envisages not only the damage that may be incurred but the opportunity that may be missed if the average American proves incapable of coping with the situation in which he finds himself as the century enters its second half. For the twentieth century has wrought for the United States something rare in the history of nations—it is given a second chance. We have come, in the Biblical phrase, "through great tribulation" to a point at which it is theoretically possible for us to retrieve the error of 1920.

Nor can it be reasonably denied that the average man has glimpsed the opportunity. Consider the ready acceptance of the United Nations. Consider the wide popular support of the Marshall Plan. Consider the steady adherence of the people to the Good Neighbor Policy. Does anyone seriously contend that these attitudes, or anything like them, were possible twenty-five years ago?

But the fact that the opportunity is present, and that we recognize it, is no guarantee of our ability to improve it. The assumption that the United States cannot fail is as idiotic as the assumption that it must inevitably fail. As between Pollyanna and the Calamity Howler there is no choice, intellectually. The assumption that the country can fail, but need not do so is the only one that justifies an American in taking thought for the future. If it cannot fail, no thought is necessary; if it is bound to fail, thought is useless.

The fact that there is any popular interest in public affairs is proof that this is the attitude of the average American; and it is certainly a more mature attitude than the spread-eagleism that prevailed as recently as 1898, when the brush with Spain inspired a ridiculous cockiness in the ordinary citizen. The determination that government shall be an instrument in the hands of the people to effect their safety and happiness is evidence that the common man has pulled up, in his political thinking, to the level of Jefferson and Hamilton, who were certainly mature. The fact that the common man regards the people as consisting of himself and his friends, not "the rich and well-born," is evidence that he is a man of the twentieth century, not of the eighteenth, as Hamilton was; the fact that he is somewhat uncertain of the virtue of the people is evidence that he is not a man of the twenty-first century, as Jefferson, in some of his aspects, undoubtedly was.

Consider, then, the case of a man born in 1920. He has known no other century but this. He has known no other international situation than war, hot or cold, or at best an armed truce. His generation is now entering the thirties; it is beginning to be effective in public affairs, but the chief burden of responsibility will not fall upon it for some years. Yet the time is close; another decade, and these will be the men who run the United States. Have their immediate predecessors anything significant to say to them, either of warning or of encouragement? Does the incredible tale of the past half-century really mean anything, or is it "a tale told by an idiot, full of sound and fury, signifying nothing"?

Surely, there is one profoundly significant remark that the ordinary American of fifty can make to the ordinary American of thirty; it is the remark of the Abbé Sieyès: "I survived."

Sieyès was in Paris during the Reign of Terror; and that gives to his laconic statement immense significance. The ordinary

American is here—still relatively free, still the final authority in public affairs, still better fed, better clothed, and better housed than the common man in any other country. If he has been here since 1900, the mere fact that he has survived means a great deal; for twice within that period a coalition of empires has risen against him to beat his political system down, once his economic system crashed about his ears, practically every year some part of his social system has given way and has had to be remodeled and rebuilt, and for the past five years his form of government, his economy, and his faith have been sternly and relentlessly challenged by the most redoubtable foreign power in existence. Yet he survives.

No great hero is this average American who is now about to turn over his authority and his responsibility to younger men, but no one can question his power of endurance. He has not proved himself master of time and circumstance. He has not proved himself master of his own folly and weakness, but has lost much blood and treasure through both. He has not discovered the answer to any of the governmental problems that worried Solon and have continued to worry rulers ever since. He has found no direct avenue to the good life, but has blundered into countless blind alleys.

Nevertheless, he has attained a certain distinction, if only the second-rate kind that has preserved Sieyès' fame. He has taken the most terrific battering, and by long odds, to which the nation was ever subjected, and he has survived. His life has been attacked by armed enemies, his living has been attacked by impersonal economic forces, his moral certainties have been wrecked by science, art, philosophy and, above all, by time and change, yet he has survived—scarred, charred, maimed, perhaps, but recognizably the same.

If the rising generation is made of material as durable—mentally, morally and physically—there is little justification for the prophecies of doom which have been so frequent recently.

But two items of the hard-won wisdom of the first half of the century the new generation must preserve if an easier time is to bear fruit in greater accomplishment. One is the fact that the efforts of great heroes to save, and of great villains to destroy, the American people are both ineffectual. The passing generation has seen four of the greatest, Wilson, Lenin, Roosevelt, Stalin, and three of the most menacing, Hitler, Mussolini, Tojo, but so much of American civilization as has been salvaged has been saved by the American people; and so much as has been lost, has been lost, for the most part, by their folly.

For they alone endure. Wilson could lead us to a high peak of rational, mature thinking about the art of government, but he died, and we swiftly descended into the Slough of Despond. Roosevelt could lead us to another; but he died, too, and if we do not descend again, it will be because the common people learned something from the first experience.

The second item of wisdom wrung from the past fifty years is that the way out of trouble is to wade straight through, not to try to turn back. We tried turning back after 1918, and again after 1929, and the result both times was confusion worse confounded. In 1945 we could not turn back because Stalin stood in the way; and by 1950 we were no worse off than we were in 1945, and in some ways better off. In Mommsen's phrase, "courage to grasp the hand which beckons to them out of the darkness of the future, and to follow it they know not whither," seems to have paid off, at least reasonably well.

This new man, then, this American, may not be remarkable at all for his beauty, or his wisdom, or his puissance; but he is unquestionably remarkable for his durability. He is a standing encouragement to believe that the worst has already happened, yet here we are; and in the next half-century, that can certainly not be fiercer, and may be far milder, it is impossible to fix a limit on what we may become. So when the next great man appears, he may outstrip all his predecessors, having better followers at his back.

But that is speculation. What is indisputable fact is that the ordinary American who is now fifty or more has been somewhere and seen something. He has escaped the most deplorable of all fates—to be born, to subsist for many years, and then to die without ever having really lived.

Index